LITERARY CRITICISM AND
CULTURAL THEORY

Edited by
William E. Cain
Wellesley College

A ROUTLEDGE SERIES

LITERARY CRITICISM AND CULTURAL THEORY

WILLIAM E. CAIN, General Editor

THE END OF THE MIND
The Edge of the Intelligible in Hardy, Stevens, Larkin, Plath, and Glück

DeSales Harrison

Routledge
New York & London

Published in 2005 by
Routledge
Taylor & Francis Group
711 Third Avenue
New York, NY 10017

Published in Great Britain by
Routledge
Taylor & Francis Group
2 Park Square, Milton Park
Abingdon, Oxon OX14 4RN

Routledge is an imprint of the Taylor & Francis Group.

Transferred to Digital Printing 2005

10 9 8 7 6 5 4 3 2 1

Library of Congress Cataloging-in-Publication Data

Harrison, DeSales, 1968–
    The end of the mind : the edge of the intelligible in Hardy, Stevens, Larkin, Plath, and Glück / DeSales Harrison.
        p. cm. -- (Literary criticism and cultural theory)
    Includes bibliographical referneces and index.
        ISBN: 0-415-97029-6 (alk. paper)
    1. American poetry--20th century--History and criticism. 2. Subjectivity in leterature. 3. English poetry--20th century--History and criticism. 4. Stevens, Wallace, 1879–1955--Criticism and interpretation 5. Glück, Louise, 1943--Criticism and interpretation. 6. Larkin, Philip--Criticism and interpretation. 7. Plath, Sylvia--Criticism and interpretation. 8. Hardy, Thomas, 1840–1928--Poetic works. 9. Meaning (Philosophy) in literature. I. Title. II. Series.

PS310.S85H37 2005
811'.509353--DC22   2005019884
ISBN13: 978-0-415-97029-7 (hbk)
ISBN13: 978-0-415-86512-8 (pbk)

Contents

Acknowledgments

Without the assistance and participation of many people, this book would never have reached completion. My advisor Helen Vendler's knowledge of poetry is equaled only by her patience, stamina, and skill in guiding an undertaking such as this out of the shadows. To have Peter Sacks as teacher and friend has been on of my greatest good fortunes, and to write in anticipation of the lucid seriousness with which he approaches a text is to write with hope. I am grateful as well to Elisa New for the vigor of her sensibility and for her subtle and original eye.

In addition to those on my committee, many other teachers and writers have offered indispensable help. To these people I extend special thanks: Phillip Fisher and Barbara Johnson for the clarity and rigor of their thought; Leo Damrosch and Marjorie Garber for modeling the liveliest integration of scholarship and pedagogy; Allen Grossman for the great gay gravity of his mind; Seamus Heaney for the great grave gaiety of his; Frank Bidart for showing with such passion and care how the page can be the site of the "intensest rendezvous." And I never would have begun in the first place had it not been for Michael Fried at Johns Hopkins, or for Richard Brodhead, David Bromwich, John Hollander, Vera Kutzinski, and Marina Leslie at Yale.

In the best circumstance, scholary work fosters a unique and intense form of friendship, and such friendships, in turn, foster better thinking than one could ever accomplish alone. I give special mention to Dan Chiasson, Nick Halpern, Virginia Heffernan, Scott Karambis, Sophia Padnos, Scott Stevens, and Douglas Trevor—and to John Everett, who would have been glad to hear that the work was finally done.

Respect and appreciation for his talents tempers the dread I feel that Siddhartha Deb, novelist and critic, will not always be at hand, as he unfailingly has been, to improve my drafts in every possible way.

I am grateful to Kyle Strimbu, whose prodigious copyediting talents have saved me from many errors in thought and execution, and at Routledge to Bill Cain, Paul Foster Johnson, Robert Sims, Rich Hale, Joyce Monaco,

Max Novick, and Jaclyn Bergeron, for their persistence, patience and unstinting care.

Special thanks to Gwen Urdang-Brown for crucial administrative and logistical assistance.

What merits this book has are the dividends of the chance to learn in the company of such people; its flaws are a part of my failure to learn enough.

My siblings, parents, and parents-in-law have offered more forbearance, reassurance, and support than a family should have to offer.

If each of these pages—however acid-free and archive-ready—must eventually crumble, may the last to go be the one which records my unpayable debt of gratitude to Isabel Gillies Harrison for her unflagging encouragement and love.

This book is for her.

She attends the tininnabula—
And the wind sways like a great thing tottering—
  Of birds called up by more than the sun,
  Birds of more wit, that substitute—
Which suddenly is all dissolved and gone—
  Their intelligible twittering
  For unintelligible thought.

    —Wallace Stevens, from "The Hermitage at the Center"

Introduction

Strange Resistances

This book is about the uses to which poetic unintelligibility can be put. By poetic unintelligibility I do not mean poetic *difficulty,* the resistance with which a text, to a greater or lesser degree, confronts the reader's desire for comprehension, or mastery, or possession. I take as my topic rather a class of features in poems that by definition cannot be assimilated into a positive account of what the poem says or of how it says it. An educated, intelligent, or divine reader could not overcome this different, absolute form of resistance any more readily than a reader ignorant, stupid, or merely mortal. Of course what is by definition unintelligible to one person—say, the night sky—might overflow with meanings for another. In light of this fact, I can specify further what this book will not be about; I will not attempt to adjudicate differences between subjective accounts of the intelligible. That is to say, I will not undertake to distinguish between the different kinds of intelligibility, those meanings, intended or not, to be perceived in the night sky, or an octagonal red sign posted at an intersection, or an infant's cry, or the sudden disappearance of a certain genus of tree frog from a certain rainforest. Instead, by the term *unintelligible* I designate a specific feature of *art,* in this case literary, poetic art. Such a feature is one where the intelligibility of the artwork, as an artwork, is not merely delayed or deferred, as in the case of difficulty, but arrested, impeded, obscured, damaged, or destroyed. Such a feature then, is to be known only by contrast to instances where the text can presume its own (present or eventual) clarity, instances where the text makes available the possibility of its assimilation to the reader's understanding. Impossibility, by contrast, is manifest as an unassimilable rupture or tear in the fabric of intelligibility, a rupture or tear in the text itself.

To express the difference between this possibility and this impossibility in the most schematic terms, one might think of a lyric by Sappho. If the text is complete and the writing legible, and the reader knows something of the language and the cultural context of the poem, then the poem is intelligible. Even if a reader knows nothing of Greek poetry or the Greek language, nothing inheres in the poem itself to disrupt this intelligibility. If on the other hand, all that remains of the lyric are six and a half words on a shred of papyrus, the poem, as an intact artifact, has been irrevocably compromised. It may now be a new form of fragmentary artifact, as Pound pointed out, but its margin is defined by an impenetrable opacity. No knowledge, short of the knowledge of where the rest of the text might be found, could restore the poem to its initial intelligibility. In this book, I am concerned with a set of instances where the *poems themselves* present the reader with sites, frontiers, or margins of unintelligibility, poems which entail, from the moment of their writing, disruptions to their internal terms of knowability, terms on which the intelligibility of their address is elsewhere founded.

Poetry is the genre in question not because this category of the unintelligible is unique to poetry, or to the poetry of the period to which I refer, but because poetry *by definition* foregrounds a perimeter of closure, not only in the closed forms of traditional prosody, but also in the ineradicable fact of closure manifest by the line itself—whether or not that line conforms to a named formal pattern. Poetry's insistence upon closure, as I will argue in this introductory essay, makes constantly visible the drama or struggle between what can and cannot be said. Even when a line fits its metrical pattern so seamlessly that the natural cadences and inflections of speech are in no way deformed, as in Elizabeth Bishop's favorite iambic pentameter, "I hate to see that evening sun go down"[1] (from W. C. Handy's "St. Louis Blues"), the line by definition exerts an external force on the utterance, so that what is most natural is also inherently framed by, and suspended in, the artificial. (One analogy would be an undisturbed perspective of pristine wilderness viewed through a window or the "window" of a photograph; even though no "external" agency has intruded upon the landscape, the framing intervenes as a formal principle.) Such formal or external influence on the line can be all but invisible—as in Handy's line—or it can be extreme, as in a line by Skelton, Dickinson, Hopkins, or cummings. It is this extreme conflict that provides me with my subject, not merely the conflict between metrical form and intelligible speech, but between speech and *any* influence, thematically or formally expressed, that brings to bear a limit condition of *impossibility* for the poetic voice, against which that voice must negotiate—or from which it must wrest—the terms of its future possibility. It is in this way that poetry, even the clearest, most transparent, most intelligible poetry, arrives in the world at a place immediately adjacent to the realm of the unintelligible. The poems I discuss here are those that explicitly allow their own precinct to be traversed, or incurred upon, by this border.

In this introductory essay, I propose a new reading of a key term in the history of modernism, *impersonality*, with a view toward including in poetic theory an account of how poems can address themselves to phenomena which stand, by definition, outside of representation. Modernism's investment in impersonality, I propose, is in part an orientation toward this region *beyond* human meaning, that realm which Wallace Stevens called "the end of the mind."

IMPERSONAL PROBLEMS

It is certain: between a person and a poem there is a difference. One might expect poetry to make peace with such a fact, if only to secure *ars longa* in the face of life's brevity. But the story of modernist poetry in English (which, in this matter, includes the story of postmodernism) is a long testament to the difficulty bedeviling this distinction. One way in which modernism sought to separate itself from romanticism was in its avowed dissatisfaction with earlier accounts of the poem-person relationship. A new account of the difference was needed, and this new account, as it evolved (slowly, erratically, fractiously), assumed a number of distinctions corollary to the difference between poems and persons: between the impersonal and the personal, objectivity and subjectivity, tradition and the individual, art and emotion. Newly in the forefront was the emphasis on a *negative* relation; the question was no longer (as it seemed always to have been) how art related to life, but how it did not, or could not, or should not. Framing the issue in a formulation both polemical and arch, Eliot's "Tradition and the Individual Talent" declared these truths to be self evident:

> In fact, the bad poet is usually unconscious where he ought to be conscious, and conscious where he ought to be unconscious. Both errors tend to make him "personal." Poetry is not a turning loose of emotion, but an escape from emotion; it is not the expression of personality, but an escape from personality. But, of course, only those who have personality and emotions know what it means to want to escape from these things. (*Selected Prose*, 43)

The right kind of *loosing* had to be achieved, not the loosing of emotion *by means of* art, but the loosing *of* art *from* emotion. But what is the value, or even the nature, of this loosing? And in the interest of what freedom is it to be sought? What specifically is to be freed from what? The voice from the body?

The artist from the person? The speaker from the poet? The immortal from the mortal? In short, what is impersonality, and what remains once impersonality has been achieved? Eliot states that the human emotion is converted through art, catalytically, into what he calls "a new art emotion" (*Selected Prose*, 43)— without specifying *whose* emotion this "art emotion" is:

> What happens is a continual surrender of [the poet] as he is at the moment to something which is more valuable. The progress of an artist is a continual self-sacrifice, a continual extinction of personality [. . . .] There remains to define this process of depersonalization. (*Selected Prose*, 40)

And it remains still. Which is to say, it remains to be acknowledged that whatever "the continual extinction of personality" may be, such a process subjects all attempts at definition (including Eliot's) to a telling defeat. What lingers most palpably now is not the veracity or even the possibility of the assertion, but the intensity of the wish—a wish strong enough to persist even in the knowledge that the desired end (surrender, sacrifice, extinction) requires, if it is possible at all, unending maintenance. This conflict renders poignant the word "continual," which seems to concede, through its very persistence and ongoingness, its own ambition's unshakeable unsuccess. Viewed together with antecedent remarks in Nietzsche and Emerson, this passage of Eliot's reveals an eagerness to affix a ballot of no-confidence to the very program it claims to advocate.

Although Emerson, in a letter written in 1832, allows that the war to achieve a vital self-transcendence may be "constant," he asserts that this war can, in fact, be won:

> The constant warfare in each heart is betwixt Reason and Commodity. The victory is won as soon as any Soul has learned always to take sides with Reason against himself; to transfer his Me from his person, his name, his interest, back upon Truth and Justice, so that when he is disgraced and defeated and fretted and disheartened, and wasted by nothings, he bears it well, never one instant relaxing his watchfulness, and, as soon as he can get a respite from the insults or the sadness, records all these phenomena, pierces their beauty as phenomena, and, like a God, oversees himself. (315–16)

The cost of this conflict is an unblinking watchfulness, and while this cost may be high, it nonetheless affords a sure antidote to being "wasted by nothings." It is a reasonable sacrifice whose end is the achievement of a God-like oversight; in the long run it is the self, the "Me," that is supplemented, enhanced, and confirmed. Emerson claims this ability for ordinary human capacity, as a part of what "each heart" can do; Nietzsche, in *The Birth of Tragedy*, conceives of it as a particular, inherent attribute of the lyric poet:

> The Dionysiac musician, himself imageless, is nothing but original pain and reverberation of the image. Out of this mystical process of *un-selving*, the poet's spirit feels a whole world of images and similitudes arise, which are quite different in hue, causality, and pace from the images of the sculptor or narrative poet. [. . . .] [The lyrical poet] himself becomes his images, his images are objectified versions of himself. Being the active center of that world he may boldly speak in the first person, only his "I" is not that of the actual walking man, but the "I" dwelling, truly and eternally, in the ground of being. It is through the reflections of that "I" that the lyric poet beholds the ground of being. (39)

A person is a lyric poet for Nietzsche when the *I* uttered refers not to the "walking man" but to the "ground of being." This "walking man" suffers an exile no less categorical than does Eliot's "personal" man, but the terms of his exclusion differ. They are the universal attribute, and not the ideal instance, of the lyric poet. In Eliot, by contrast, as the optative mode calls constant attention to itself, the notorious "extinction" seems less the focus of his argument than the principle of the "continual" in which "extinction" remains inextinguishable, and in which the self is never wholly sacrificed or surrendered. That we may "want to escape" from emotion and personality, and that poetry may offer the means for this escape, says nothing of how one might avail oneself of the offer—at least insofar as Eliot's escape would in some way entail an escape from one's location in the world, whether that location is called one's physical body, one's historical coordinates, or one's cultural affiliations. The impersonal problem, then, is not how impersonality may be attained, but how it relates to the personal in the first place, and how it should be that an impersonal voice seems simultaneously so desirable and so impossible to achieve.

WHO'S SPEAKING IF NOBODY IS SPEAKING?

It was Yeats who understood better than anyone else that the discourse of impersonality, if it was to get anywhere at all, must take into account the fact of physical embodiment. Far from being the corporeal antithesis to the impersonal, the physical body (wholly subject to the external powers of mortality, history, and desire) represented another axis of impersonality distinct from that offered by art. For Yeats, the address of personhood enunciated itself at the point of intersection of these two axes of impersonality, and it was a set of terms for this impersonal personhood that "Among School Children" proposed. The "body swayed *to* music," at once distinct from and subsumed by music, becomes *manifest in* the dance that it performs. It is the nature of the Yeatsian paradox that the soul so swayed is most itself, and has most fully recovered "radical innocence" and knit "its own sweet will" with "Heaven's will." The moment of "the body swayed to music" resembles—but ultimately stands in complete antithesis to—the kind of two-dimensional determinism to which impersonality has sometimes been reduced, as in Charles Olson's call for

> the getting rid of the lyrical interference of the individual as ego, of the "subject" and his soul, that peculiar presumption by which western man has interposed himself between what he is as a creature of nature (with certain instructions to carry out) and those other creations of nature which we may, with no derogation, call objects. (24)

What Yeats argues, and Eliot concedes, is that there is no "getting rid of lyrical interference" as Olson states it.

The term best qualified for dual-citizenship in the realm of the personal and impersonal was, for the New Critics, the *speaker*. "Depersonalization," Jonathan Culler points out, "instead of eliminating the category of person, leads [in the Anglo-American New Criticism] to the construction and explication of a speaker" (191). The advantages that speakers have over persons, in this approach, is that their identity is defined solely in relation to speech, in which the poem also has its being. A speaker in this sense, as distinct from a person, is not merely a person-who-speaks, or the person-who-happens-to-be-speaking; it is, rather, what a person would be if persons *were made of speech*—what a person would be if speech were the only ground in which identity could be established. Speech (and not, in this instance, *language*, in the Saussurean formulation) is, as it were, the matter which achieves a form in utterance; only at the moment of utterance is a speak-*er*, a self-contiguous and distinct agency, designated. It is in this way that theory of the "speaker" does not stipulate a distance from the body; rather, it sponsors the coherence of what could be called the lyric body, if the body is the site of self-contiguity and distinct agency.

The impersonal, by this account, does not register a qualitative difference from the personal but one of degree. The impersonal emerges not as the anti-personal or the non-personal, but as a condition of *minimal* personhood, whereby all the multifold attributes sedimented into the cultural category of the person are stripped, sanded, or purged away until only speech is left, given form by the least, frailest tissue of specificity capable of distinguishing one speaker from all others. Speakers, then, are derived through a process of relinquishing not accretion: *per via di levare* not *per via di porre* (Loewald, 226). Chief among the attributes to be relinquished is that of *autonomy*. An impersonal aesthetic is one that declares its willingness to relinquish as fully as possible the agency of the speaker, to converge as fully as possible upon that point where the–*er* in *speaker* designates a property in speech itself and not the idiosyncratic will of the walking man.

According to Northrop Frye, this willingness, this desire, is at play in the medium of poetry itself:

> Poetry is the product, not only of a deliberate and voluntary act of consciousness, like discursive writing, but of processes which are subconscious or pre-conscious or half-conscious or unconscious as well. . . . It takes a great deal of will power to write poetry, but part of that will power must be employed in trying to relax the will, so making a large part of one's writing involuntary. . . . Creation, whether of God, man, or nature, seems to be an activity whose only intention is to abolish intention, to eliminate final dependence on a relation to something else. . . . [360]

What this trajectory of abnegation points toward, as Andrew Ross has remarked (214), is a formal extreme, an expressionism, for which other plastic media, perhaps painting in particular, appear more ideally suited. Paint, unlike printed text, can be employed to reveal the yielding of the artist's gesture to those material properties inherent in the paint itself: its thinness, viscosity, translucence, luster, its tendency to drip, pucker, dull, or crack. When Jackson Pollock declares "I am Nature" (O'Connor, 26) he is arrogating to himself the position of the lyric poet that Nietzsche describes; his paint—dripped, dropped, dabbled, dribbled, splattered, streaked, and flung—is applied in a rhetoric of *ceding* or *yielding* utterly to the inherent fluid properties, the *nature,* of the medium; this rhetoric—and it is a rhetoric because spontaneity is always alien to composition—implies a painter whose will has been "knit to Heaven's will" to such an extent that the seam between man and nature is no longer visible. While this is most apparent in, or easily arrogated to, the procedures of expressionist painting, Frye claims that it is no less present in poetry itself, or rather, poetry is the proper term for this yielding of intention to the medium, whatever the medium might be. If in New Criticism, the intending author is supplanted by the speaking speaker, Frye merely extends the New Critical formulation. He agrees that there is an essential split between author and artifact, but that the split makes itself known not merely at the instant the poet removes pen from page. The split is always there; the very act of taking up the poetic instrument is by definition a passing over of the limits of one's intentional will. What was for the New

Critics a practical exigency in *describing* poems, was, according to Frye, an inherent characteristic of poetry itself.

For J. Hillis Miller, in *Poets of Reality*, this abnegation is most properly
understood as an attribute not of poetry in general but of modernist poets in
particular. The phenomenon that Frye describes is a procedure that became
visible—and available to theory—only after a certain number of writers,
artists, and philosophers undertook, in the twentieth century, to avow and describe these goals:

> To walk barefoot into reality [the program that a strain in modernism
> conceives and encourages] means abandoning the independence of the
> ego. Instead of making everything an object for the self, the mind must
> efface itself before reality, or plunge into the density of an exterior world,
> dispersing itself in a milieu which exceeds it and which it has not made.
> [. . . .] [T]he will must will not to will. Only through an abnegation of
> the will can objects begin to manifest themselves as they are, in the in-
> tegrity of their presence. When man is willing to let things be then they
> appear in a space which is no longer that of an objective world opposed
> to the mind. In this new space the mind is dispersed everywhere in things
> and forms one with them. (8)

This is not Eliot's surrender of the self "to something that is more valuable,"
even the something that Pollock calls "Nature." It is not a surrender to, but a
surrender *of*, specifically of the Cartesian dualism between subject and object.
Whether such an account is in fact a credible description of modernist lyric
practice matters less than the visible discomfort with any notion of agency in
the first place. What is surrendered is not *the* self in the interest of a higher
value, which is to say, the higher self of Man, God, or Nature; what is surrendered is the claim to any agency separate from the medium itself. By comparison, the expressionist yielding of the artwork to Nature is an act already
intelligible to romanticism; paint becomes the visual manifestation of the
Aeolian lyre, to be played by Nature. The agent (Nature) and the medium
(paint) remain distinct. When the speaker is posited as the only agency, however, this distinction breaks down. To say that the poem is spoken by (only) a
speaker is to propose a state of affairs romanticism could not have imagined.
The ceding of the poem's agency to *speech itself*—is an act for which only a
modernist sensibility, Miller implies, can account.

If speech by this account is what speaks through, or by means of, the
person, then the speaker's agency is limited to the act of invitation, welcoming, or admission that ushers in another agency. It is this greater agency of
speech for which the "immortal" predecessors of any poet stand as the sign.

Their immortality points not toward their greater human strength and its undying fame, but toward a different immortality, the non-mortality of speech (for which the muse also is a figure), a non-mortal realm to which they were accorded special access. That this access is not determined by human will suggests why the voices audible in a strong poem, as Eliot models such a poem in "Tradition and the Individual Talent," must be the voices of the dead:

> One of the facts that might come to light in this process is our tendency to insist, when we praise a poet, upon those aspects of his work in which he least resembles anyone else. We dwell with satisfaction upon the poet's difference from his predecessors, especially his immediate predecessors; we endeavor to find something that can be isolated in order to be enjoyed. Whereas if we approach a poet without this prejudice we shall often find that not only the best, but the most individual parts of his work may be those in which the dead poets, his ancestors, assert their immortality most vigorously. (*Selected Prose*, 38)

The immortality asserted, then, is not just an assertion of poetic *virtu*. Rather, it is an insistence on the externality of poetic speech to the personal, unique, individual, historical life. It is in this way that modernism establishes a kind of radical classicism, where poetry is not personal except in the most literal, most etymological sense, as a *speaking-through*, where the mouth is not a source, but that point at which an outside speech passes through the local, mortal, enunciating body.

While each of these passages claims for itself the authority of mere description, however, their recourse to paradox and gnomic formulation ("continual extinction," "making... writing involuntary," "the... will not to will") reveals beneath the declarative rhetoric an underpinning of utopian or mystical polemic. Despite their protestations, intent persists, as does the spectral presence of the mortal body. An act of surrender or of abnegation presumes a subject no less than an act of resistance or affirmation. As long as speech is understood as utterance, as a moving outward from somewhere, that somewhere tenaciously implies some *body*, whose mouth is shaping sound—or whose hand is shaping a line—into speech. Even if—or especially because—this body presents itself as unnamed, immortal, or impersonal, it must trouble any account of how the poem speaks for itself.

TRANSMUTATIONS OF THE BODY

For Allen Grossman, a contemporary theorist of radical impersonality, poetry is that means of representation uniquely privileged with the ability to give access to impersonal principles of speech, which are both implied by and manifest in the abstract prosody of the poetic line. It is through invocation of these impersonal principles that poetry achieves its deepest purpose, which is, paradoxically, the preservation of what Grossman terms *personhood.* Personhood, as Grossman defines it, is distinct from selfhood—artifactual, the result of a special kind of human work. It is not prior to human agency but the "inscription" thereof:

> Now, I am making a distinction which I think is alien from the way you think about things: a distinction between *selves* and *persons.* I believe that poetry is fundamentally antipsychological, and I would summon as my witness the High Modern poets with their advocacy of impersonality, which led them all, each in his own way, to reject the analysis of the "real" self that we find in Freud. I am in effect saying to you that poetry has a destiny not in selves, but in persons; and that, whereas selves are found or discovered, persons and personhood is an artifact, something that is *made,* an inscription upon the ontological snowfields of a world that is not in itself human. (19)

Whereas Eliot had distinguished impersonality from the personal, Grossman, in the interest of a related project, distinguishes *persons* from *selves.* For Eliot, the impersonal was that field wherein immortal voice could be most clearly heard; for Grossman, it is the person, the bearer of the human name, which is sponsored by an immortal principle inherent in poetry itself. In *The Sighted Singer* he articulates this principle, propositionally and aphoristically, in a series of "commonplaces":

> 1.4 The poem facilitates immortality by the conservation of names.

> 1.5 The features of the poem which are instrumental toward its immortalizing function are those which distinguish it from other forms of words, its prosody (for example, meter and line). (212–213)

> 14. Immortality (poetic immanence) is the descent of the speaking person into the ground of language as a collective possession. (240)

Grossman's theory takes care to define personhood itself as an outcome of those undertakings which, in Eliot, achieved impersonality and immortality. For Grossman the remainder term is the term *self* which assumes the vulnerable, outcast position that the "personal" had occupied for Eliot, or the "walking man" had for Nietzsche. (Grossman, revising Nietzsche, substitutes "ground of language" for "ground of being.") The self, then, corresponds to what is mortal about the human, what must be left behind before the descent into the ground of being can be made. Another way of stating this is to say that the self is that part of the will which cannot be the speaker, that part which cannot be relinquished to the medium.

Why would it be, though, that in these two closely linked theories of impersonality, a term as central as *person* could be valued so differently? I suggest that it is not merely causes difference in local context that to the *person* occupies antithetical positions in Eliot's and Grossman's formulations. This slippage or treachery in the word is symptomatic of a problem at the very heart of lyric theory, a problem that both Eliot and Grossman, for the sake of their arguments, must elide. The problem that remains is what to do with the body. In this sense, the history of modernist poetic theory reads like *Oedipus Rex, Hamlet,* or any other murder mystery, a plot unfolding as the body, or the body of evidence, resists disposal or erasure. It is the body that insists upon itself in the figurative textures of both Eliot's and Grossman's accounts. For Eliot, the description of the "transmutation" into art entails a startling shift in metaphor toward the corporeal:

> [. . . .] [T]he more perfect the artist, the more completely separate in him will be the man who suffers and the mind which creates; the more perfectly will the mind *digest and transmute* the passions which are its material. (*Selected Prose* 40, emphasis added)

That *transmutation* and *digestion* are not distinct acts in this account suggests that the perfection of the art may involve a return to the body and a reliance on certain processes (corporeal, unwilled, suffered, invisible) that by definition resist translation into representational form. The path toward art is not away from the bodily selfhood of the "walking man" but somehow *through* the body and *of a piece* with its inner workings. How this might be true is not a question that Eliot strives to answer; the implication persists in the passage only under the auspices of a contrary and unexplicated metaphor. Grossman, aligning a theory of poetic line with a theory of respiration, binds together artistic and bodily processes more directly:

> There are two breaths or breathings which poetic analysis takes into account: the Greater or Feeding Breath is the breath taken in, during which there can be no speech. This breath comes to an end with the *limit of expansion,* when the body is as full as can be of the nurturant air. This silent feeding on the world to the limit of expansion precedes or prepares for *the line opening* (or, in appropriate degree, the lesser medial caesura). The Lesser Breath is the breathing out, during which speech occurs as the

reticulation of the dead breath. This Lesser, or Dead, or Speech breath explores the opposite limit, the limit of contraction—at which limit is *the
line ending.* The strong sense of the contradiction of speech and feeding
lends weight to the preference of silence to speech, and adds a further bitterness to the paradox of storytelling [. . . .]

Speech is obtained by *inscription* upon the dead breath, a meddling with
the exhausted air as it is pushed from the body outward. The terminal
caesura is the point of turning (*vertere*), as at the end of a furrow, the beginning of the inbreathing which carries the burden of the process from
preceding line-close to following line-opening. (279)

Inscription designates a relation of figure to ground between the "meddling
reticulations" and the exhaled, exhausted, "dead" breath and recalls its earlier
appearance in the "inscription upon the ontological snowfields" of the non-
human world. This figure-ground relationship is a precondition of speech.[2]
In order for there to be speech, there must be a breath (or a snow-field) available to receive a reticulation, to be meddled with. The vector is an outward
one, away from the body which requires nurturing and extracts it from the
"feeding" breath. However, just as the body had lingered in the term *digestion*,
it lingers for Grossman in the vocabulary of respiration and nurturance. The
breath cannot be employed as speech until something has been depleted, until
the nourishment has been extracted from the air, making it available for reticulation or meddling. It is at this point that the dead breath differs from the
snowfields. The snowfields were never alive and stand for the aspect of the external world that can sustain human marks. They are a ground wholly alien
to the human figures whose imprint they receive. The breath, on the other
hand, is not wholly alien. Because it had been life-giving and nurturant, it was
alive. Now it is dead because it has been subdued to the internal processes of
the body's own continuation (which, like digestion, is a form of metabolism).
The breath manifests the negative contour of the body; to the extent that the
body has been filled, the breath has been emptied, and to the extent that it has
been emptied, it is now fit for reticulation. This negative relation of breath to
body is not the same as the difference between mortal concerns ("self," or
"person" or "walking man") and non-mortal facts ("snowfields," or Yeats's
"murderous innocence of the sea" [185]). It is a relation to something that has
been marked, before it has received specific *marks*, with the human or mortal
form. The air must become breath and bear the body's hollowing mark before
the hollowed breath in turn can bear the marks that give it its value as speech.
    This prior mark, the non-specific, non-representational mark of the
body is the mark that Eliot's and Grossman's accounts elide in the interest of

privileging their central terms, immortality and impersonality.[3] They establish, nevertheless, a point of intersection with the body, and imply a definition of what "the body" is in this context. This definition is a specialized and restricted one, to be distinguished from a simplified and sentimental understanding of the body as "merely" the mortal human form or the address of selfhood. The body is indistinguishable from its representations, and never manifests itself in naked and unmediated presence. It is the "body" after all that simultaneously resists and enables representation: it is on account of the body that one cannot wholly enter "the ground of language," even while it is the peremptory needs of the body, made known in the infant's first cry, that draw the means of representation into the body's precinct.

SIGNATORY GESTURES

One difficulty that attends upon this association of language with the body is the fact that no class of words is inherently more bodily than any other; "digestion" is no more "bodily" a word than "immortal." All intelligible words stand at an equal distance from the body that utters them. This is why the signature, that sign which is meant to attach inextricably a verbal sign to a physical body, requires a deviation toward the illegible, toward a uniquely peculiar and nonrepresentational deformation of the written name, a peculiarity which corresponds to the unique, embodied, and non-substitutable personhood as acknowledged by law. The extent to which a signature is reproducible (by forger or machine, or because it is inscribed in black ink instead of violet ink or blood) is the extent to which it falls short of its function as signature. The signature in this respect must bridge the great distance between the substitutable, recombinatory field of verbal representation, made up of marks which are by definition infinitely repeatable, and the physical body of the social person, which is the only one of its kind. Reversing Grossman's formulation, the signature's deformation of the written name is the body's "meddling" with or "reticulation" of the inscription.

The effect the signature secures in the eyes of the law is one which lyric speech must secure without recourse to the particular deformations that can be imposed upon it by a single body. Just as the signature fails to the degree that it is reproducible, to the degree that it can be detached from the singularity of the body, the poem fails insofar as it is *not* able to detach itself. The poem in order to be a poem must be an utterance, an *outer-ance,* separating from the sentient body of its author and passing over into the non-sentient realm of text (of which, in this case, the spoken word is a subset). This utterance, however, in order to succeed, must manifest an irreproducibility of voice.

The poem, then, for Eliot and Grossman, comes into being in the field of tension between two conflicting imperatives. The first is the imperative to detach and become a part of the commonwealth of art. The second is to achieve the specificity, the singularity of utterance that not only distinguishes it from all other works of art but that makes reference, as the reticulated signature makes reference, to a singular body. It is in this effect, in this deformation out of intelligibility back toward the singular opacity of the body, that the work's status as lyric inheres.

To utterances most felicitously established in this field of tension, R. P. Blackmur assigns the term *gesture*. Such an utterance would be

> [. . . .] a poem which, using alliteration and rhyme and meter and refrain, using symbol and making symbol, playing upon its words as it runs, escapes all the mere meaning in words and reaches the pure meaningfulness of gesture. You can do with it whatever you will, for with poems of this order all things are possible. [. . . .] [W]e feel almost everything that deeply stirs us as if it were a gesture, the gesture of our uncreated selves. (24)

Like Eliot and Grossman, Blackmur employs the rhetoric of escape, not the escape that art enables from emotion or personality, or the escape of the inscribed breath from the mortal body, but the escape a poem might make from "all the mere meaning in words." This escape, successfully accomplished, "reaches the pure meaningfulness of gesture," a gnomic term whose invoking of purifying powers recalls Eliot's "transmuted material" of the passions. As "the gesture of our uncreated selves" it designates a realm of pure incipience, a realm itself unfallen yet constantly falling into "mere meaning" as these gestures are made known in representation.[4] This realm of the uncreated is analogous to the eternal newness that sponsors Pound's "news that stays news" (29) or the eternal outpouring of "the sacred well / That from beneath the seat of Jove doth spring" (Milton, 120). As much, however, as it partakes of a world of purity or immortality, Blackmur implies, it is not imaginable without the body as the source (or the spring) of all gestures. Gesture for Blackmur is a way of imagining the body as it might be present in the body's absence: pure gesture distinct from the gesturing form, just as pure meaningfulness can be separated, as he hypothesizes, from "all the mere meaning in words." The question that Blackmur raises is what endeavor poetry might be engaged in if it intends an escape from "mere meaning." It is to this question that this book proposes a response.

A STRANGE RESISTANCE IN ITSELF

What Blackmur imagines is a terrestrial version of Blake's "Sublime Body" which replaces the "false body: an Incrustation over my Immortal / Spirit; a

Selfhood, which must be put off & annihilated always / To cleanse the Face"
(141). Like Blake, he seeks to preserve the body, but in spiritualized or abstracted form—to rescue the body from the realm of "mere meaning" and
translate it into a realm of pure force or pulsion.[5] Unlike Blake's sublimation,
this spiritualization is not sponsored by divine intervention; his account
takes its place, therefore, in the general modernist undertaking to theorize an
artistic form that has been successfully (but not unrecognizably) isolated
from the body itself. The provision of an emblem for un-bodied form is the
central task of Frost's "West-running Brook," in which the speakers describe
a standing wave in a stream, a wave which is not only a meddling with the
flow of the water, but also a personified gesture—a gesture both of greeting
and of valediction:

> [. . . .]
> 'Speaking of contraries, see how the brook
> In that white wave runs counter to itself.
> It is from that in water we were from
> Long, long before we were from any creature.
> Here we, in our impatience of the steps,
> Get back to the beginning of beginnings,
> The stream of everything that runs away.
> Some say existence like a Pirouot
> And Pirouette, forever in one place,
> Stands still and dances, but it runs away,
> It seriously, sadly, runs away
> To fill the abyss' void with emptiness.
> It flows beside us in this water brook,
> But it flows over us. It flows between us
> To separate us for a panic moment.
> It flows between us, over us, and with us.
> And it is time, strength, tone, light, life, and love—
> And even substance lapsing unsubstantial;
> The universal cataract of death
> That spends to nothingness—and unresisted,
> Save by some strange resistance in itself,
> Not just a swerving, but a throwing back,
> As if regret were in it and were sacred.
> It has this throwing backward on itself
> So that the fall of most of it is always
> Raising a little, sending up a little.
> Our life runs down in sending up the clock.
> The brook runs down in sending up our life.
> The sun runs down in sending up the brook.
> And there is something sending up the sun.
> It is this backward motion toward the source,

> Against the stream, that most we see ourselves in,
> The tribute of the current to the source.
> It is from this in nature we are from.
> It is most us.' [. . . .] (257)

For the stream to sustain the unbreaking wave, it must in fact be two streams. The first is the dominant current, the "universal cataract of death" which like the sun's path through the sky runs westward. The second is a countercurrent, lesser than the first but nonetheless an ineluctable flowing. This eastward countercurrent through which the stream tends backward toward its spring is both elegiac and sacrosanct: "some strange resistance in itself / [. . . .] As if regret were in it and were sacred." In arriving at the conclusion that "It is most us" the speaker imagines that the primary emblem of identity is to be found, not in one's own nature, but outside in an impersonal realm, a region not of the "we" (because "we" are *not* "most us") but of the "it," that stream prior to the mortal lives of the speakers, a stream, like Yeats's in "The Wild Swans at Coole" (131) both companionable and cold. The wave, (literally, because it is a *waving* wave) is the gesture without the body, or to put it differently, the body of the gesture itself. It is the body of the gesture in the way that the "speaker" in the New Critical account is the voice of the poem and not the voice of the poet.[6]

The wave, to the extent that it disturbs the smooth, reflecting, mimetic surface of the water, constitutes a step outside "mere meaning" (if that is what the purely mimetic promises, in its fidelity and its flattening) and into a "pure meaningfulness." This step is another instance of "substance lapsing insubstantial," but it is not a lapsing toward the abyss of emptiness, but toward a pure form, one that lacks specific content. It is the work of describing that resistance and its "strangeness," that disruption beneath the smooth mimetic surface, in which theorists of modernist impersonality, one way or another, find themselves engaged. David Bromwich, in "An Art Without Importance," employs terms that recall both Frost and Blackmur:

> It is hard to take all communication out of language. What one can take
> out are the cues, the frames, the signals, the gesticulations. The aesthetic
> that seems to me compelling in modernism was mostly improvised from
> a rhetoric of understatement [. . . .] Words written in this discipline con-
> vey, by the adjustment of accent or by repetition, a disturbance under the
> surface of the events of narrated action. (3)

Whereas Blackmur had situated his remarks in reference to a horizon of pure meaningfulness, Bromwich points out the difficulty of imagining language without communication; what can be removed, on the way toward gesture, the pure meaningfulness on the far side of communication, is "gesticulation." This removal is accomplished in the service of the "rhetoric of understatement," which seeks to influence not by violation or intrusion but by a "disturbance" registered from beneath the surface. It is in this disturbance that credible personhood is established as "a site of resistance" (29). This disturbance, this "strange resistance" is the disturbance of Frost's stream "flung backward on itself in one white wave," a disruption that conceals its cause. While Frost's narrator makes plain that the wave is the "the black stream, catching on a sunken rock," the husband is not so quick to ascribe causes, pointing instead to the water's *inherent* contrariness. (In this designation of an inherent attribute, the rock is edited out, or rather, becomes a Stevensian *Rock,* impenetrable and incapable of being known.)

Bromwich ascribes this preference for understatement (or undercurrent, or "oversong") to modernist poets in particular, because he wishes to describe those features which distinguish modernism from other procedures. However, while Bromwich's pragmatism partakes in its own way of a "rhetoric of understatement," it necessarily implies a positive belief in or avowal of certain aesthetic criteria—criteria that necessarily underlie such large-scale judicial assessments of what "it" is that is "most us." It is with reference to higher-order criteria of this sort that Allen Grossman articulates his theory of the dead and living breaths into a broader account of "resistance," those "reticulations" or "disturbances" that poetry makes in what he has elsewhere termed "the stream of speech" (292):

> The business of the poet, as I understand it, is, first, to reconstruct in the artifactual space of the poem those rules resistance to which constructs our humanity, because our courage and capacity for self-evaluation are invested in *our resistance to those resistances*. And then, second, to enact the presence of the human voice, inscribed in such a way as to supply a case of the endurance and the momentary overcoming of those laws (replicated in the poem as metrical laws) which resist us whenever we undertake to meet and love. (165, emphasis added)

For Grossman, the voice as it comes into being in a poem is a resistance to certain laws replicated in metrical pattern, laws which resist our inclinations toward one another. Lyric voice, in this context, is a "resistance of resistances," that which comes into being when one force pushing against the will meets a counterforce. In this "momentary overcoming" the credible presence of a speaker is attainted. Credible presence, however, is not the content of expression or disclosure (or the "turning loose of emotion") but the manifestation of resistance and counterpressure.

Frost's poem, then, considered through the lens of these theories of resistance, offers a thematization of *the stream of speech* as it is resisted and reticulated while passing through the poetic aperture. The brook, like Grossman's "dead breath," is an exhalation, a movement out of the world "to fill the abyss' void with emptiness," but like the dead breath it too has been meddled with. Its movement, a running away that nonetheless entails "not just a swerving, but a throwing back," repeats the movement of verse itself, whose flowing works around and through that contrary force—*line*—which throws the stream of speech back upon itself and "sends up" the poem even as speech flows down the page.

Elaine Scarry in *Resisting Representation* demonstrates that resistance is serviceable not only to general theories of line in the abstract but to the discourse of the specific and unmistakable as well. The singularity of the voice, its credible specificity, inheres in the particularity of the reticulations and resistances it sustains:

> Precisely because each writer needs to solve a different problem of representation, each requires a sentence bearing a different grammatical shape. That shape, the "acoustical signature" of the resistance the sentence must overcome, holds visible within a small compass the larger shape of the scene as a whole. (6)

Scarry's remark manifestly concerns prose fiction, and proposes a part-whole homology between small and large elements in a narrative. The sentence, however, does not assume its unique shape because it is a part of a particular scene, but because a particular resistance, *external* to both scene and sentence, shapes the story's largest and smallest elements. Because poetry articulates itself in sentences as well as lines, and is not, in this regard, distinct from narrative, Scarry's term "acoustical signature" pertains as much to lyric as to narrative itself. The struggle against resistance marks the line as it marks the sentence with an "acoustical signature" which is at once the mark of the poem's unmistakable specific locality and of those pressures acting on the poem *from the outside,* which can never receive representation within the precinct of the poem itself. The singularity of voice the poem seeks to manifest, that which "is most it," is, like the wave, not derived from the poem's inherent nature but only as a force acting upon the poem from the outside. The resistance is "strange" because it remains estranged, a stranger to the poem, an outsider.

VERSE AND THE OBVERSE

Placed alongside the cited passages from Blackmur, Frost, Bromwich, and Grossman, Scarry's claim makes visible in the verbal surface of poetry the tension inherent in the signature between an intelligible name and those alterations, distortions, or deformations that estrange the name from the intelligible. The signature and the poem both provide instances where the impersonal and the personal, as Eliot would define them, intersect inextricably—instances where the dance, to frame the matter in Yeats's terms, is embodied in the dancer, and the dancer is danced by the dance. For Eliot the aesthetic imperative was in its essence an ethical one, to show how art, and therefore life, could be improved, in an act of conscious choice, by exercising a preference for the impersonal. What has persisted, for chiefly polemical purposes, is the ethical context in which Eliot situated the issue. This same ethical imperative is visible in affirmations (explicit and implicit) of Eliot's formulations, Grossman's or Bromwich's, as well as in those accounts that take a stance in opposition to Eliot, arguing for the privileging of the personal. This counter-argument derives from the conviction that the impersonal entails a rationalization of oppressive ideologies enshrined and perpetuated by High Modernism. While this position amounts to a transvaluation of Eliot's contention, it does not alter the fundamental ethical presuppositions underlying the issue. Arguments for the social and ethical privileging of the autobiographical or the confessional refute only Eliot's conclusions, not the ethical axis on which the issues are to be adjudicated.

In "West-running Brook," however, as in "Among School Children," the imperative is not to adjudicate the role of the personal and impersonal, only to isolate the intersection of the two and to designate it as an insoluble condition of the poets' art. The proposition implied in the two poems is that the relation of the impersonal to the personal is not approachable in ethical terms, or at least not in the specific ethical terms hitherto invoked. It is a relation less adaptable to the sort of polemical position assumed by Eliot, his advocates, and critics, and, I suggest, one whose exploration constitutes the major accomplishment and contribution of the poets I consider in this study.

The nature of this accomplishment, however, calls for a reconsideration and reassessment of the central terms in question. In *Totality and Infinity,* Emmanuel Levinas develops a model for the relation between the personal and impersonal—or more specifically, between the region of the *I* and the region of all that is other—a model uniquely suited to such a reconsideration. Levinas is particularly concerned with the radical limits of the self, limits beyond which the self, by definition, cannot "escape":

> The Other remains infinitely transcendent, infinitely foreign; his face in which his epiphany is produced and which appeals to me breaks with the world that can be common to us, whose virtualities are inscribed in our

nature and developed by our existence. Speech proceeds from absolute difference. (194)

It is the absoluteness of the difference between the *I* and Other on which Levinas insists, a difference inherent in the relation between them. This relation entails a fundamental refusal of integration or comprehension into (mere) intelligibility, that which can be *known,* that which can be appropriated into the *self.* Speech is not employed in the service of this intelligibility but is predicated by the absolute difference between the *I* and the Other. The point of derivation of this difference, the spring from which speech derives, is *le visage,* the face:

> This attestation of oneself is possible only as a face, that is, as speech. It produces the commencement of intelligibility, initiality itself, principality, royal sovereignty, which commands unconditionally. The principle is possible only as command. (201)

Speech, insofar as it calls into view a face-to-face relationship, inscribes and re-inscribes this absolute difference. What I wish to draw out in Levinas is his specific employment of the term *resistance* in his account of *le visage,* for it his elaboration of *resistance* that lends a coherence to the term's somewhat more arbitrary usage in the previous accounts I have cited.

> The face resists possession, resists my powers. In its epiphany, in expression, the sensible, still graspable, turns into total resistance to grasp. This mutation can occur only in the opening of a new dimension. For the resistance to the grasp is not produced as an insurmountable resistance, like the hardness of the rock against which the effort of the hand comes to naught, like the remoteness of a star in the immensity of space. The expression the face introduces into the world does not defy the feebleness of my powers, but my ability for power [*mon pouvoir de pouvoir*]. The face, still a thing among things, breaks through the form that nevertheless delimits it. This means concretely: the face speaks to me and thereby invites me to a relation incommensurate with a power exercised, be it enjoyment or knowledge. (197)

For Frost, for Grossman, Scarry, and Bromwich, resistance is inherently oppositional, one force turbulently moving against another. [7] For Levinas, the chief quality of this resistance is its slipperiness, its elusiveness to grasp. If "attestation of oneself is possible only as a face," it is the nature of the face always to elude appropriation by the self and to assume a facing position. The self, then, it may be said, is that face which presents itself as other to the other. The other eludes the grasp of the self because the self is always defined against the ground of what it is not, just as the *I* and the *you* cannot, at any single instant, be appropriated by one subject in discourse. It is this eternal eluding of appropriation, Levinas argues, from which speech springs, and to which all intelligibility is subordinate. This theory, however, is distinct from structuralist and poststructuralist theories of an inherently self-displacing signifier because it posits a relation in the world prior to that between signifier and signified, or between sign and sign. Signification is always secondary to the primary difference between the *I* and the Other [8]; a break separates the *I*, which Levinas aligns with the will, from the intelligible, which he aligns with the other (because it is only with reference to an other that the *I* enters into intelligibility in the first place). The face then is the term Levinas chooses for that which stands at the border of what the *I*-as-will can encompass:

> If the subjectivity were but a deficient mode of being, the distinguishing between will and reason would indeed result in conceiving the will as arbitrary, as a pure and simple negation of an embryonic or virtual reason dormant in an I, and consequently as a negation of that I and a violence in regard to oneself. *If on the contrary the subjectivity is fixed as a separated being in relation with an other absolutely other, the Other, if the face brings the first signification, that is, the very upsurge of the rational, then the will is distinguished fundamentally from the intelligible, which it must not comprehend and into which it must not disappear,* for the intelligibility of this intelligible resides precisely in ethical behavior, that is, in the responsibility to which it invites the will. (218, emphasis added)

The will is not a deficient rationality, but constituted "as a separated being in relation with an other absolutely other." The *I*-as-will maintains and is maintained by this separation, this fundamental distinction. I invoke this claim to show how an alternative relation can be elaborated between the personal and impersonal (for which Levinas' terms are the will and the intelligible, or the subjective and Other). What Levinas seeks to emphasize is not a *value* difference to be established between two categories, but the nature of the *formal* relationship between them. He names this formal relationship an "inevitable orientation":

> The differences between the Other and me do not depend on different "properties" that would be inherent in the "I," on the one hand, and, on the other hand, in the Other, nor on different psychological dispositions which their minds would take on from the encounter. They are due to the I-Other conjuncture, to the inevitable *orientation* of being "starting from oneself" toward "the Other." The priority of this orientation over

the terms that are placed in it (and which cannot arise without this orientation) summarizes the theses of the present work. (215)

It is this orientation and its "priority over the terms that are placed in it"
that best describes the abstract tendency embodied by the "strange resistance"
in the west-running brook. It is what is at work against the west-running current, what *orients* it back towards an east from which it sprang and rushes
away. In giving the poem its title, Frost makes playful reference to that specifically American cultural orientation, that "destiny" manifest in the westward
push across the continent, a push which entailed (in addition to the naming
or re-naming of the landscape's features) an inevitable, eastward yearning back
toward a European "origin." He is, however, making another reference, simultaneously more abstract and more material, toward the poem's spatial orientation on the page. This orientation is the orientation of each line toward its
ending, located (cartographically speaking) at the poem's "eastern limit."[9] The
poem's flowing, its principle of narrative and continuity, is downward and
westward, inhering in its ability to devise, down and to the left or west, ever-
new points of beginning. The eastern or right contour of the poem is that circumscribed by the principle of limit, the limit imposed by metrical pattern,
which is also—because Frost's poem is a meditation on origins and ends, on
"sending up" and "running down"—the fact that we can never be so far away
from our origins as to say that we have lived forever. The poem, in order to be
a poem, must end.

This eastern mark is a mark of radical limit, the formal manifestation of
the end of meaning. It is a poem's way of thematizing that horizon beyond
which it cannot extend but with reference to which it assumes its form. It is a
limit to meaning the poem invites into itself, and which reciprocally invites the
poem, through the line's constraint, into its status as poem. This limit is a principle of verse which by definition can be known only negatively, and stands in
relation to the poem in that way that Levinas' "other-absolutely-other, the
Other" stands in relation to the self. That it simultaneously defeats and constitutes poetic speech is the fundamental thesis on which this argument rests. This
principle is one which I propose to call *the obverse*. I choose *the obverse* for its
dual designation of a face or aspect that simultaneously stands away from what
is in view ("that which answers to something else as its counterpart") while remaining prior and constitutive (as the obverse of "a coin, medal, [or] seal" is the
side "on which the head or principal design is struck [and remains] opposed to
[the] *reverse*" [OED, X, 673]). *The obverse* is the means available to *verse*, sponsored by the fact of line itself, that enables a poem fictively to register gestures
not only of the uncreated, but of *the uncreating* and *the uncreatable* as well, to

modify Blackmur's formulation. The obverse is that which can be known only as the articulations and "reticulations" of resistance, a meddling which works against and gives form to "the universal cataract" "that spends to nothingness," but which (by Frost's leave) brooks no representation.

The phenomena discussed in this book partake of what I call the *obverse.* It is under its auspices that I see each of the poets sharing an undertaking, however widely they may otherwise differ. What I mean to designate by the term, however, is not a procedure or set of procedures, such as minimalism, or abstraction, or even impersonality in any of the ways it has been programmatically adopted by poets in the last century. I seek rather to clarify an aspect of poetic practice that inheres, varying only by degree of visibility, in lyric.[10] I elaborate my account with respect to modernism because it is during the last century that the obverse emerges from a predominantly implicit and unacknowledged position. (Although, of course, the point of view established by modernism makes prior instances visible in any literary period.)

The term, as will be noted, is not one that I employ liberally throughout these chapters. To do so would, I believe, not only colonize the poems with alien terminology, but would too closely align certain strategies in, say, Hardy's poems, with those in Larkin's—whereas, in that instance, Hardy and Larkin employ their crafts with respect to the obverse to significantly different ends. I raise the term over my argument, then, as an orient point, one against which certain ratios of distance and proximity may be triangulated, but which remains remote from the precinct of any particular poet.

Thomas Hardy

Hardy is, I suggest, the first poet to search out—in an extended, even obsessional, undertaking—terms for those regions of experience which by definition defy representation. A fundamental narrative of discovery in Hardy's lyrics is that story whereby such regions are first intimated with fear, then glimpsed, then denied, and finally accepted with recognition and acknowledgment. The first recognition, as I describe in my account of "The Darkling Thrush," is the recognition of an essential difference separating the speaker from his natural surround, that Nature of which the romantics felt the self to be so freely a part. In making this recognition Hardy also encounters a limit to his own contiguity with romanticism, a limit which I describe by considering the evolution of a topos (Landscape with Songbird) as Hardy appropriates it from precursor poems by Shelley, Keats, and Wordsworth. Although Hardy effectively repudiates his affiliation with "the egotistical sublime" or the several tropes comprised by "the pathetic fallacy," he does not, as Stevens later will, seek to give an account of the world *outside* the human world, the world that does not yield itself to human terms of intelligibility. What Hardy finds instead, and seeks tirelessly to account for, is a world irreparably marked by the departure of the human, a world, in short, shaped around an absence.[11]

Confronted with this absence, even the customary offices of poetry falter and break down—particularly the elegiac offices of praise, commemoration, and repair of a rent world. In response to this threat he seeks to devise ways of accounting for these absences, ways that do justice not only to what has been lost—the former lover, the beloved wife—but to the persistent and unshakable fact of the rent into which these objects of love and regard have vanished. What he devises is a way of writing which proceeds not only as a commemorative act of inscription—a writing-in—but also as an effacement, an erasure, a burning away, a displacement, in short, a *writing-out*. Those figures then, for which Hardy searches with greatest intensity, accommodate, or bring together, both presence and absence, signification and meaninglessness, the *here* of inscription and the *there* that stands outside of it, verse and its obverse. Hardy's most powerful figure for his art is the "broken lyre," a damaged instrument, tuned to discord and shaped around an absence, and for these reasons, all the more suited to the poet's purposes.

Wallace Stevens

Like Hardy, Stevens found himself situated uneasily in a world bereft of the consolations of romanticism, but whose modernity he could not embrace wholeheartedly, at least if espousing modernity meant writing in a way that resembled more closely the works of Pound or Eliot or Williams. As had been true for Hardy, this discontent manifested itself in the interrogation of figures for poetic speech, such as birdsong or specific musical instruments (harmonium, blue guitar). There is, however, a fundamental difference between Hardy's and Stevens' approaches. For Hardy, the world was never unmarked by the presence of the human, although this presence was often registered in negative or ghostly ways. Stevens, on the other hand, contemplates a world *wholly alien to the human*. Whereas Hardy had been fascinated with specific *human* absences, a principal fascination in Stevens lies in the absence of any human meaning whatsoever.

This fascination with the absence of the human, as central as it is to Stevens' identity as a poet, in many ways worked against the grain of his sensibility, attuned as it was to the opulence of the world and the exquisitely various sensations it afforded. Both tendencies, working thus against each other, imbue Stevens' work with a quality of unresting dissatisfaction importantly different from, for instance, Larkin's pessimism or Glück's relentlessness. When

Stevens writes "it can never be satisfied, the mind, never" (218), he paradoxically designates a kind of sufficiency in the world's implacable incompleteness—because the experience of desire (in spite of its foundations in lack) is the only state in which the Stevensian mind can achieve full being. This dissatisfaction compels him to carry forward his poetic labors into a powerful late period (to which my chapter gives special attention) and fosters an account of poetic making more subtle and rich than would have been possible had either his most astringent or his most lavish impulses taken the upper hand.

This *via negativa* in his work mortifies the complacencies of both the aesthete and the ascetic. Stevens undertakes to strip away whatever deflects attention from the "Rock" of reality, the *ding an sich,* while at the same time resisting the stony sentimentality of a world from which all value has been willfully withheld. Just as order and disorder in "Connoisseur of Chaos" partake of one another, so too do opulence and poverty, Stevens learns, much complicating his search for a vital primary realm of meaning at the foundation of the world, a primary vigor or "gaiety of language." Unable to locate positively a sponsoring principle for poetic utterance, he seeks out figures for voice that account for its doubleness, its simultaneous poverty and vigor. In this search, his attention turns increasingly toward the limits of speech, toward those moments where speech seems least transparent or least meaningful. In the late poems, this attention is most concentrated, particularly in his consideration of utterances articulated as though *outside* human meaning, in the cry of birds, for instance, or the crepitation of dead leaves agitated by autumn wind.

What I seek to describe is Stevens' deepening interest in a poetics of foreignness. While Hardy writes to give a voice to his lost Emma, a voice that inscribes absence as well as presence, Stevens writes not to establish a place in the world for a lost person but to establish the place within speech for those moments where speech most fails to sponsor human knowing; he writes to find terms for a register "without human meaning, / Without human feeling, a foreign song." It is this *withoutness,* both in the sense of lack and of exteriority, that most manifests the obverse in Stevens' poetry. It is in orientation toward this frontier "beyond human meaning" that Stevens devises a way to describe the "romance" between human intelligibility and those conditions that remain foreign to it.

Philip Larkin

While Larkin, by his own account, claims a deep affinity for the work of Hardy, his own interest in the world beyond or without the human establishes a closer affinity with Stevens' concerns than has been commonly recognized. His chief preoccupation is not (as it had been Hardy's) with the repair of the human world, but with the rupture or corrosion of the "human" as it encounters forces oblivious or inhospitable to its interests. The human world finds itself fundamentally at odds with the absence of care for human concerns that the wider world manifests. Knowledge of this absence of care is for Larkin both unavoidable and violent—violent in the sense that it engenders, within his own sensibility, a destructive relation to those terms of meaning, those primary affirmations, which the mere act of writing poems at all would appear to entail.

It is in this way that Larkin's work is a poetry of damage, not only the damage that the human world sustains, but the damage sustained by poetry itself. This fact is for Larkin both the fundamental impediment to his work and its most fruitful occasion. While this damage is not always explicitly thematized, it remains the primary preoccupation of his work. Even in his more relenting poems, which praise the world's sufficiency to itself, this sufficiency is obtained by the act of the exclusion of the viewer, to the point where Larkin raises as an ideal a poetry of anonymity—not of a poetry of impersonality, where associations to specific persons have been *elided*—but of anonymity, where the poem seeks the *removal* from itself of associations to any persons *whatsoever.* On the other hand, in his *least* relenting poems, the poetry of anonymity—of the removal or occlusion of the human name—gives way to the poetry of effacement and defacement—the violent destruction of the human countenance.

It is in this poetic of effacement that Larkin's poetry extends Hardy's topos of the broken lyre toward a radical extreme. The *there* of Hardy's poetry is a *there* comprehended on a human scale of loss; when Hardy outlines the absence of Emma or his father, his portrayal presumes a world shaped, even constituted, by the care that grief implies. Larkin, on the other hand, draws Hardy toward the non-human extreme of Stevens' world, and undertakes to explore those conditions under which human grief, or human care, are rendered "meaningless," a pivotal Larkinian term. This *there* is the site of the obverse in Larkin's work; Larkin's accomplishment is to apprehend this *there* precisely at the point where the poems most seem to falter, undermine themselves, or lapse into silence. While it is for this formal and political conservatism that Larkin's poems have been both praised and blamed, in this struggle with damage and failure they take a place alongside those projects least contented with the traditional resources of the craft.

Sylvia Plath

If for Hardy the world is by definition a site of human care, and if for Stevens, the central task is to imagine a world beyond human pathos, and if, for Larkin, the task is to write into human meaning an account of meaninglessness and meaning's defeat—for Plath, then, the world is that place in which the term *human* itself breaks down. Her work is, I argue, an extended inquiry into the dismantling of the speaking subject by the very medium wherein it seeks its image. Plath's deepest fascination is with the non-congruity of the *I* with those powers and passions it seems at first to designate. Whereas most critical accounts and debates concerning Plath are based on the primary assumption that her work manifests—successfully or unsuccessfully, justly or scandalously—a selfhood, I suggest that the accomplishment of the poems is to mount a critique of the very notion of a coherent lyric selfhood as mediated by the lyric. Another way of putting this is to say that Plath proposes in her work a theory of the lyric as that medium in which subjectivity surrenders the effect of unitary coherence—whether that coherence is understood in psychological, historical, political, or narrative terms.

Plath's central trope is one of reduction and abstraction, by means of which she refracts the speaking *I* into a variety of componential arrangements as rider and horse, patient and iron lung, Nazi and Jew, engine and track, to name only a few, and numerous others that do not yield themselves to neat dyadic formulation. That the self might be fragmented is an idea neither surprising nor novel, but Plath's accomplishment lies in the detailed account she gives of the *outcome* of this fragmentation of the unitary will. The fragments at first resemble a million filaments or particles, and finally, in their smallness, come to establish a sort of mirroring surface. The *I*, in the very act of confronting its image, comes to the recognition that it has yielded itself to destructive and disintegrative forces at work in the poetic medium.

It is in this complex account of the poetic surface (for which her work is an archive of figures) that Plath arrives at her greatest achievement. While the self, as it approaches the surface of the medium, comes to know itself as divided, the division it discovers is not between object and image, or between original and copy. The division is between a reflection and a *fundamental absence* to be found at the point from which the image seemed at first to derive. To express this formulaically: the central testimony of Plath's work is that the image of the self, the eidetic presence, is orphaned in the medium that sustains it; the recognition of the self, the *I*, in the poetic surface, is simultaneously the recognition that the *I* is not the sign of, but the sole instance of, the cohesion it appears to designate. The *there* then to which Plath's verse is oriented is a *there* located not outside but at the center of the speaking self. It is this origin whose absence forms the "mouth hole," the aperture of enunciation.

Louise Glück

While Plath's poetry is indeed an experiment in extremes, and while it proposes a theory of subjectivity in which the *I* is founded on a radical absence, her work nonetheless manifests an intense longing for the coherent subjectivity it critiques. It is for this reason that her poems narrate the finding and perpetual refinding of the absence, or point of disintegration, into which they stage their own disappearance. This longing gives her work its characteristic eschatological or apocalyptic orientation, where the speaker is always approaching another world, a world beyond, in which the "woman is perfected." Like Plath, Glück mounts a critique of a unitary "selfhood," but Glück cannot espouse Plath's eschatology of extremity. In fact, her first four books narrate, in part, the relinquishing of those presuppositions, postures, and mannerisms that had lent Glück her superficial resemblance to Plath in the first place. The movement that these books trace is the movement away from an apocalyptic worldview toward one more resigned to the persistence of irony and contingency in human experience.

Like Plath, Glück concerns herself with the limits of the will as they are expressed in the lyric, but for her these limitations are not imbued with Plath's dire fatality. For Glück, what the world threatens is not annihilation but the ongoingness of "impassive process"; the *I* of lyric asserts itself not in a flare of self-extinguishing but through a series of subtle negotiations with the things of an implacably worldly world: gardens, flowers, marriages, divorces, cheese shops, and bird's nests, to name some. The sign of transcendental otherness inheres not in the self's extinction but in the elements of the contingent quotidian, those bits and pieces ("souvenirs") that constitute one's memory and experience, but that also insist, as they had in Stevens, on their alien and accidental nature. For this reason a central figure in Glück's poetry is the figure of the dream, because the dream makes itself known simultaneously as a gesture of the deepest passions and as the unwilled emergence of a foreign body within consciousness.

The obverse, then, in Glück's poems, is manifest in the tenacious phenomenological otherness or outsideness of the world in which the speaker dwells. In this regard, her work most resembles Stevens', particularly his concern with the externality of reality and the externality of voice. But unlike Stevens, Glück sees the inner world and its native forces, including the force of imagination, to be an outside in its own right. It is in order to register this otherness, including the otherness of one's own memories, feelings, and mind, that Glück seeks to embody, rather than theorize, the "mereness" of experience. The limits at which Plath and Larkin sought the terms for subjectivity were those at which the mind was most subject to damage or dissolution; the limit toward which Glück inclines is a different limit, the limit of *least* deformation in the stream of the quotidian, the registration of the faintest disturbances and the frailest discords in experience. What she achieves is not so much a minimalism, nor an avowed objectivity or impersonality, but a perspective whereby the speaker comes to know itself—not as it looks at or into the west-running brook—but as it perceives that it is *a part of* the brook itself, a local disturbance in the stream's ongoing flow.

Chapter One
Thomas Hardy: The Broken Lyre

MISMARRIAGES: IMPEDING SUCCESS

Was Hardy an incompetent poet? Ever since he published his first poems, the *yeas* and the *nays* have scrimmaged, and a broad rift has divided his critics. While some have dismissed his work outright, others have argued not only for his goodness but his greatness, and a few have proclaimed him not only great but the greatest.[1] This difference is not merely the natural separation between those who take a writer seriously and those who do not; adjudicatory concerns have preoccupied Hardy's apologists as well, who have sought to distinguish credibly the good poems from the bad. No consensus, however, has emerged, either with regard to the composition of the Hardy canon or to the criteria by which such a canon could be established. For a poet so unshakably installed in the pantheon of English letters, then, the critical assessment is uniquely preoccupied with questions of basic merit. I rate Hardy's poetry among the best of his era; what I propose here, however, is not yet another justification of yet another opinion, but a consideration of *why* evaluative concerns have remained inextricably central to Hardy's critical legacy—for it is, I suggest, the *persistence* of these disputes, and not any final judgment upon them, that illuminates Hardy's uniquely fraught management of his poetic resources. This resistance to evaluative assimilation is one of an array of impediments—formal, thematic, evaluative—with which Hardy's poetry confronts the reader. This chapter will seek neither to remove these impediments in the service of assimilating Hardy's poetry to accepted criteria of value, nor to remove Hardy from acceptance on the grounds that such impediments are unassimilable to such criteria. Rather, it will seek to elucidate certain specific uses to which Hardy puts these impediments, uses unattempted yet in prose or rhyme.

Without pursuing the subtler implications of his formulation, T. S. Eliot perhaps got as near to the problem of Hardy's impediments as anyone has:

> He was indifferent even to the prescripts of good writing: he wrote some-
> times overpowerfully well, but always very carelessly; at times his style
> touches sublimity without ever having passed through the stage of being
> good. (*After Strange Gods*, 54)

Although this is a grudging and isolated admission of merit in a passage otherwise intent upon arraigning Hardy for his "decadence," it does Hardy the
service of segregating his best accomplishments, his "sublimity," from the category of "good writing." To write sublimely, to write "overpowerfully" well,
Eliot implies, is something *qualitatively* different from writing *merely* well; it
is as though one of the virtues of Hardy's achievement is its escape from virtue.
For all Eliot's disdain, he concedes more to Hardy than do many of Hardy's
other detractors (e.g. Richard Ellmann, who dismisses Hardy's poetry as "that
blend of cliché and ineptitude" [34]). More importantly, Eliot concedes more
than many of Hardy's proponents, to the extent that such proponents argue
that his roughness is deployed in the service of verisimilitude, authenticity, or
sincerity—which is to say, in the service of values inextricable from the constitutive values of realism itself. Examples of this argument abound:

> Hardy's awkwardness, whether completely deliberate or inadvertent or
> even a funny mixture, comes from a concern for *authenticity*. It usually
> succeeds when his stylistic concern is subordinated to his concern for
> *exact depiction of his subject*. [. . . .] The small imperfections have their
> own sweetness when they are a genuine part of his subject-matter, be-
> cause they indicate a *faithfulness to its humanity*. (Gunn 101)

> [The poems] show at their best an originality that springs from *deeply felt
> and tested* experience in the ways of human ordeal. Their devices of stanza
> and rhythm, of verbal oddity and surprise, begin to lose the inhibiting ef-
> fect of a personal convention and to take on the qualities of a genuine con-
> tribution to English diction and meter. In their finest development [. . . .]
> they arrive at *an authentic poignance and wholeness of style*. (Zabel 31)

> For the poet to have broken a rule he set such store by is another *"guar-
> antee of integrity."* For nothing but *fidelity to feeling* could have caused
> him to do so. (Davie 26)

> If we speak of Hardy's "ultimate quality," we must mean that *utterly de-
> fenseless sincerity* which never stops to reckon the cost of what must be

said; but in the poems themselves this sincerity is realized through his awkward and drooping rhythms, the music of loss and reconciliation. (Howe 185)

The effect of the poem springs from *the reality of normal everyday experience honestly recorded and felt:* the moment of insight into our relationship to the rhythms of the universe from the unflinching response of Hardy's senses to all facets of the objective world. Lyric ecstasy gives way to *loving fidelity to what he sees and hears;* yet this very devotion to fact produces lyric emotion. [. . . .] In the simple but precise diction, the natural speech rhythms straining against metrical rigidity, in the verse form itself, he has found the means to infect his readers with those intuitions. (Brooks 51)

For his purpose of seeking to make us wonder at the usual, Hardy's harshness of style is invaluable. [. . . .] Lines pronounced with difficulty *reflect* the more than simply verbal difficulties that attend the discovery and expression of truth. The idiosyncrasies of Hardy's poetic style are *perfectly fitted* to convey a sense of the anomalous position, in his view, of consciousness in a universe of nescient striving forces. (Grundy 8, all emphasis mine)

It is easy enough to argue that Hardy is a poet of immense mimetic talent, and easy enough to do so without troubling oneself as to *how* such mimetic effects are achieved. But to say that Hardy's irregularities of style reflect the irregularities of the outer world, or even of his private inner world, is to ignore the fact that Hardy's way of writing disrupts the mimetic surface of his poems as often as it smooths them to perfect-seeming reflectivity. If some state of affairs is being faithfully or authentically represented by his poems, the nature of that state of affairs is assumed rather than defined by his critics. The "exact depiction" of the thrush's *blast-beruffled plume* manifests a "fidelity" to a reality very different from that "honestly recorded" by *the century's corpse outleant* ("The Darkling Thrush," 150).

Something of the problem becomes visible in F. R. Leavis' landmark response to Hardy's poems:

If one says that he seems to have no sensitiveness for words, one recognizes at the same time that he has made a style out of stylelessness. There is something extremely personal about the gauche unshrinking mismarriages—group-mismarriages—of his diction, in which, with naïf aplomb, he takes as they come the romantic-poetical, the prosaic banal, the stilted literary, the colloquial, the archaistic, the erudite, the technical, the dialect word, the brand-new Hardy coinage. (86)

There is one sense in which the word "mismarriages" could not be more right. To read Hardy is very often to contend with discord, with the harsh or forced conjunction of different registers and modes of address, as though the poem were an arena wherein distinct voices or agencies or sensibilities struggled for control. And there is another sense in which "mismarriage" is also xactly right, but an entirely different one. Hardy is, of course, the writer *par excellence* of mismarriage, not only formally, in the tonal disjunctions so characteristic of his work, but thematically as well; one of his greatest and most persistent topics is that of the star-crossed, tragic, misjudged, repented-but-irrevocable union or contract, of which marriage for him is the signal example. And unavoidably, because Hardy was so unhappy in his life with Emma Gifford Hardy, and so unexpectedly torn by her death, the word brims with an intense biographical irony as well. While it is impossible, then, not to take Leavis at his word, it is equally impossible not to take him at *more* than his word. What he offers as an evaluative assessment of Hardy's work becomes instead a description of its most inherent attributes. To say that Hardy's tone is flawed is to suggest how Hardy could have been better; to say that he is a poet of mismarriage is to describe—both merely and complexly—precisely *what he was*.

This local event in Leavis' assessment is not a mere accident or felicitous infelicity of phrase; it is, I suggest, symptomatic of the uniquely complex relation between the limits to Hardy's success and his success. This relation, startling in the intense, pinprick irony of Leavis' term, finds fuller expression in the multiple usages of the term *impediment* itself as it appears in the critical record. Like *mismarriage*, it is employed to denote both a limitation and an inherent attribute to Hardy's poetry. With it, Ellmann assails the poems: "Awkwardness is in him sometimes a kind of inverted narcissism—see how unbeautiful I am!— and a serious impediment to articulation" (34). Davie, with reluctance, concedes that Hardy's impediments compromise the poems: "And yet if this is the nerve of the poem, the hidden form of its unfolding, that form is (I think) not merely hidden and decently cloaked but positively *impeded* by the overt form with its intricate symmetries" (59). Zabel, more approvingly, sees impediment as a crucial pressure against which the poems achieve their success:

> [The poems'] authentic poignance [. . .] is not only a matter of their delicacy of suggestion and tone or their candor in restoring personal appeal to poetry in the face of the impediments which modern sophistication and experiment have set against that appeal. It is a matter of Hardy's gradual mastery of effects: of subtle turns and balances of phrasing, of fine shadings he is able to put on traditional emotions, of the sure hand with which he succeeds in justifying, by the time a poem ends, its apparently faltering progress from stanza to stanza. (395)

The faltering that Zabel sees in the poem is only "apparent," not in the end a limitation to Hardy's "mastery." Similarly, Irving Howe sees the impediment as a point of access to the poem's deepest center: "[. . . .] It is also true that impediments can be energizing, and whatever it is that blocks our profoundest speech may also serve as an agent for releasing it" (176). Samuel Hynes, refuting Ellmann, has given the fullest account of how Hardy's success might derive from his handling of impediments:

> It seems to me that Ellmann is here describing not Hardy's badness, but the central properties of his excellence: that the "narcissism" (which I would call "inwardness" or simply "privacy") creates the essential Hardy relation to reality, and that the "awkwardness," *if it is an impediment to articulation, is a necessary impediment, and creates the essential Hardy relation to language.* (74)

> I suggested, in commenting on Richard Ellmann's remarks, what I thought the true nature of that gift was: that it was a mode of inward discourse, an impeded, unmellifluous articulation of private feelings. (77)

> Though the poems are rooted in the actual, they do not readily reveal its meaning: there are, as Ellmann observed, *impediments.* [. . . .] The best poems have a hovering mysteriousness about them. No doubt this is in part a consequence of the private nature of the discourse. [. . . .] But the mysteriousness is more than simply personal; it is in Hardy's world, which withholds the satisfactions of order and meaning—*the impediment, that is, is out there.* In Hardy's world, feelings exist, but they exist independently of meaning; the subjects of his poems are those feelings, including most prominently the feeling of the absence of meaning. (78)

> "The Division" is not a particularly awkward poem, but it is nevertheless an *"impeded"* one. It says very little, it is not vividly metaphorical, and its language seems strained without being "poetic"—as though the poet had to make do with a small and randomly selected vocabulary, not especially appropriate to the occasion. It has, you might say, a slightly strangulated quality: it is working as hard at not saying things as most poems do at being eloquent. In all of these ways, it is a representative good Hardy poem. (79, all emphasis mine)

Hynes' remarks elaborate the claim that *impediment,* like *mismarriage,* is a word that designates not so much a stylistic or evaluative limitation—a failure in the work—but a pervasive attribute of Hardy's formal and thematic style. The poems are not only impeded *from* success, they are impeded *in their execution* ("working hard at not saying") and lastly *about* impediments.

In the attempt to adapt Hardy's impediments to variously defined categories of "good writing" (those very categories that Eliot placed to one side in his own critique) the critics cited above ignore, perhaps inevitably, how the category "good writing" or "poetic success" must shift in order to accommodate the inclusion of these impediments. What remains to be described, then, is, on the one hand, how Hardy's negotiation of impediments is *not* undertaken in the interest of successful speech or of finding ways in which speech can be made to succeed under the most adverse of conditions, and, on the other, how he devises means for considering and including failures of speech in the fabric of his poems. It is this inclusion and assimilation of *failure* that shows Hardy to be engaged in an aesthetic undertaking more radical than commonly thought, an undertaking whose success inheres in its rupture with those terms of success by which it has so frequently been judged. It is only through such radical means that Hardy is able to offer an account of his experiences of radical impediment. He describes the problem most succinctly in "The Division":

> But that thwart thing betwixt us twain
> Which nothing cleaves or clears,
> Is more than distance, Dear, or rain,
> And longer than the years" (221).

Even if, like Philip Larkin, we would not wish the collected poems a page shorter (*Required Writing* 174), it is difficult to imagine that such vigorous appreciation would not entail an equally vigorous effort to find a way of liking certain poems that are resolutely absurd, forced, bathetic, gawky, bilious, or glib. The separation of the poems into those that hold the interest of a particular reader and those that do not will always be inevitable—and inevitably idiosyncratic. For that reason, I will forgo further discussion of evaluative criteria in favor of a consideration of the central *thematic* impediments in Hardy's poems: pivotal instances of lack, breakage, faltering, loss, blindness, and silence, instances whose relation to successful speech is one of essential or inherent resistance. I give particular attention to poems addressing an absent or unintelligible other, for it is at the point of closest proximity to absence and unintelligibility that Hardy devises his most original strategies to include or assimilate negative presence. The impediment is, I hope to show, the means—not properly a *representational* means—by which the poem bears the mark of its contact with, or derivation from, this realm outside of speech.

BROKEN LYRES: "THE DARKLING THRUSH" AND THE LIMITS OF REFLECTION

If one says that Hardy is a poet of impeded relationships, one must include among these Hardy's complex relationship to his literary inheritance. It is (in part) this relationship to which "The Darkling Thrush," one of Hardy's earliest major poems, addresses itself. In it, the speaker finds himself in a solitary, desolate landscape, a landscape which appears at first to reflect the "fervourless" countenance of its human occupant. This appearance, however, this impression of pathos exhibited by the surroundings themselves, is what the poem ultimately calls into question. The reflective responsiveness of the landscape is broken when an unexpected, surprising bird-voice breaks through the gloom:

> I leant upon a coppice gate
> When Frost was spectre-gray,
> And Winter's dregs made desolate
> The weakening eye of day.
>
> The tangled bine-stems scored the sky
> Like strings of broken lyres,
> And all mankind that haunted nigh
> Had sought their household fires.
>
> The land's sharp features seemed to be
> The Century's corpse outleant,
> His crypt the cloudy canopy,
> The wind his death-lament.
>
> The ancient pulse of germ and birth
> Was shrunken hard and dry,
> And every spirit upon earth
> Seemed fervourless as I.
>
> At once a voice arose among
> The bleak twigs overhead
> In a full-hearted evensong
> Of joy illimited;
>
> An aged thrush, frail, gaunt, and small,
> In blast-beruffled plume,
> Had chosen thus to fling his soul
> Upon the growing gloom.
>
> So little cause for carolings
> Of such ecstatic sound

> Was written on terrestrial things
> Afar or nigh around,
>
> That I could think there trembled through
> His happy good-night air
> Some blessed Hope whereof he knew
> And I was unaware. (150)

Although "The Darkling Thrush" reveals direct kinship to Keats's "Ode to a Nightingale," Shelley's "To a Sky Lark," and the prologue to Book III of *Paradise Lost*, the poem is neither expostulation, effusion, nor ode and falls securely in what Thom Gunn has called the reflective tradition in English lyric (101). In this regard it anticipates Robert Frost's "The Wood-Pile" or "The Oven Bird" and reveals a strong precedent in Wordsworth as well. It is Wordsworth's poem "There Was a Boy" to which "The Darkling Thrush" bears the most striking resemblance. In both poems a person encounters a landscape composed, as it were, of echoes or reflections, and both poems describe a breakdown of this reflecting, reduplicative capacity accompanied by a breakthrough of new awareness:

> There was a Boy; ye knew him well, ye cliffs
> And islands of Winander!—many a time,
> At evening, when the earliest stars began
> To move along the edges of the hills,
> Rising or setting, would he stand alone,
> Beneath the trees, or by the glimmering lake;
> And there, with fingers interwoven, both hands
> Pressed closely palm to palm and to his mouth
> Uplifted, he, as through an instrument,
> Blew mimic hootings to the silent owls,
> That they might answer him.—And they would shout
> Across the watery vale, and shout again,
> Responsive to his call,—with quivering peals,
> And long halloos, and screams, and echoes loud
> Redoubled and redoubled; concourse wild
> Of jocund din! And, when there came a pause
> Of silence such as baffled his best skill:
> Then, sometime, in that silence, while he hung
> Listening, a gentle shock of mild surprise
> Has carried far into his heart the voice
> Of mountain-torrents; or the visible scene
> Would enter unawares into his mind
> With all its solemn imagery, its rocks,
> Its woods, and that uncertain heaven received
> Into the bosom of the steady lake [. . . .] (362)[2]

"There Was a Boy" narrates a shift from one activity to another, or more precisely, from activity to exquisite receptivity, from skill to revelation. The first half of the episode describes a playful technique for engaging owls in a certain form of conversation. By blowing through cupped hands ("as through an instrument") the boy is able to elicit a responsive chorus of hoots and shrieks. When he joins the owls in music thus, the entire vale itself becomes a sort of "instrument," overflowing not only with mimic hootings and authentic "halloos" but with "echoes loud / redoubled and redoubled." For a brief span, nature yields itself to the boy's control. When the owls stop responding, however, the instrument breaks down. At that crucial moment there intrudes "a pause / Of silence, such as baffled his best skill." The silence opens an aperture into which pours the "voice / Of mountain-torrents," and through which "the visible scene" enters "unawares into his mind." Technique at this instant is supplanted by perception, by a deepening and enrichment of consciousness. At first, the boy had called up the cries of the owls as though the cries were extensions of his own voice. That echoing chorus, however, is replaced by the voice of torrents, a voice the boy receives rather than summons. The crucial change that the poem narrates, then, is the one registered in the boy's "heart," not that response elicited from nature at his behest.[3]

This act of in-flowing or reception into the boy's heart is accompanied by, and depicted emblematically, by a parallel act of reception: "that uncertain heaven received / Into the bosom of that steady lake." The relation of skill to willed effect has been replaced by the fixed relation of starlight to its reflection in a smooth lake. The exchange between nature and a reflective consciousness, unsponsored by personality, occurs as though determined by the laws of optics. Wordsworth employs this story, in essence a narrativized pun on the word "reflection," in the service of a fiction of unmediated lyric authority. The heart is as helplessly obliged to receive the impressions of the outer world as the "bosom of the steady lake" is obliged to reflect the stars above it. By extension, the poet who gives utterances to these perceptions, Wordsworth implies, speaks with an inspired, neo-Platonic, objective authority.[4]

Like Wordsworth's poem, "The Darkling Thrush" narrates a central reversal parallel to Wordsworth's, but with a radically different outcome. Just as the boy from Winander turned the wilderness into a din of voices echoing his own, Hardy perceives his surroundings precisely to the degree that they reflect his faltering spirit. He sees the dregs of the ebbing year not only as an emblem for the end of an age—the nineteenth century with all its convulsive progress and violence—but also as a harbinger of his own death. To this degree the scene around him becomes the extension of his own body. Although it is *Hardy's* vision that fails as dusk and late age close around him, he describes day itself as having a "weakening eye." There the "pulse of germ and birth" is "ancient"—not because it is an eternal regenerative force, but because it is the desiccated remnant of an extinguished potency. What subsists is a posthumous lingering, a "haunting" in the "spectre-gray" of winter. Hardy, anticipating the end of his art, sees in the leafless creepers the "strings of broken lyres" and envisions his song drowned in the wind's "death-lament." Thus, it is as much his own sharp-featured form as the body of the century that he sees laid out beneath the leaden sky. These correspondences confirm themselves in the phonetic resonance between the initial, unprepossessing description of the poet, "*leant* upon a *coppice* gate," and the later, phantasmagorical image of "the Century's *corpse* out*leant.*"

The most important resemblance is that which Hardy posits between himself and the thrush; the bird is "aged . . . frail, gaunt, and small," and like Hardy, engaged in "fling[ing] his soul upon the growing gloom." The thrush, however, is happy, or at least seems to be, and it is this difference that prods Hardy out of despair: "If a thrush so like me can manage to sing a full-hearted evensong, then I must allow the possibility that something I know nothing about might justify hope and fervor." But the thrush's song is different from Hardy's not merely because it is cheerier. It is different in kind, and this essential difference places Hardy at the edge of a region radically and disruptively beyond the interpenetrating correspondences of romantic poet and romantic nature. "There Was a Boy" describes a chain of reflections: heaven received into lake, lake received into boy. In "The Darkling Thrush," there is no such continuity of correspondence. In Wordsworth's passage, the pouring-in of sounds and scenes is an expansion of the self toward heaven, even as heaven extends itself into the self. What Hardy encounters in "The Darkling Thrush" is a strangeness that cannot be encoded or reflected, which cannot be assimilated into the tissue of resemblances out of which he has been trying to fashion an image of his despair.

One way of illustrating this is to indicate how Hardy's thrush differs essentially from Shelley's skylark and Keats's nightingale. Although Shelley's bird, like Hardy's, sings outside the capacity of the human poet, the difference for Shelley is one of degree. Shelley wants to get as close as humanly possible to that supernal height of song which is the bird's natural element: "Teach me half the gladness / That thy brain doth know, / Such harmonious madness / From my lips would flow / The world should listen then—as / I am listening now" (229). While it is this unalloyed gladness of the skylark to which the thrush's song most directly alludes, Hardy's poem bears an even fuller resemblance to Keat's. Common attributes include a speaker on the verge of a spiritual swoon, dim and shadowy trees, growing darkness, spectral features, a bird with a soul capable of ecstasies, and finally, a crucial difference between what bird and poet know. For Keats, the desire to take wing with the bird is the desire to "leave the world unseen"—not only to depart unnoticed from earthly responsibilities, but to avert his own gaze from sickness, age, and disaffection. In the end the poem concludes with a cruel separation from the bird's seemingly effortless powers of song and flight, but a different, successful flight has been made on the "viewless wings of poesy" (369): the singer has been praised, a desire has been recorded. Although Keats cannot leave the world of human meaning and enter into the ecstasy of the bird's song, an equivalent of that song has been derived from it in human terms, terms necessarily mournful and bittersweet.

Both Shelley and Keats undertake to show how something of a bird's song can be translated into poetry—disagree though they may on how partial or costly such a translation might prove. Hardy, however, does not endow the bird's song with the transcendent power ascribed to it by Keats and Shelley. In his predecessor's poems, the reader must take for granted that the nightingale and skylark are in fact possessed of ecstasies of intense feeling. They stand as apotheoses of the poets' own desires and abilities, ideal versions of capabilities the poets themselves claim for their medium. It is in this way that ecstasy is part of the poems' *donnée*. The thrush's song , however, is only "ecstatic" insofar as Hardy claims it to be so. Hardy acknowledges that he may be merely *ascribing* ecstasy anthropomorphically to the bird: "So little cause for carolings/ Of such ecstatic *sound* / Was written on terrestrial things / Afar or nigh around / That I *could* think. . . ." By this acknowledgement, he admits the possibility of a fundamental difference between himself and the thrush precisely at that moment where he manifestly disavows the difference. This admission indicates a world outside the landscape of likenesses in which Hardy had sought to establish a correspondence between self and environment. To this degree, "ecstasy" designates literally and etymologically the state of being outside or beside oneself. In the local context of the poem, this ecstasy indicates a world outside of self-resemblance, projection, and simile, a region of meaning explicitly exterior to the poet's assimilating consciousness. At this moment writing itself (as opposed to singing or speaking) assumes a position in the foreground. The attribution of identity breaks down exactly at that moment where Hardy realizes that "So little cause for carolings / [Is] *written* on terrestrial things." Writing becomes an expression for doubt, for an order dubiously imposed or *ascribed* by simile or metaphor. As such, "writing" designates that form of representation which excludes speech even while it points toward it, toward the untranslatable speech of the thrush and its testimony to the possibility of *something else,* the possibility of an awareness essentially different from the awareness of the speaker.

Hardy, then, is drawn toward the thrush's song as much for what it with-holds as for what it suggests. In this way the song takes its place among those voices, traces, and apparitions in Hardy's poetry that resist description and hover on the cusp of intelligibility. The thrush establishes a site in the poem, in the re-flective, reflecting surface of the poem's rhetorical progression, for what reflec-tion and reflectivity cannot accommodate. The mere *designation* of a voice external to the *I*, however, is the point at which "The Darkling Thrush" ends. This affords the poem its clarity and restraint but also its limitation. Hardy ar-rives at his most lasting accomplishment when he moves beyond this point of mere acknowledgment and considers what happens when fundamentally differ-ent worlds intersect, astonish, penetrate, and disquiet one another.

OLD FLAMES AND UNWRITTEN HISTORIES:
BURNING THE DOCUMENT

Hardy, like Frost, takes pains to cultivate the rhetoric of plainspoken fidelity to his immediate surroundings, a rhetoric claiming no loftier virtue than rigorous accountability to the material world. It is possible to appreciate Hardy for noth-ing more than the crisp felicity of his depictions. A description of "hares print[ing] long paces" ("The Haunter," 345) or of a deer peering through a win-dow "fourfooted, tiptoe" ("Fallow Deer at the Lonely House," 598) invites the reader into a moment of bracing assent, where the startling and the precise unite in tingling collusion. In the "Darkling Thrush," the bird's stalwart weathering of the wind's assault "with blast-beruffled plume" solicits unambiguous admira-tion—the tiny victory of his holding on!—ruffled but undaunted! Entire poetic careers have been dedicated to the pursuit of such fine isolated verisimilitudes. But Hardy takes pains to note the private quality of these registrations: each local correspondence denotes not a larger comprehending order (man and thrush united, leaning into the wind of an uncertain future) but a local partic-ularity verging toward hermetic isolation. The final awareness in "The Darkling Thrush" is an *unawareness*, the knowledge of limit rather than a sharing of knowledge. In this inheres Hardy's disconsolateness; for all his attention to nat-ural phenomena, he remains reluctant to read nature as a book of wisdom. He does not find in birdsong a rich figure for poetic craft, as Shelley and Keats had in the past, or as Stevens and Glück would in the future. The dominant figure for his art is the voice of the absent person, lost or dead. "Thoughts of Phena, At News of Her Death," confronts such an absence, and struggles to find in ab-sence itself a form of austere consolation:

> Not a line of writing have I,
> > Not a thread of her hair,

No mark of her late time as dame in her dwelling, whereby
    I may picture her there;
And in vain do I urge my unsight
    To conceive my lost prize
At her close, whom I knew when her dreams were upbrimming with light,
    And with laughter her eyes.

What scenes spread around her last days,
    Sad, shining, or dim?
Did her gifts and compassions enray and enarch her sweet ways
    With an aureate nimb?
Or did life-light decline from her years,
    And mischances control
Her full day-star; unease, or regret, or forebodings, or fears
    Disennoble her soul?

Thus I do but the phantom retain
    Of the maiden of yore
As my relic; yet haply the best of her—fined in my brain
    It may be the more
That no line of her writing have I,
    Nor a thread of her hair,
No mark of her late time as dame in her dwelling, whereby
    I may picture her there. (62)

A "phantom" must stand as the only "relic" of this lost woman. Both of these terms describe something importantly different from memory or recollection. Just as a chip of bone says nothing specific about the saint to whom it once belonged but radiates instead a sanctified and sanctifying presence, this phantom relic manifests mute, indistinct powers. What description the poem does offer tells us nearly nothing of Phena. What she dreamed or why she laughed remain unknown. Hardy argues that this absence may prove a blessing, particularly if life has betrayed Phena's hopes and subjected her dreams to the corrosions of anxiety and doubt. He embraces his ignorance as a protection against knowledge he would rather not have. The poem, then, offers itself as a form of anti-elegy, a shrinking away from knowledge and memory rather than a commemoration.

In a moment that resembles the central discovery of "The Darkling Thrush," Hardy contends once again with a region of experience that writing cannot reach. The line "Not a line of her writing have I" names an absence that seems at first quite dolorous, as if his anguish would be relieved if only he had a single line of her writing, a lock of hair, anything at all. By the end of the poem, however, when he writes "It may be the more / That no line of her writing have I," he fills or covers this absence with his own words. He has, in a literal way, written her out of his life; there is no "picture" of her, only words that protect him from the picture he would rather not see. "Fined" in this context takes on the sense not only of "confined" but of "refined" and the more archaic meaning of "finished, completed." The poem completes a process of purification, purging, and quittance.

When Hardy writes "It may be the more / That no line of her writing have I," what he does not make clear is *why* it would necessarily be "the more." A later poem, "The Photograph," indicates that the "more" of absence might prove in fact to be more than Hardy can endure:

> The flame crept up the portrait line by line
> As it lay on the coals in the silence of night's profound,
> And over the arm's incline,
> And along the marge of the silkwork superfine,
> And gnawed at the delicate bosom's defenseless round.
>
> Then I vented a cry of hurt, and averted my eyes;
> The spectacle was one that I could not bear,
> To my deep and sad surprise;
> But, compelled to heed, I again looked furtivewise
> Till the flame had eaten her breasts, and mouth, and hair.
>
> "Thank God, she is out of it now!" I said at last,
> In a great relief of heart when the thing was done
> That had set my soul aghast,
> And nothing was left of the picture unsheathed from the past
> But the ashen ghost of the card it had figured on.
>
> She was a woman long hid amid packs of years,
> She might have been living or dead; she was lost to my sight,
> And the deed that had nigh drawn tears
> Was done in a casual clearance of life's arrears;
> But I felt as if I had put her to death that night! . . .
>
>   *   *   *
>
> Well; she knew nothing thereof did she survive,
> And suffered nothing if numbered among the dead;
> Yet—yet—if on earth alive
> Did she feel a smart, and with vague strange anguish strive?
> If in heaven, did she smile at me sadly and shake her head? (469)

Like "Thoughts of Phena," "The Photograph" seeks to re-establish an equilibrium sponsored by the absence of the beloved's countenance, the very absence that was at first the cause of anxiety—and like the earlier poem, "The Photograph" concerns an absent souvenir. This absence, however, is not a passive absence but the result of an erasure. The "casual clearance of life's arrears," intended as the deletion of a record or the amortization of a debt, instead backfires alarmingly, overwhelming the speaker with a surge of grief and guilt (recalling Shakespeare's "sad account of fore-bemoaned moan / Which I new pay as if not paid before" [Sonnet 30]). What was meant to be a lessening or a closing out becomes an anguishing inversion of "the more" for which Hardy had expressed his gratitude in "Thoughts of Phena."

The poem appears at first to unfold in two distinct parts or phases, a flaring up and a dying down of feeling, but this backfiring deprives it of simple resolution. The "cry of hurt" and the "deep and sad surprise" are indeed followed by "great relief of heart when the thing was done," but the "ashen ghost" of the card remains a looming source of dread for Hardy. He attempts to justify the act of burning, arguing that the gesture intended nothing more than a "casual clearance," but is reminded anew of his act's painful consequences. Once again, he seeks consolation (she "knew nothing" and "suffered nothing"), but once again ("Yet—yet—") he is beset by doubts. In this way the manifest two-part structure of the poem breaks down into a series of smaller intervals, into a cyclical, unresolved oscillation between attempted consolation and resurgent doubt. This oscillation is compressed to maximum intensity in the poem's central, redoubled conjunction, "Yet—yet—." If the poem were, so to speak, a single "yet" poem, it could be summarized in the sentence, "I was afraid I might have burnt an actual person, yet such a thing is not possible, so I was mistaken." Every "yet" juncture in the poem, however, is followed by a second countervailing "yet": "I thought I might have burnt her, yet that couldn't have happened, yet there remains the possibility that it might have happened, yet that would be a wild surmise" and so on. "Yet," therefore, lends both of its senses to the poem. Implying both "but" and "still," it excludes possibility ("but there is no way she could have felt anything") and admits possibility ("still, somehow, somewhere . . .") at the same time.

The most notable effect of this oscillation is a blurring of the distinction between one sensorium and another. No longer distinct from the woman, Hardy becomes both agent and victim of his own thoughtlessness. At the moment the flame begins to "gnaw at the delicate bosom's defenseless round" it is Hardy who cries and flinches with pain, as though he himself had been burnt. Although it is Hardy who contemplates the woman's immortal soul, his own soul is "set aghast" by the burning. Moreover, this conjunction of "soul" and "aghast" suggests that Hardy himself has undergone a transformation into ghostliness. In this context, the word "ashen" refers doubly to the burnt paper reduced to a fluttering ash and to the anguished countenance of the speaker himself; Hardy, like the card, has been left an "ashen ghost." It is Hardy then and not the woman who ends up feeling the heat of the flame. Conversely, Hardy wonders whether the woman will respond to the photograph in a manner that would be, under less phantasmagorical circumstances, more appropriate to Hardy himself. Had he not been so vulnerable to the harassment of his own imaginings, Hardy and not the woman might merely have smiled and shaken his head upon finding the picture.

By these means Hardy attributes to pain a commutative property. As a consequence, the site of agency in the poem is uncoupled from Hardy's intending will. This dislocation is manifest most visibly in the flame itself. Although at first the flame is merely the means by which Hardy undertakes to destroy a photograph, it quickly assumes an agency of its own. It tears into the image, "creeping" across, "gnawing," and "eating" the breasts, arms, hair, and silk, as though the flame were a monstrously gorging and engorged version of Hardy's own desires. As both a magnification and a distortion of those desires, the flame both stands for and stands away from Hardy's "self-held qualities" ("Not Known," 917). The flame becomes Hardy's agent, but as his agent, it also becomes something that is not Hardy, possessed as though of a will of its own. In this way its action repeats that of the poem itself, which manifests Hardy's voice but also his absence. The troubled autonomy of the flame, and the elision of the difference between writing and burning are in fact thematized centrally within the poem. "The flame [creeps] up the portrait line by line" in a mirror image of the poem's own incremental progress, as it is composed or read, line by line, down the page. Concretely, the poem presents itself as a burning-in or branding, wherein burning and writing are not distinct acts; it is the flame, moving "line by line" that traces the poem's progress. In this way, "The Photograph," like "The Darkling Thrush" and "Thoughts of Phena," foregrounds writing and situates it in an equivocal position, as an act of marking and as an act of exclusion or destruction. Like the flame, writing itself simultaneously extends and overrides the poet's intentions, and like the flame, it is capable both of burning in and burning out an image.

If "The Darkling Thrush" asserted difference between the speaker and an external agency, then "Thoughts of Phena" and "The Photograph" assert the complexity of this difference, a complexity that inheres, Hardy suggests, in the act of writing itself. "The Photograph," because it pivots around a specific, sudden, special occasion, must compress all this complexity into the single nodal point of the "yet—yet—" moment, that access of emotion or apprehension which lifts the speaker out of reflection into wild surmise. It remains for some of Hardy's greatest poems to open this complexity to a closer and more illuminating account—*The Poems of 1912–13*, written after the death of his first wife, Emma Gifford Hardy, and grouped under the heading *Veteris Vestigia Flammae:* "Traces of an Old Flame."

A BURNT CIRCLE: EPITAPH AND ANTI-EPITAPH

In the *Poems of 1912–13*, Hardy is haunted by the memory of his dead wife. The twenty-one poems in the sequence comprise a rough arc, tracking a progression from astonished disbelief and dismay, through anguished encounters with her seeming presence (either as voice or flitting apparition), towards a more resolved acceptance of her death. This loose narrative records the poet's struggle to repair a world after it has been torn by loss. To this degree, it represents a "clearance" similar to that described in "The Photograph." And as in "The Photograph," the "clearance" results not so much in a repair as in a radical complication of the world. The complication is that presented by impeded discourse—an impediment first manifest within the marriage itself, then permanently and cruelly "hardened" by Emma's unexpected death. A just account of loss, Hardy implies, is not the final articulation of what had been unspoken, but a registration, painfully derived, of what must forever remain just beyond the grasp of speech; it is this impediment "past amend" which the sequence seeks simultaneously to resolve and preserve.

The tension between what may and may not be articulated is maintained in part by the central rhetorical tension shaping the sequence's progression, the tension between rhetorics of closure and of irresolution. The dominant rhetoric, as Sacks points out, is toward closure (235 and n. 356). The first poem, "The Going," about the evening preceding Emma's unexpected death, establishes this expectation, tracing in miniature an arc from dismay to resignation. This arc is composed of smaller question-and-response units that mirror the larger pattern of alternating address in the sequence, the poet's repeated turning toward and away from the haunted or fraught absence of his wife:

> Why did you give no hint that night
> That quickly after the morrow's dawn,
> And calmly, as if indifferent quite,
> You would close your term here, up and be gone
> > Where I could not follow
> > With wing of swallow
> To gain one glimpse of you ever anon!
>
> Never to bid good-bye,

Or lip me the softest call,
Or utter a wish for a word, while I
Saw morning harden upon the wall,
Unmoved, unknowing
That your great going
Had place that moment, and altered all.

Why do you make me leave the house
And think for a breath it is you I see
At the end of the alley of bending boughs
Where so often at dusk you used to be;
Till in darkening dankness
The yawning blankness
Of the perspective sickens me!

You were she who abode
By the red-veined rocks far West,
You were the swan-necked one who rode
Along the beetling Beeny Crest,
And, reining nigh me,
Would muse and eye me,
While Life unrolled us its very best.

Why, then, latterly did we not speak,
Did we not think of those days long dead,
And ere your vanishing strive to seek
That time's renewal? We might have said,
'In this bright spring weather
We'll visit together
Those places that once we visited.'

Well, well! All's past amend,
Unchangeable. It must go.
I seem but a dead man held on end
To sink down soon. . . . O you could not know
That such swift fleeing
No soul foreseeing—

Not even I—would undo me so! (338)

In the odd-numbered stanzas, the first two lines in tetrameter address a question to the dead wife. The even-numbered stanzas, beginning with trimeter lines, turn away from this direct address toward more solitary registers, first in a lament for the poet's ignorance, then in elegiac commemoration of Emma's radiant youth, and finally in exhausted resignation to the fact of her death. The questioning lines with their additional foot more closely approximate spoken discourse and presume the possibility of a reply. The shorter, declarative lines, in their terseness, foreclose this possibility and "harden" Hardy's unalterable solitude. It is on this note of grieved resignation that the poem closes. The poem, in this sense, is a poem about fate, and the inability to predict the future. It is a matter of fact, Hardy says, that he could not have foreseen his wife's sudden death; it is a matter of tragedy that he was also unable to have foreseen how deeply he would feel the loss.

Manifestly, it is this tragedy, and this final acceptance of fact, that the *Poems of 1912–13* work through, venturing address, posing questions, acknowledging loss, and assuming an attitude of final resignation, in a larger-scale pattern of turning toward and away from Emma, who appears sometimes as a ghost, sometimes as a memory, sometimes as a sheer absence. This manifest progression, then, is from address to record. After "The Haunter," "The Voice," "His Visitor" (345–7)—the eighth, ninth, and tenth poems in the twenty-one-poem sequence—the woman never speaks again, and the poems strive, or seem to strive, toward a greater reconciliation with loss. In "After a Journey" (349) Hardy accepts the fact that the ghost is a mere apparition, a weaker presence than he'd previously surmised: "Soon you will have, Dear, to vanish from me." In "At Castle Boterel" (351) the apparition is a figure less in the present than in the past:

> And to me, though Time's unflinching rigour,
> In mindless rote, has ruled from sight
> The substance now, one phantom figure
> Remains on the slope, as when that night
>   Saw us alight.

In "Places" Hardy claims outright that these phantasmagorical imaginings are his and his alone: "Nay: one there is to whom these things, / That nobody else's mind calls back / Have a savour that scenes in being lack. . . ." (352). "The Phantom Horsewoman" establishes that the phantom is in fact "A phantom of his own figuring" (353). In "St Launce Revisited" the woman is definitively gone, "banished into naught" (356). Finally, "Where the Picnic Was" locks the past irrevocably into the past (357). The landscape is no longer a disorienting panoply of echoes and resemblances but the site of the past's distinct, extinguished imprint:

> Where we made the fire
> In the summer time
> Of branch and briar
> On the hill to the sea,
> I slowly climb

Through winter mire,
And scan and trace
The forsaken place
Quite readily.

Now a cold wind blows,
And the grass is gray,
But the spot still shows
As a burnt circle—aye,
And stick-ends, charred,
Still strew the sward
Whereon I stand,
Last relic of the band
Who came that day!

Yes, I am here
Just as last year,
And the sea breathes brine
From its strange straight line
Up hither, the same
As when we four came.
—But two have wandered far
From this grassy rise
Into urban roar
Where no picnics are,
And one—has shut her eyes
For evermore. (357)

"Where the Picnic Was" alights at a terminal point. The designation of a stable, specific, commemorative mark marks the extinguishing of the voices, flittings, and glimmerings that haunted Hardy earlier in the sequence. As such,
it stands at the end of a progression toward inscription—not verbal inscription, but the making of a precise, circumscribed imprint. This mark is that
unambiguous designation of mere *site* to which the voices, flittings, and glimmerings have finally been subdued. It marks not only the site where Hardy
and his wife had been, but defines negatively all of the places where Emma is
no longer. The shutting of the eyes that concludes both poem and sequence
is not only the shutting of Emma's eyes by death, but the end, for Hardy, of
his phantasmagorical envisioning. The burnt circle, then, is the closest thing
to an epitaph that the series proposes. Peter Sacks shows how it stands emblematically for the elegiac accomplishment of all the poems: ". . . the
branded circle points to the *flammae*, the passion and its ruin, of which these
elegies have been the vestige" (259). It is in this way that the manifest work of
Poems of 1912–13 has been the conversion of apparition to inscription.

This end point in Hardy's journey, however, turns out to be only the half-way point in the sequence's accomplishment. One may agree that the mark eventually comes to fill or heal the "yawning blankness" that so dismays Hardy in "The Going," but such a formulation does not take into account how the burnt circle is signficant both in what it says and in what it does not say; if it is an inscription, it is an anti-inscription as well. Like "The Photograph," it marks both the burning out and the burning in of a presence. The poems of the sequence have enabled Hardy to write an epitaph without in fact *writing* an epitaph.

The poem that most visibly manifests this conflict between representation and its opposite is "The Voice":

> Woman much missed, how you call to me, call to me,
> Saying that now you are not as you were
> When you had changed from the one who was all to me,
> But as at first, when our day was fair.
>
> Can it be you that I hear? Let me view you, then,
> Standing as when I drew near to the town
> Where you wait for me; yea, as I knew you then,
> Even to the original air-blue gown!
>
> Or is it only the breeze, in its listlessness
> Traveling across the wet mead to me here,
> You being ever dissolved to wan wistlessness,
> Heard no more again far or near?
>
> Thus I: faltering forward,
> Leaves around me falling,
> Wind oozing through the thorn from norward,
> And the woman calling. (346)

In one sense "The Going," the earlier poem recalling Emma's sudden death, conforms to the "yet—yet—" structure of "The Photograph," an invocation of immediate presence followed by its denial, followed by a renewed invocation, coming to rest at last on a final denial. Similarly, "The Voice," turning toward and away from the evanescent presence of the wife, hinges on a key conjunction. This key conjunction, however, is not the "yet" of "The Photograph" but the "And" of the final line; the poem's considerable rhetorical complexity is comprehended in this shift from "or" to "and." At first, tormented by the voice of his beloved, the poet implores her to make herself visible as she once had been. (The "air-blue" of the "gown" suggests, however, that no great difference ever separated "original" woman from substanceless ghost.) But doubt intrudes, and Hardy wonders if he might be hearing nothing more than the breeze, a solvent flux, nothing more than a "listless" response to his own desperate listening. The final stanza, its attenuated form deviating markedly from the preceding three, is both a "faltering" and a moving "forward." In this stanza both the wind *and* the voice are present, forcing Hardy to persist in his journey, gripped between belief and doubt. In "The Going" the movement had been the shifting or strophing back and forth between these two alternatives. In "The Voice" the alternatives exist side by side, enabling the poem to embody Hardy's grief with more nuance than "The Haunter" or "His Visitor" could, based as those poems are on the fictive premise that the dead woman is in fact possessed of a voice. It is not difficult for Hardy to speak in the voice of a ghost; the real problem is how to find terms for a voice that is both present *and* absent at the same time. The burnt circle, that mark which is both inscription and anti-inscription, manifests this tension between presence and absence at a point of maximum compression.

WRITING SHADES

The trope of writing-that-is-not-actually-writing is put forward early in the sequence. The first instance occurs in the second poem, "Your Last Drive," in which Hardy deplores his inability to have "read the writing on [Emma's] face," writing that portended her imminent death. The figure posits a sort of invisible script, present but unreadable; because Emma was to die so soon after the narrated incident, surely something somewhere indicated this fact, even though Hardy knows that he would have been powerless to see it. Hardy is posing for himself a version of the tree-falling-in-forest conundrum. If signs exist, but are invisible, are they properly signs at all? And what are the ramifications of this question for a speaker who is in fact a writer? The problem matters for Hardy precisely because the world in the wake of Emma's death now brims with signs neither wholly intelligible nor unintelligible, neither wholly legible nor illegible, neither wholly present nor absent. Writing, then, particularly when it comes to the writing of an epitaph, strikes Hardy as a peculiarly treacherous medium. By definition too invested in distinctions to depict adequately the rupture of distinction brought about by Emma's death, writing is, in short, too black and white. Faced with this difficulty, Hardy undertakes to write in shades of gray.

Hardy's poetry shows from its earliest instances a preoccupation with the concept of blurred distinctions, of neutral, gray, or intermediate tints. Anticipating by decades the ashen encaustics of "The Photograph," Hardy's early poem "Neutral Tones" evokes in explicitly chromatic terms a landscape whose desolation is both physical and psychological:

> We stood by a pond that winter day,
> And the sun was white, as though chidden of God,
> And a few leaves lay on the starving sod;
> They had fallen from an ash, and were gray.
> [. . . .] (12)

The winter of the poem is not merely a season but the aftermath of devastating divine retribution. Hardy takes pains to specify that the "few leaves" fell from an "ash," as though the leaves were ashes of the "chidden" sun. (The "few leaves" also recall the "few" leaves and the "ashes" of youth in Shakespeare's Sonnet 73.) Love, its fires extinguished, shakes out a pall of ashen grayness over the whole world, although the ash remains the preserving vestige of the flame that produced it. The neutrality of the gray, rather than being the hue of inert indifference, is a field of intense but static tension between the force of passion and passion's inevitable extinction.

In the *Poems of 1912–13*, this grayness is the field of tension between the realms of the ghostly and the actual; in "His Visitor," it is the natural or friendly element of the ghost herself, who speaks the poem:

> I come across from Mellstock while the moon wastes weaker,
> To behold where I lived with you for twenty years and more:
> I shall go in the gray, at the passing of the mail-train,
> And need no setting open of the long familiar door
> As before.

As in "Neutral Tones," the landscape is one of "wastes" and grayness, but in this instance, the gray is the cast of light in which the shade can "come across" into the world of visibility; a sort of mercuric medium, it sponsors, *per amica silentia lunae*, a passage between worlds. The ghost, however, finds that she does not like what she encounters in her formal dwelling:

> The change I notice in my once own quarters!
> A formal-fashioned border where the daisies used to be,
> The rooms new painted, and the pictures altered,
> And other cups and saucers, and no cozy nook for tea
> As with me.
>
> I discern the dim faces of the sleep-wrapt servants;
> They are not those who tended me though feeble hours and strong,
> But strangers quite, who never knew my rule here,

> Who never saw me painting, never heard my softling song
> > Float along.
>
> So I don't want to linger in this re-decked dwelling,
> I feel too uneasy at the contrasts I behold,
> And I make again for Mellstock to return here never,
> And rejoin the roomy silence, and the mute and manifold
> > Souls of old. (347)

When the ghost says, "I feel too uneasy at the contrasts I behold," she is saying she objects not only to the nature of the contrast but the *fact* of contrast in its very essence. The poem is a poem of border-crossing, not only between different realms of being, but between the world of distinctions and a region beyond it, beyond any distinctions whatsoever. Topoi of difference and distinction pervade the poem, in the threshold over which the ghost passes effortlessly, in the "formal-fashioned border" in the garden, in all the specific changes of the "altered" household, and most importantly, the distinction between the world of utterance ("softling song") and the "roomy silence" of "mute" death. In the final stanza the shade makes clear that her greatest relief will be to leave the world of form itself, the world of distinct shape and distinct voice.

The ghost's struggle is in fact a version of Hardy's struggle in the sequence at large, the struggle to depict Emma in terms accountable simultaneously to her form and her formlessness. In "After a Journey" the compromise he devises is the distribution and dissolution of her features in the general features of the landscape, where her "gray eyes, and rose-flush" are absorbed into the colors of the gray and rose-tinted dawn itself and she "[faces] round about [him] everywhere." The greatest negotiation of this challenge, however, occurs in the poem "At Castle Boterel":

> As I drive to the junction of lane and highway,
> And the drizzle bedrenches the waggonette,
> I look behind at the fading byway,
> And see on its slope, now glistening wet,
> > Distinctly yet
>
> Myself and a girlish form benighted
> In dry March weather. We climb the road
> Beside a chaise. We had just alighted
> To ease the sturdy pony's load
> > When he sighed and slowed.
>
> What we did as we climbed, and what we talked of
> Matters not much, nor to what it led,—

Something that life will not be balked of
Without rude reason till hope is dead,
                And feeling fled.

It filled but a minute. But was there ever
A time of such quality, since or before,
In that hill's story? To one mind never,
Though it has been climbed, foot-swift, foot-sore,
                By thousands more.

Primaeval rocks form the road's steep border,
And much have they faced there, first and last,
Of the transitory in Earth's long order;
But what they record in color and cast
                Is—that we two passed.

And to me, though Time's unflinching rigour,
In mindless rote, has ruled from sight
The substance now, one phantom figure
Remains on the slope, as when that night
                Saw us alight.

I look and see it there, shrinking, shrinking,
I look back at it amid the rain
For the very last time; for my sand is sinking,
And I shall traverse old love's domain
                Never again. (351)

Hardy's "look behind" the waggonette concretely enacts his looking back at a fading past. Although that past is obscured by drizzle and the passage of time, he can still "see" himself and a "girlish form" on the slope, "distinctly yet." [5] Later, the girlish form is described as a "phantom figure" (like the "phantom of his own figuring" in "The Phantom Horsewoman") the substance of which has been "ruled from sight." Thus, he both sees her and does not see her. She is distinct "yet," yet indistinct. It is the imprint of this present-absence that the hill receives, recording not in writing but "in color and cast / . . . that we two passed." The passage to which this phrase refers is in fact two passages, the passage that can be recorded or remembered, and the passage into oblivion already made by the "transitory in Earth's long order." Hardy wants the rocks to record not a moment of presence, but the shifting between presence and absence, the gradient, as it were, embodied in the "sinking sands" (and indeed in the slope of the hill itself, which Hardy has just descended). This is the "traversal" that the poem seeks to narrate, a traversal oriented explicitly toward a region outside of writing, a region designated also by the burnt circle in "Where the Picnic Was." What the rocks record in "color and cast" is "that we two passed," a recording distinctly different from "we were here" or "we are here no longer," which is to say, different from a pronouncement made by an epitaph or a line of graffiti. Thus "At Castle Boterel" opens a field of conflict between the thematic recording "in color and cast" that it describes and the written, typographic enactment of the recording itself in the poem, whose verbal constraint entails the requirement that "color and cast" be removed. Color and cast cannot be said properly to record, but require instead an interpreter or rememberer whose memory is evoked by their "quality."

Hardy represents the shifting between presence and absence not merely through assertion (by *declaring* that the rocks make a record), but through a strategy of splitting, a strategy central to other pivotal poems as well. Locally, this splitting opens up a number of dramatically crucial divisions—between the present self and the past self, the viewing self and the visible self, and the visible girlish form and the invisible phantom. It is another instance of this strategy that allows Hardy to hear in "The Voice" both a human call and mere sound in the wind. The fictive predicate of the poems is the coexistence of each split element in the same temporal and dramatic frame. It is in this way that Hardy discovers the deictic act of the poem, the poem's "we were here" to be a split act, in which the point of the *here* reveals itself to be a gradient or traversal toward a delocalized *there*.

Hardy's discovery of this is in fact a rediscovery of the myth of Echo and Narcissus. Hardy alludes manifestly to this myth in "The Voice," both in the woman's call itself and in the echoic attenuation of her call in the progression of the central rhyme: "How you call to me, call to me, all to me." In the spatial orientation of the poems, however, in their overlaying of present and past landscapes, in their depiction of present and absent forms, they invoke the myth on its more essential, formal level, the level at which it comments directly on the essential slippages entailed in self-declaration, in the complex demand placed on a speaker by the question "Is anybody here?" The question is Narcissus's, when he first realizes that he has lost sight of his hunting party. "Here!" Echo replies, her *here* signifying both *here* and *there* (where Narcissus is) and ultimately *nowhere* at all. What Narcissus encounters when he hears this voice is a version of what he encounters in his reflection, the belief that a representation of himself is in fact a separate person, capable of being approached and addressed, not as an image but as an other. The wit of this passage inheres in its self-conscious enactment of the displacement of the site of speech, the phatic "here" presumed at any moment of utterance.

For Narcissus, the act of speaking is not the designation of a specifically localized subjectivity, but the designation of a dislocation inherent in subjectivity. For Hardy, this dislocation is not solely a property of grief, although grief may emphasize it; it is the fate of whosoever undertakes to speak at all. Just as Narcissus's voice is thrown back on him as the voice of Echo, Hardy's projections of memory onto landscape are thrown back upon him as the "yawning blankness" of Emma's absence or as phantoms of his own figuring. And it is precisely a throwing-back of this same kind that the burnt circle, the sequence's terminal image, accomplishes.

While it suggests manifestly that Hardy himself has come "full circle," arriving at acceptance after traversing the haunted territories of his grief, it throws into sudden retrospective emphasis the earlier circle-poem in the series, "A Circular," a poem wholly resistant to resolution and consolation. It is this retrospective thrust that converts the manifest arc of consolation into a cycle of radical unrest:

> As 'legal representative'
> I read a missive not my own,
> On new designs the senders give
> For clothes, in tints as shown.
>
> Here figure blouses, gowns for tea,
> And presentation-trains of state,
> Charming ball-dresses, millinery,
> Warranted up to date.
>
> And this gay-pictured, spring-time shout
> Of Fashion, hails what lady proud?
> Her who before last year ebbed out
> Was costumed in a shroud. (347)

With deceptively mechanical dispatch, this poem treats the trivial but cruel irony that a person's death does not prevent mail from arriving at her address. Each time a circular arrives, Hardy, as "legal representative," is thrust anew into painful awareness of all the things Emma will no longer do—choose blouses, make purchases, drink tea, read, hear, see, or hold. The starkness of this irony recalls the crude ironies of Hardy's *Satires of Circumstance* but resonates with a deeper complexity than those more superficial poems. In fact, it is the circular's very vacuity that imbues it with its weightiest import. With a reticence similar to that of "At Castle Boterel," Hardy explicitly excludes description in favor of the language of the copywriter. The ball-dresses are "charming," but their charm is asserted and not described. The nature of the designs' newness is not revealed. The "tints as shown" are in fact not shown, nor are they named. They "figure here" to the precise degree that they do not figure at all. In this way, the dresses form representational lacunae that mirror Emma's absence. A gap opens between, on the one hand, the words "designs" and "tints," and on the other, the actual designs and tints denoted. "Figured here" in this gap is the unbridgeable distance between the name *Emma* (such as one might write on an envelope) and the absence into which she has passed.

It is this gap that links "A Circular" to better-known poems in the sequence. "The Haunter," "The Voice," and "After a Journey" place between Hardy and the ghost an immovable obstacle to full presence. In "The Haunter" the ghost can hear the man but cannot respond. In "The Voice" Hardy believes he can hear the ghost but cannot see her. In "After a Journey," the ghost is "voiceless" and lacks distinct form. Whereas the limit to full presence in these poems is a fictional or dramatic premise, in "A Circular" the limit is an inherent quality of abstract speech. It is the very writing of the poem, its very ink, so to speak, that excludes from the words "design" and "tint" the specific quality of design or tint. Writing itself manifests the problem of the mourner, the seeming presence of the beloved indicated everywhere and embodied nowhere. In this regard, this poem directly recalls Hamlet's first speech:

> 'Tis not alone my inky cloak, good mother,
> Nor customary suits of solemn black,
> Nor windy suspiration of forced breath,
> No, nor the fruitful river in the eye,
> Nor the dejected 'haviour of the visage,
> Together with all forms, moods, shapes of grief,
> That can denote me truly; these indeed seem,
> For they are actions that a man might play;
> But I have that within which passeth show,
> These but the trappings and the suits of woe. (1674)

The "rose-flush" of Emma's countenance has in the setting and the very writing of this poem hidden itself in the "inky cloak" of the printed circular. For Hardy, however, there is not a clear distinction, as there is for Hamlet, between false surfaces and true denotation. Each of the articles of clothing (costumes and "customary suits" of daily life), along with the circular itself, piece themselves together to form a shroud that both indicates and obscures Emma's departure. This doubleness inheres in the irony of the phrase "costumed in a shroud." The shroud, that fabric or textile concealing the remains of the dead, becomes the text that lends to Emma her only remaining presence now that she herself "passes show."[6]

A central discomfort then that persists through the sequence, and resists the assimilating work of elegy, is this discomfort with writing itself. For Hardy, at this stage in his career, the doubt remains whether what he writes can ever be anything more than the circular he receives as Emma's "legal representative." What if all writing shrouds as much as (or more than) it discloses? What if his medium does not embody the voice of his beloved, but relegates that voice to the suspended condition of "tints" and "designs," shown but not shown? Faced with these radical questions, what the poems strive to "record" is the mark of what they must perforce fail to record. This failure is a special form of incapacity for Hardy, an incapacity which deforms or disrupts the representational surface of the work, occluding its representational transparency. Hardy's most "successful" impediments are those in which this deformation or occlusion achieves the effect of encrypting—and thereby preserving a hold upon—that which it cannot yield to representation. This encryption registers itself as a fault, in the literal sense of a fold, rift, cleft, or crease in the representational field of the poem. It is such a fault, such a crease or cleft, that Hardy's impediments bring into being. The surface of the poetry is damaged because it is within these instances of damage that what cannot be shown can be retained.

The *Poems of 1912–13,* Hardy's greatest poetic achievement, affords him an extended occasion to consider how this act of preservation may inhere within the capacities of poetic speech itself. Having negotiated the unique representational demands that Emma's death placed upon him, he is at this point free to give more abstract consideration to the nature of this damage. To do so he returns to a central trope from "The Darkling Thrush," the trope of the "broken lyre."

EFF-HOLES AND WORM-WOUNDS: DAMAGE AND FIGURATION

Paul de Man, discussing Rilke's poem "Am Rande der Nacht" ("At the Borderline of Night")[7] gives particular attention to the figure of the violin, a figure which appears at first to model a way for the poet to mediate between his subjectivity and an outer "world of things" (33–36). De Man argues that this appearance is illusory; rather than disclosing any inherent relation between poet and world, what it reveals instead is an inherent property of figurative language itself. The violin, then, is ultimately not a metaphor for a relation in the world, but the "metaphor of metaphor":

> The metaphorical entity is not selected because it corresponds analogically
> to the inner experience of a subject but because its structure corresponds

to that of a linguistic figure: the violin is *like* a metaphor because it trans-
forms an interior content into an outward, sonorous "thing." [. . .] The
musical instrument does not represent the subjectivity of a consciousness
but a potential inherent in language: it is the metaphor of a metaphor.
What appears to be the inwardness of things, the hollow inside of the box,
is not a substantial analogy between the self and world of things but a formal and structural analogy between these things and the figural resources
of words. (35)

De Man's reading (and Rilke's poem) depend for their coherence on the violin's perfection as an instrument, not only for the flawless tone of the instrument assumed within the premise of the figure itself, but for its perfect
adaptability *as* a figure to Rilke's and de Man's purposes. The violin, harmo-
nizing between worlds, is in this sense a celestial instrument, its music a version of the perfectly harmonized music of the spheres:

The coming into being of metaphor corresponds point by point to the
apparent description of the object. But it is not surprising that, in evoking the details of the metaphorical instrument or vehicle (the perfect fit
of the string to the box, the openings in the sounding-board, etc.), the
metaphor comes into being before our eyes, since the object has been
chosen exactly for this purpose. The correspondence does not confirm a
hidden unity that exists in the nature of things and of entities; it is rather
like the seamless encasement of the pieces in a puzzle. Perfect adjustment
can take place only because the totality was established beforehand and
in an entirely formal manner. (37)

In sum:

The poem, which first appeared to be a confrontation between man and
nature, is in fact the simulacrum of a description in which the structure
of the described object is that of a figural potential of language.
Moreover, one should not forget that the metaphor of the metaphor is
represented as an acoustical process; the metaphorical object is, literally,
a musical instrument. The perfect encasing of the figures makes language
sing like a violin. (37)

It follows, perforce, for de Man that to sing "like a violin" is to sing perfectly,
its tone by definition sterling like silver, because, in his account, the poem is
perfectly figural, not a figure for something else but a figure for its own figurative process. De Man's account is predicated on a break, that separation or
segregation from referentiality which girds like a moat all literature within the

precinct of the figural order. As Joseph Riddel puts it, "De Man [interprets] literary language as that which forever names the void lying between sign and meaning" (10). What becomes clear in the reading of Hardy proposed here is that de Man could never have derived his particular account of figuration from Hardy's poetry, because the metaphoric instrument for Hardy is in a fundamental sense always broken; a rift does not separate it from "the world of things" but rather traverses it laterally as a fault, the mark of damage. To this degree, "perfect adjustment" and "perfect encasement" are idealized and idealizing terms which Hardy's art cannot countenance. His great poem of "the broken lyre" is "To My Father's Violin":

> Does he want you down there
> In the Nether Glooms where
> The hours may be a dragging load upon him,
> As he hears the axle grind
> Round and round
> Of the great world, in the blind
> Still profound
> Of the night-time? He might liven at the sound
> Of your string, revealing you had not forgone him.
>
> In the gallery west the nave,
> But a few yards from his grave,
> Did you, tucked beneath his chin, to his bowing
> Guide the homely harmony
> Of the quire
> Who for long years strenuously—
> Son and sire—
> Caught the strains that at his fingering low or higher
> From your four thin threads and eff-holes came outflowing.
>
> And, too, what merry tunes
> He would bow at nights or noons
> That chanced to find him bent to lute a measure,
> When he made you speak his heart
> As in dream,
> Without book or music-chart,
> On some theme
> Elusive as a jack-o'-lanthorn's gleam,
> And the psalm of duty shelved for trill of pleasure.
>
> Well, you cannot, alas,
> The barrier overpass
> That screens him in those Mournful Meads hereunder,
> Where no fiddling can be heard

In the glades
Of silentness, no bird
Thrills the shades;
Where no viol is touched for songs or serenades,
No bowing wakes a congregation's wonder.

He must do without you now,
Stir you no more anyhow
To yearning concords taught you in your glory;
While, your strings a tangled wreck,
Once smart drawn,
Ten worm-wounds in your neck,
Purflings wan
With dust-hoar, here alone I sadly con
Your present dumbness, shape your olden story. (451)

Like de Man's Rilkean violin, Hardy's invites self-referential, metapoetic understanding. It cannot, however, be a metaphor of metaphor, a metaphor of language's ability to "sing like a violin," except insofar as that metaphor takes into account the violin's wounds, the damage it sustains. Acknowledgement of this damage is something fundamentally different from acknowledgement of the fact of mortality, the fact of the father's death. It begins, however, with a traditionally elegiac struggle to face death. What starts as a flight of fancy—premised on the notion that a dead person can still enjoy violin music—ends in an unconsoled recognition of mortality. At first, the mode of address presumes that Hardy's father carries on his life in an afterworld. Playing this violin would not so much memorialize the dead as it would provide a diversion for someone locked temporarily, say, in the engine room of a ship, "where he hears the axle grind / round and round." By posing the question of *what* the father might like to hear, the poem turns away from the harsher question of *whether* the father can hear at all. The awareness of death, however, creeps into the poem, announcing itself with a bodily vividness in the physical description of the violin itself. What this description reveals is a stark similarity between the violin's condition and the imagined condition of the father's body once it has been unstrung by death, eaten by worms, and reduced to dust. By the poem's end, to sit in the presence of the violin is to sit, as it were, in the presence of a corpse. The violin does not "speak his heart"; it speaks his absence and his silence.

The violin then, like the song of the darkling thrush, calls Hardy's attention to a realm that writing cannot reach. This division is on the first level the difference between written and improvised music, as printed or "charted" music gives way to improvisation when duty is "shelved" as a psalter might be.

Standing in antithesis to codified duty and printed music is a group of related elements—"heart," "dream," and a "theme / Elusive as a jack-o'-lanthorn's gleam." This indeterminate, heartfelt, flitting theme recalls the *Poems of 1912–13*, particularly "After a Journey," where the ghost disorients Hardy and leads him astray, "facing round about [him] everywhere," or the unquantifiable "color and cast" that the rocks record in "At Castle Boterel." The violin stands for a group of "colors and casts" of experience that writing—the "book" and "chart" and the "story" the poem itself "cons"—can register only negatively. The greater negative presence to which all these smaller instances refer is the negative presence of the dead father. The position the violin "fills" is the father's unfillable absence.

As the poem progresses, then, a predictable slippage occurs, an elision of difference between father and violin. This elision is most visible in the fluid valence of the pronoun "you," which denotes the violin but comes to imply the father as well. Insofar as the violin was the father's instrument, a means of extending the father's living gestures into the world, this displacement is inevitable; it is the father, by means of the violin, who guided the choir, and it is the father who employed the violin to speak his heart. As a mere possession, however, it is not different from any other souvenir, such as the absent "thread of hair" or "line of writing" in "Thoughts of Phena" or the burnt image in "The Photograph." Hardy, however, chooses the violin (and not a letter, or a lock of hair, or a photograph) because the violin's capacity to be touched and played resembles the emotive and sensual capacities of a human being, his responsiveness to the world of sentiment and sensation. In this way, the muteness of the violin corresponds to the deafness of the dead. "No fiddling can be heard" in the underworld not because the "glades / Of silentness" are surrounded by a tune-proof barrier, but because the father himself can hear nothing. "No bird / Thrills the shades," not because Avernus is by etymological definition a place without birds, but because to be a "shade" is to be dispossessed of sensoria. "No viol is touched for songs and serenades" not because violins are prohibited in the "Mournful Meads," but because the dead themselves can no longer touch or be touched. "No bowing wakes . . . wonder" because no one wakes the dead. The violin cannot be "stirred" because the father himself cannot stir. What Hardy imagines in the poem is a violin that shares, as it were, the father's body; what the father feels, the violin feels, and likewise, what the father's body suffers, the violin suffers as well.

Hardy thus ascribes to the violin those very capacities which death has taken from the father. The violin, therefore, stirred to life by a skillful player, could afford the father a sort of afterlife. Such an instrument, like Rilke's violin, would be an Orphic lyre, a poetic instrument, such as one imagined by

Allen Grossman in *The Sighted Singer,* capable of conferring a form of immortality in representation (364). The violin, however, is broken—"unstrung," "wounded," "wan," "hoar," a thing of "dust." The only voice it has is the voice that Hardy, faced with its "present dumbness," furnishes in its stead. Thus, the poetic instrument that the violin figures, is a *damaged* instrument, one subject to the same mortal vulnerabilities to which the father, and all people, are subject; what the violin manifests is not music or resonance but damage itself.

If the violin shares the body of the father, it also shares the body of the poem as well. Likewise, as the violin is unstrung because the father is unstrung by death, the poem too is wounded in its own way. Just as the violin's silence, its brokenness, is of a piece with the silence and brokenness of the dead father, it is also of a piece with the silence of the poem itself, the silence that inheres in its writtenness, in its inability to manifest the "elusive theme" and the "trill of pleasure" which remain always beyond the poem's margin. It is this silence that the poem's foregrounded "holes" figure. At first the "eff-holes," those letters shaped from an absence, appear to be the apertures of utterance of the perfect instrument, as imagined by Rilke and de Man. They suggest the elegiac possibilities for which the poem at first expresses a yearning, the possibility that a hollow or an absence could be converted into a resonant chamber in which the "theme" and the "trill" can take refuge from death and enunciate themselves anew. In the course of the poem, however, the eff-holes in the body of the violin give way to the "worm wounds" in the violin's neck, wounds which are not "out-flowing" apertures of utterance but the mark of the instrument's disrepair. These wounds exchange the outward, overflowing vector of "out-flowing" song for a reverse trajectory directed toward the "netherworld," the "glades / Of silentness," and ultimately the demythologized state of "present dumbness." What had at first seemed to be an open or full throat becomes in the end a neck pierced with grievous wounds.[8]

It is this woundedness that the poem "cicatrizes," to use Larkin's term (*Collected Poems* 184); this writing as cicatrice both records and occludes the wound itself, which is in this instance the wound to speech effected by the father's death. It is not, however, the wound brought about by one loss only that the poem negotiates. Instead, the poem contends at its deepest level with the woundedness of speech as such, which the poetic instrument, as Hardy conceives of it, necessarily makes present. What this woundedness represents, or rather embodies, is a maximal proximity to the body itself, that proximity achievable only when the text bears the marks, and sustains the damage, that the body itself sustains. If the effect that Hardy's impediments secures is still, in the strictest sense, an effect of representation to the extent that it necessarily takes place on the page, then the point within representation at which this effort is secured is that point closest to the opacity and unspeakableness of the body's interior, an opacity and unspeakableness for which death is only the most obvious emblem. The wound, the fault, the impediment, is that way of including this opacity and unspeakableness within the text—or more properly, the texture—of the poem itself.

While later in the century, Larkin will pursue the ramifications of this approach to the outer limits of possibility, and Louise Glück will recall the broken lyre as she undertakes to "make a harp of disaster," it is Wallace Stevens who takes up most directly (although in almost entirely different terms) the topic of the inherent limits to speech, and of the influences and deformations to which these limits subject the poem.

Chapter Two
Wallace Stevens: A Foreign Song

The imaginary map of Hardy's world, as I have described that world in the preceding chapter, is a perforated map, a map that marks, in the most precise terms, *sites* of lack or absence: a particular "yawning blankness," a specific "burnt circle," the exact address where a certain woman may no longer be found. Hardy in this way is an unexportable feature of his landscape; for Hardy, to experience the world is to see it marked indelibly with the "record" of one's passage and to be marked indelibly in return. The basic fictive premise on which his poems rest is the premise that to read Hardy is to imagine oneself with Hardy in his landscape, looking at *that* hill, *that* crossroads, *that* gate. What would the map of Wallace Stevens' world look like? Stevens does not invite his reader, as Hardy does, to witness with him *that* particular scene, to experience *this* particular sensation. You can purchase a package tour to Hardy's Dorset, but what would it mean to pay a visit to Stevens' Key West, his Hartford, or his New Haven? How do you get to Oxidia if "Oxidia is Olympia" (149)? Stevens' world, unlike Hardy's, is not arranged around sites; it is a world oriented toward a *frontier,* an edge or a limit which simultaneously solicits and resists the poet's approach. Although this frontier takes many local names throughout his work, it is in its most basic form the frontier of human meaning, the frontier of the intelligible, specifically the intelligible as it is both extended and withheld in poetic making—which is to say that for Stevens, poetry always has a stake in the "end of the mind" (476). The "ends" that preoccupy Hardy manifest themselves in historical, didactically inflected terms, each soliciting an ethical understanding; Hardy's satisfaction was in learning (and teaching) the hard lesson. Anyone, he suggests, whose fate it was to live a life as long and as disconsolate as his could expect to draw the same conclusions. While Stevens' poetry is no less didactic ("Begin, ephebe . . ." [329]), *his* hard lesson imposes the burden of paradox; while it is true the poet must always be an "ephebe," a "marvelous sophomore" (29) one of the things the ephebe will learn is something about what he cannot learn, cannot know, cannot do with words.

In saying that his poetry is a poetry oriented toward the frontier of the intelligible, I am specifying the place this argument takes in the wider expanse of Stevens criticism. While I believe that Stevens' central interest is in finding terms for his experience of this frontier, I do not join those who say that his poems ultimately assert only their being-in-language, their inherent rhetoricity or figurality.[1] It is I think fundamental to his work to acknowledge this proposition but to resist its embrace; while he sought ways to write an unconsoled poetry, the poetry of a "spirit without a foyer" ("Local Objects" 473)[2], such an assertion entailed for him a kind of negative romanticism, a too-easy elision of the resistance between the "local objects" of the world and "the creations of sound" or of language (274). What would come to be known as a Poststructuralist account was not one in which he could find the "absolute foyer beyond romance" that he sought. Conversely, claiming for Stevens a primary interest in the frontier with the unintelligible places me at a remove from the countervailing argument that describes Stevens as fundamentally a Pragmatist or Epicurean, whose stake in the world—the peculiar pleasures it could afford, the orders it could reveal—cast him in the role of an eccentric Adam dedicated to finding "fresh names" for his "local objects," a tireless tester of the applicability and utility of his hypotheses.[3] This chapter takes a position between these two poles; my fundamental argument is that chief among his local objects, "the few things / For which a fresh name always occurred" is this frontier, the "end of the mind" itself.

The category of the unintelligible that I seek to outline here, then, is that fundamental Beyond toward which Stevens' poetry turns, with increasing urgency and singlemindedness, in the last and strongest years of his writing. Stevens is aware of such a region from early on, but as his career progresses, his interest in theorizing poetic powers of Heroic, Gigantic, or Solar magnitude gives way to a sharpened focus on the poverty, smallness, and withoutness underlying or coinciding with these more massive potentials. Such poverty points toward that region "beyond the last thought" where even the mind's perceptions and the senses themselves have been revoked from "the integrations of feeling" that comprise an identifiable self (476, 473). It is a property of such a radical poverty that it can find no place within the poems themselves; as such, it differs from the other unintelligibles for which Stevens does find a place in his writing, specifically those "unfamiliar escapades: whirroos / And scintillant sizzlings such as children like," the *ohoyahos* and *zay-zays*, the "pleasant outbursts on the ear" that enact an exuberant overflowing of sense into nonsense (377). This nonsense, however, is not the opposite of sense but its elevation into pure gestural expressiveness.[4] Stevens' inclination toward a region truly "beyond human meaning," in spite of early polemical feints in that direction such as "The Snow Man" (8), begins to gather force only in *Transport to Summer,* and attains its final force only in the poems written between 1950 and 1955, some of them not collected until after Stevens' death. For this reason, my focus will be on the last three books and the posthumously collected work.[5] In these late texts Stevens engages the difficult challenge of articulating, in human terms, what a realm beyond human intelligibility might be.

THIS MANGLED, SMUTTED SEMI-WORLD HACKED OUT OF DIRT: STEVENS' TRASH

In "The Darkling Thrush" Hardy draws a boundary between his own awareness and a region beyond it; the thrush's song is the song of the region beyond. In drawing this boundary, Hardy seeks to refute the romantic postulate of a self capable of unlimited expansions outward into nature. While Hardy insists on a difference, however, the gradient of difference that interests him most is that between *similar* terms—between the human and the not-quite human, particularly as the not-quite-human is manifest in the animal and ghostly realms. Stevens' world, like Hardy's, is traversed by a difference, but one that cannot be expressed in terms of similarity or resemblance. He is drawn toward the category of the unassimilably non-human, and therefore suggests a radical deepening of the limit to self-expansion that Hardy insists on in "The Darkling Thrush." (Paradoxically, in offering such an extension, Stevens ends up looking something like a negative image of Wordsworth; against the Wordsworthian capacity for infinite expansion, Stevens propounds a capacity for infinite contraction or particulation.) Wordsworth in "There Was a Boy" describes a scene which could have been labeled "Poet with Birds in Landscape." The subtitle for "The Darkling Thrush" adjusts the formulation to "Landscape with Poet *and* Bird (Not to Be Wholly Confused with Poet)." The scene of Stevens' "No Possum, No Sop, No Taters" could be called "Landscape with Two Crows and No Poet at All, If Such a Thing Can Be Imagined":

> He is not here, the old sun
> As absent as if we were asleep.
>
> The field is frozen. The leaves are dry.
> Bad is final in this light.
>
> In this bleak air the broken stalks
> Have arms without hands. They have trunks

Without legs or, for that, without heads.
They have heads in which a captive cry

Is merely the moving of a tongue.
Snow sparkles like eyesight falling to earth,

Like seeing fallen brightly away.
The leaves hop, scraping on the ground.

It is deep January. The sky is hard.
The stalks are firmly rooted in ice.

It is in this solitude, a syllable,
Out of these gawky flitterings,

Intones its single emptiness,
The savagest hollow of winter-sound.

It is here, in this bad, that we reach
The last purity of the knowledge of good.

The crow looks rusty as he rises up.
Bright is the malice in his eye . . .

One joins him there for company,
But at a distance, in another tree. (261)

Stevens' poem, placed beside Hardy's, reveals itself to be a variation on
Hardy's themes. In "The Darkling Thrush," dated "December 1900," the
speaker cannot help but see in the "land's sharp features" "the century's
corpse outleant"; the poem looks backward into the nineteenth century and
forward into the twentieth. For Stevens this desolate moment of looking
Janus-like into both past and future is the poem's "deep January." Part of the
poverty of Stevens' landscape is a radical solitude, abandoned even by the
sun, a solitude which echoes Hardy's, isolated as he is from the "household
fires" of the surrounding dwellings. The encroaching sightlessness of
Hardy's "weakening eye of day" reappears in Stevens' poem as "eyesight
falling to earth / Like seeing fallen brightly away." The landscape of "The
Darkling Thrush" is a place damaged by an obscure and silencing violence:
"The tangled bine-stems scored the sky / Like strings of broken lyres." This
violence is at work in "No Possum," and the human form itself is not pro-
tected from its ravages. Branches and tree trunks become maimed arms and
torsos: the "arms without hands," the "trunks / Without legs or, for that,
without heads." The figure for poetic voice for Stevens is not a lyre but the

meaningless "moving of a tongue." Both scenes reveal an infertility from which the world, it seems, will never recover. For Hardy "the ancient pulse of germ and birth" is "shrunken hard and dry," while for Stevens the field of fecundity and growth is starkly "frozen," not a field covered in snow, but a depth and expanse of permanent frost: "The stalks are firmly rooted in ice." For each poet, this bleak surround sustains a voice, the voice of the thrush or the voice of the crow, whose "syllable . . . / Intones its single emptiness, / The savagest hollow of winter-sound," and in each voice, the poet finds a kind of minimal companionship. Hardy finds it in his *semblable,* the thrush, "frail, gaunt, and small," and for Stevens it is in the austere company of the crow, although this company is only to be enjoyed at the wary remove offered by a separate tree. As I have suggested in my imaginary subtitle, however, to call the crow a companion is to impose upon the poem a Frostian or Wordsworthian social context that the poem does not invite. "No Possum" takes up the project begun as early as "The Snow Man" (8) and "A Postcard from the Volcano" (128); it is to conceive of a world without Stevens. Sociability is supplanted by the (non-romantic) "solitude" and "bright malice" of the crow, whose cry neither addresses a person, nor proclaims a "Hope," but assumes a position among the fragments of its fragmented world no more replete with sense or intent than the scraping of the leaves or the rattling of the desiccated tongue. One can "join" the crow in this landscape (which is otherwise a bleak testament to the failures of joining and of integration), but to do so, one must become a crow as well, and rise up "at a distance" into an independent "single emptiness." In choosing "single" Stevens endeavors to isolate solitude, removing it from a social field. This "single emptiness," which isolates what is not human, stands in opposition to Wordsworth's, Frost's, or Hardy's solitudes, which serve to isolate the elementally or irreducibly human.

This is not to say that such a landscape resists ethical understanding. To the unrecoverable finality of this "bad" (an adjective amputated from its referent, like all the other parts strewn throughout the poem) Stevens ascribes a "last purity of the knowledge of good." It is an amoral or inhuman good that has infused and valorized the bad, like the brightness that sharpens and vivifies the "malice" of the crow's eye—a Nietzschean gaiety beyond a human understanding of good and evil. The purification that sponsors the "purity" is this purging of romantic sympathy from the world, or more accurately, the cleansing of sympathy itself so that it sponsors a mode of perception that does not confuse "The savagest hollow of winter-sound" with a human meaning. This form of Stevensian sympathy, then, is an attunement to the presence not of a human other but of an explicitly *inhuman* other.[6]

It is both a problem and a boon to Stevens that the world is so prone to fall into parts, that human sympathy is not irreducible but can be factored out into inhuman affinity. At times he recoils from desolation such as he describes in "No Possum"; at other moments he undertakes to ascribe to this desolation a good in its own right, an inhuman but inalienable value. "World without Peculiarity" is a poem of recoiling, one that seeks its solace in the thought that such desolate states are transient and that human meaning, like spring itself, is incapable of permanent absence:

> [. . . .]
> It is the earth itself that is humanity . . .
> He is the inhuman son and she,
> She is the fateful mother, whom he does not know.
>
> She is the day, the walk of the moon
> Among the breathless spices, and sometimes,
> He, too, is human and difference disappears
>
> And the poverty of dirt, the thing upon his breast,
> The hating woman, the meaningless place,
> Become a single being, sure and true. (388)

Perhaps—but the reader's sense of how or why such a transformation should occur is neither "sure" nor "true." "Sometimes" expresses resigned acknowledgement that one must wait, more or less helplessly, for the moment when difference seems "for small reason" to disappear (444). When Stevens is not content with acquiescence, when he engages more vigorously the demands and differences inherent in reality—its persistent meaninglessness, its resistance to integration—he finds himself in the grip of a Manichaean struggle. Devising a set of terms for this struggle—at times violent, at others erotic, at others banal—is the central work of "The Man with the Blue Guitar" (135) and an undertaking which dominates Stevens' attention throughout *Parts of a World*.[7] It is this culture of conflict that incubates one of the most familiar Stevensian figures, the poet-hero: Redwood Roamer, the pine spokesman, MacCullough, Major Man, and the "rugged roy" of "Chocorua to Its Neighbor."

Neither struggle for struggle's sake, however, nor towering, puissant giganticisms are sufficient for Stevens, at least the Stevens who seeks to accomplish for the idea of *repose* what he accomplished for the idea of sympathy—to place it at a remove "beyond romance" like the foyer in "Local Objects." This search for the "serene he had always been approaching" (473) leads him to another strategy for the containment of desolation, in which he devises post-apocalyptic revivifications and magical enlivenings in which the rusty wings of the crow take on more mythic volition as the wings of a resurrected muse. In "God is Good. It is a Beautiful Night" the damage portrayed as unredeemable in "No Possum" is in fact redeemable. Stevens imagines an "absolute foyer beyond" desolation:

> Look round, brown moon, brown bird, as you rise to fly,
> Look round at the head and zither
> On the ground.
>
> Look round you as you start to rise, brown moon,
> At the book and shoe, the rotted rose
> At the door.
>
> This was the place to which you came last night,
> Flew close to, flew to without rising away.
> Now, again,
>
> In your light the head is speaking. It reads the book.
> It becomes the scholar again, seeking celestial
> Rendezvous,
>
> Picking thin music on the rustiest string,
> Squeezing the reddest fragrance from the stump
> Of summer.
>
> The venerable song falls from your fiery wings.
> The song of the great space of your age pierces
> The fresh night. (255)

The obdurate and oxidized qualities of the malicious crow are distributed and mitigated here, appearing as the "brown" plumage of the bird-moon and the "rustiest string" that can still pluck out a tune of "celestial / Rendezvous," whose thin music can still squeeze "the reddest fragrance from the stump / Of summer."[8] Despite its arresting formulations, however, and the subtlety with which it recalls "Phosphor Reading by His Own Light" (240) and anticipates the "intensest rendezvous" of "The Final Soliloquy of the Interior Paramour" (444) the poem fails precisely to the degree that it must appeal, Ezekiel-like, to a celestial breath in order to reassemble the dry bones, the dismemberments, of the world; by no other agency, the poem implies, could the thin music and the litter turn into the "venerable song," the "great space," and the "fresh night" of the final stanza. What is lost is a sense of tension, a sense of the resistance to integration that suffuses the world with a perverse or malicious energy, the joy of "pulling the day to pieces" (185).

Such a force provides the purifying intensity of "No Possum's" "final bad." In "Montrachet-le-Jardin" it is this force that resists the consoling and consolidating affirmations on which the conclusion of "God is Good" rests. It is this force that showers "The Man on the Dump" with such a joyously anarchic and paratactic petal-fall of trash:

> Day creeps down. The moon is creeping up.
> The sun is a corbeil of flowers the moon Blanche
> Places there, a bouquet. Ho-ho . . . the dump is full
> Of images. Days pass like papers from a press.
> The bouquets come here in the papers. So the sun,
> And so the moon, both come, and the janitor's poems
> Of every day, the wrapper on the can of pears,
> The cat in the paper-bag, the corset, the box
> From Esthonia: the tiger chest, for tea.

It is only because the man is on the dump and is a part of the general entropic desolation that he manages not to succumb to revulsion or despair.

> Now, in the time of spring (azaleas, trilliums,
> Myrtle, viburnums, daffodils, blue phlox),
> Between that disgust and this, between the things
> That are on the dump (azaleas and so on)
> And those that will be (azaleas and so on),
> One feels the purifying change. One rejects
> The trash. (185)

"One feels the purifying change" in a purification akin to the encounter with "the last purity of the knowledge of good" in "No Possum." This purification is experienced in rejecting the trash, but this rejection is not the recovered embrace or recuperation of values that had forsaken this landscape, which would make the poem a sort of Stevensian version of Eliot's waste land. Rather, to reject the trash is to turn the trash into trashier trash, to purge it of pathos, whether that pathos is the pathos of *The Waste Land*, of Bartleby's dead letter office, or of the abandoned playthings in Frost's "Directive." This effort can succeed, Stevens suggests, if the extravaganza of entropy can somehow be folded into a display of incipience, a freshening of freshness, and a recovery of the "dewiest dew." Such a freshening inevitably requires an element of irony, in which the poetic voice of the nightingale and the pragmatic voice of the grackle each stand as a critique of the other and reflexively undermine the other's claim to sincere univocal authority. In the syntax of the poem's conclusion, this irony expresses itself in interrogatives, in questions that generate possible replies and possible affirmations, indiscriminately, almost mechanically, "like papers from a press." The answers to each of these questions is an un-convinced "Sort of," "Not really," "Maybe," or "That's plausible, in certain circumstances." What is important is not the affirmation but the generation of profuse possibilities, not what is specified but the vital and ultimately arbitrary act of specifying itself:

> One sits and beats an old tin can, lard pail.
> One beats and beats for that which one believes.
> That's what one wants to get near. Could it after all
> Be merely oneself, as superior as the ear
> To a crow's voice? Did the nightingale torture the ear,
> Pack the heart and scratch the mind? And does the ear
> Solace itself in peevish birds? Is it peace,
> Is it a philosopher's honeymoon, one finds
> On the dump? Is it to sit among mattresses of the dead,
> Bottles, pots, shoes and grass and murmur *aptest eve:*
> Is it to hear the blatter of grackles and say
> *Invisible priest;* is it to eject, to pull
> The day to pieces and cry *stanza my stone?*
> Where was it one first heard of the truth? The the. (185)

For the obsessional intensity of interpretation it has received, the last line rivals the conclusions of "Among School Children" and "The Quaker Graveyard in Nantucket." Bloom comes closest, I feel, to the spirit of Stevens' entropic *copia:*

> I myself would say that "The the" is not a specific experience or a present moment, not oneself in any anti-Transcendental sense, and not a poetry of the irreducible minimum. "The the" is any object whatsoever, outside the self, which is in the process of being taken up again into language. Or, ironically, "The the" is a necessarily failed fresh attempt to avoid figuration, another incipient realization that there are no proper meanings in the language of poetry. (*Climate* 146)[9]

"The the," I suggest, can be read not only as "the *The*," (as it is most often interpreted), not only as a designation and a specification, but as a hesitation, a shying away from the definition promised by the definite article, in short as "the—the—."[10] "The the" enacts a pull backward from designation, away from the image, away from the "pages from a press" which both reveal and bury the poet's words. It is this force that establishes a "strange resistance" to the "universal cataract . . . that spends to nothingness" which Frost describes.[11] By pushing designation back into a realm prior to specificity, prior to intelligibility, Stevens counters the force, to which the dump is a mountainous testament, that pulls all forms of human and natural making out of intelligibility into a state of decay. What is ultimately asserted, to employ Bloom's terminology, is not so much the lack of "proper names in the language of poetry," but the "incipient realizations" accomplished by such a pull away from intelligibility. If all images end up on the dump, then, Stevens dedicates himself to the task of determining how his writing can preserve a degree of "imagelessness," of hesitation on the brink of representation. This is what "the the" accomplishes.

In "Montrachet-le-Jardin" Stevens invites these states of "imagelessness" explicitly into the poem. The poem pivots around a visitation similar to that narrated in "God is Good. It is a Beautiful Night":

> To-night, night's undeciphered murmuring
> Comes close to the prisoner's ear, becomes a throat
> The hand can touch, neither green bronze nor marble,
>
> The hero's throat in which the words are spoken,
> From which the chant comes close upon the ear,
> Out of the hero's being, the deliverer
>
> Delivering the prisoner by his words [. . . .]
>
> He hears the earliest poems of the world
> In which man is the hero. He hears the words,
> Before the speaker's youngest breath is taken! (234)

This hero is heroic because he gives access to the world of infancy or incipience "Before the speaker's youngest breath is taken." To this degree, the hero is a "deliverer," not a decipherer. His role is to release the senses to an early nakedness, a state of innocence prior to representation. The conclusion grapples with the problem of how such an innocence can be expressed in the representational space of the poem:

> Item: The wind is never rounding O
> And, imageless, it is itself the most,
>
> Mouthing its constant smatter throughout space.
> Item: The green fish pensive in green reeds
> Is an absolute. Item: The cataracts
>
> As facts fall like rejuvenating rain,
> Fall down through nakedness to nakedness,
> To the auroral creature musing in the mind.

> Item: Breathe, breathe upon the centre of
> The breath life's latest, thousand senses.
> But let this one sense be the single main.
>
> And yet what good were yesterday's devotions?
> I affirm and then at midnight the great cat
> Leaps quickly from the fireside and is gone. (234)

The wind is "itself the most" precisely because it is "imageless." The challenge for the poet is to find a way to keep the wind a "never rounding O," to preserve within the letter "O" an attribute of voicelessness, of the zero, or the surd. The wind, the spiritus or afflatus prior to spoken voice, maintains thereby its identity and nakedness as fresh fact, not as received idea. It is this unarticulated factuality that sustains the "auroral creature musing in the mind." The minute Stevens formulates this relationship in intelligible terms, however, the minute he "rounds" the O, it becomes a part of "yesterday's devotions" and ends up on the dump. The sense of reality always evades a fixed image; the "great cat" that embodies its force has only stopped by for a visit. At midnight, "Chome! clicks the clock" and it "Leaps quickly from the fireside and is gone." For this reason Stevens dedicates himself to finding a means not of *describing* or *affirming* imagelessness, but of enacting or embodying it.

THE A B C OF BEING AND THE "HERE" OF WRITING

The figure of the wind as a "never rounding O" is a felicitous finding for Stevens, a "mouthing" that is not quite an utterance, a piece of the "constant smatter." Its never-roundingness anticipates the endless flowing of the rivers in "This Solitude of Cataracts" (366), "The Countryman" (368), "Metaphor as Degeneration" (381), and "The River of Rivers in Connecticut" (451). Most importantly, it suggests a certain use that can be made of the elemental forms of written language, the alphabetical elements that maintain themselves in a kind of abstract infancy prior to specific instances of speech. Perhaps, Stevens muses, figures for this incipience are afforded by the figures of the letters themselves, the O's, the X's, the Z's—the A B C's of the poem's printed countenance on the page. This is the literally *literal* "here" of speech toward which Stevens turns in an attempt to locate within the material presence of writing such a primary nakedness. Stevens considers how letters themselves, as the most basic and elemental "particulars" of written speech, might manifest what in "Crude Foyer" he describes as "An innocence of an

absolute" (270). Such an absolute can present itself for consideration only
after one acknowledges that

> [. . . .] we use
> Only the eye as faculty, that the mind
> Is the eye, and that this landscape of the mind
>
> Is a landscape only of the eye; and that
> We are ignorant men incapable
> Of the least, minor, vital metaphor, content,
> At last, there, when it turns out to be here. (270)

The "here" then, in Stevens' most concretely literal of moods, is the "here" of
the page itself, the "landscape only of the eye," the surface that gets looked at
in order to get read. When Stevens pushes the single letter, not articulated into
a unit of sense, to the surface of the poem, he attempts to isolate this moment
of looking prior to the moment of reading. He makes this attempt in the service of creating an undeciphered imagelessness prior to the deciphering which
turns marks on a page into words, sentences, metaphors, and images. "The
Motive for Metaphor" ruminates on the possibility of a primary region, ex-
pressible in alphabetical terms, from which all metaphors derive and deviate,
but which cannot itself be brought into metaphor:

> You like it under the trees in autumn,
> Because everything is half dead.
> The wind moves like a cripple among the leaves
> And repeats words without meaning.
>
> In the same way, you were happy in spring,
> With the half colors of quarter-things,
> The slightly brighter sky, the melting clouds,
> The single bird, the obscure moon—
>
> The obscure moon lighting an obscure world
> Of things that would never be quite expressed,
> Where you yourself were never quite yourself
> And did not want or have to be,
>
> Desiring the exhilarations of changes:
> The motive for metaphor, shrinking from
> The weight of primary noon,
> The A B C of being,
>
> The ruddy temper, the hammer
> Of red and blue, the hard sound—

Steel against intimation—-the sharp flash,
The vital, arrogant, fatal, dominant X. (257)

It is in one's nature to "shrink from / The weight of primary noon," to desire not the fully "expressed" but the "exhilarations of changes," taking refuge in what Stevens called earlier "The Pleasure of Merely Circulating" (120). This safety comes at a cost, and the cost is a lameness—the wind crippled, the words depleted of meaning. A lameness of sensibility, however, serves as an inoculation, a prophylactic wound, a shield against the fatal thrust of "primary noon." Stevens' challenge to himself is to shake free of the anesthetizations of metaphor and step into the brilliance of primary noon, even though to do so is to expose oneself to a danger; as Eliot wrote in "Burnt Norton," "Human kind / Cannot bear very much reality" (*Complete* 172). What "The A B C of being" stands for is a primary parentage, or meaning's primal scene, on which one cannot look without risking the steel and the flash of the *X.* This *X* I take to be the first point of origin, without form and void, from which these original parents first sprang: the *X* that begat the A B C that begat all the words of the world. (In "An Ordinary Evening in New Haven" the *X* is "the big *X* of the returning primitive [405].) For Stevens the *X* is a figure for the "parentage" of human meaning (459), a "parent before thought, before speech" which itself stands outside of, and before, intelligibility ("The Irish Cliffs of Moher" 427).[12]

Of course, by expressing his primary terms alphabetically, Stevens is drawing attention to the fact that states prior to language have to be expressed in linguistic terms, even if those terms are the purely alphabetical "A B C" or the purely algebraic *X.* By using the *X* to denote something that by definition cannot be here in the "here" of speech, Stevens acknowledges the impossibility of finding terms for proto-linguistic phenomena outside of language itself. It has been said that this is the profound moment toward which all Stevens' poems tend, that moment where every imaginary effect is shed to reveal the "primary noon" of the poem's fundamentally linguistic being. Miller seizes the opportunity to take Stevens' literal mode most literally. Referring to "The Rock," (another poem of A's and B's) Miller sees Stevens' work revolving in a frictionless and endless linguistic medium:

Beginning with the word *cure* in "The Rock," the interpreter is led further and further into a labyrinth of branching linguistic connections going back through Whitman and Emerson to Milton, to the Bible, to Aristotle, and behind them into the forking pathways of our Indo-European family of languages. Stevens' poem is an abyss and the filling of the abyss, a chasm and a production of icons of the chasm. Its textual richness opens abyss beneath abyss, beneath each deep a deeper deep, as the reader interrogates its elements and lets each question generate an answer that is another question in its turn. Each question opens another distance, a perspective begun at A that begins again at B, without ever reaching any closer to the constantly receding horizon. Such a poem is incapable of being encompassed in a single logical formulation. It calls forth potentially endless commentaries, each one of which, like this essay, can only formulate and reformulate the poem's receding abysses. The linguistic momentum of the poem generates a corresponding momentum in the commentaries on the poem. (422)

Such a formulation—with its labyrinthine "endlessness," its "constantly receding horizons" valorized as forms of "deepness" and "richness"—excludes from Stevens' sensibility the very conflict upon which the poems themselves are predicated, the "heavy difference" between the "rock" and the "fiction of the leaves" (446), between the "exhilarations of changes" and the "weight of primary noon." What such an account leaves out is Stevens' basic predicate that reality as manifest in the poem is in fact an affair between incompatible realities. In the earlier books, he had sought to theorize and thematize this incompatibility. The later poems, of which "The Motive for Metaphor" is an early example, seek instead to dramatize the incompatibility, to include in the surface of the poem the sort of tear or pucker in speech that can be managed by *writing* X instead of *saying* what X stands for.

What X means for Stevens, then, is not anything that X can be said to mean, which would make X a kind of blank to be filled in with whatever description of the "returning primitive" one's mood should dictate. Even if one acknowledges that any description of reality is by definition at a remove from reality (a leaf that obscures the rock and not the rock itself [446]), such a focus on the (joyous, infinite) possibilities of profusion distracts from the X's inherent opacity, the fact that the X stands for something which it, by definition, cannot be. The X is not a site to be filled with any number of possible substitutions, but the site of a removal, a fundamental absence, by definition undecipherable, imageless, a "never-rounding O" from which the metaphors of the poem stand at an irreducible remove. "From the Packet of Anacharsis" models this negative center in chromatic and schematic terms:

> [. . . .]
> In the punctual centre of all circles white
> Stands truly. The circles nearest to it share
>
> Its color, but less as they receded, impinged
> By difference and then by definition
> As a tone defines itself and separates

> And the circles quicken and crystal colors come
> And flare and Bloom with his vast accumulation
> Stands and regards and repeats the primitive lines. (317)

The blank is both vacuum and source. As a vacuum, it draws description toward itself, though it can never be filled. As a source, it resembles a white-hot solar origin, like "the inconceivable idea of the sun" (329), whose emanations cool first to "difference" and then to "definition," in a small narrative of what happens to the primitive when it falls into the secondary forms of the world; first it is recognized in an alienated, differential state—*that* primitive and not *this* articulable and therefore secondary sense of the world; next it is expressed in whatever speech seems most apt at the time, by Bloom speaking "the floridest reality." These terms do not *reflect* this blank central punctum, but refer to it in an attitude of orientation, arranging themselves around it, descending from it, their attitude an inclination or a "leaning" toward this center.[13] This center is not a site of absence such as one finds everywhere in Hardy's work, but an internal horizon, a blank point of origin, an umbilicus or omphalos. With it, Stevens provides a model for the relation of language to "reality" more apt to his purposes than the imposed model of an infinitely proliferating network of associations and "branching linguistic connections."

ANONYMOUS COLOR AND THE DOMINANT BLANK: THE "RADIAL ASPECT" OF DESIRE

The trope of this central blank, both source and absence, plays a primary role in Stevens' work in the last three books. Such a figure provides a way of designating a "first idea" without having to specify and therefore restrict what this first idea is meant to be. The last long poem that Stevens wrote, "The Sail of Ulysses," locates this central absence at the origin of desire, and concentrically locates desire at the center of all the self's experiences:

> It is the sibyl of the self,
> The self as sibyl, whose diamond,
> Whose chiefest embracing of all wealth
> Is poverty, whose jewel found
> At the exactest central of the earth
> Is need. For this, the sibyl's shape
> Is a blind thing fumbling for its form,
> A form that is lame, a hand, a back,
> A dream too poor, too destitute
> To be remembered, the old shape
> Worn and leaning to nothingness,
> A woman looking down the road,
> A child asleep in its own life. (466)

The self as sibyl is a self of gradients, of inclinations. It is constituted in lack; the central blank in "From the Packet of Anacharsis" appears here, transformed, as the "poverty, whose jewel [is] found / At the exactest central of he earth." The self comes into being oriented toward this poverty, as a "blind thing fumbling for its form." As the passage begins, the self is a blind, unmade thing that directs its fumbling toward a future in which it might achieve its destiny, but Stevens shifts the temporal perspective mid-sentence, and ends by portraying the self as a wasted element of the past, "A dream too poor, too destitute / To be remembered, the old shape / Worn and leaning to nothingness." The self gropes simultaneously toward an unachievable future and an irrecoverable past. If it is in infancy, its infancy is a second childhood, such as that described in "A Discovery of Thought" (459).[14] Self-expression, in this account, always makes reference to this central formlessness, and makes visible that "leaning to nothingness" required by the central poverty of need, that poverty in which the self comes to be. Such expressions, then, all take on what Stevens refers to in "An Ordinary Evening in New Haven" as "a radial aspect." They radiate outward from this central need, figured in that poem as the luminously blank face of the moon. ("It is fatal in the moon and empty there," he writes earlier in section X [402]. Somewhat more benign are "the moon Blanche" in "The Man on the Dump" [185] and "the absent moon" in "Blanche McCarthy" [529].)

> The moon rose in the mind and each thing there
> Picked up its radial aspect in the night,
> Prostrate below the singleness of its will.
>
> That which was public green turned private gray.
> At another time, the radial aspect came
> From a different source. But there was always one:
>
> A century in which everything was part
> Of that century and of its aspect, a personage,
> A man who was the axis of his time,
>
> An image that begot its infantines,
> Imaginary poles whose intelligence
> Streamed over chaos their civilities.
>
> What is the radial aspect of this place,
> This present colony of a colony
> Of colonies, a sense in the changing sense
>
> Of things? A figure like Ecclesiast,
> Rugged and luminous, chants in the dark
> A text that is an answer, though obscure. (408)

"The colony of a colony / Of colonies" takes its place at an extreme periphery. But the very fact of its peripheral location presumes a center. The center, as in "The Sail of Ulysses," is poverty or need. The chant in the dark—the text of "need" and of the self-constituted-in-need—must bear the inflection of this "radial aspect"; inclining toward the inexpressible, it stands "as an answer, though obscure," an imageless or unspeaking image, "an image that begot its infantines."

As anticipated in "From the Packet of Anacharsis," such a passage makes pivotal use of color, particularly color that "shares [the] color" of the "punctual white center of all circles." As a "radial aspect" the face of the earthly surroundings reflects the blank light of the "fatal" moon; thus "public green" turns "to private gray." This "private gray" recalls Hardy's "grays," as in "His Visitor," "Neutral Tones," and "Where the Picnic Was."[15] Hardy's grays in these poems proposed a potential escape from denotation by achieving a "shade" compounded of presence and absence alike. Like Hardy, Stevens is drawn toward registers of meaning that stand on the edge of meaning; "private" here appears as a radial aspect of the privation and withoutness that is the subject of the poem, a privation that includes the privations of meaning or of "intelligence" that result in obscurity and chaos. Shades of gray, however, do not capture Stevens' imagination in the way they capture Hardy's. A brighter spectrum interests Stevens more. Colors, the hues of the visible spectrum, provide Stevens with the means of representing the "radial aspect" of desire in a way that embodies not so much presence and absence (so starkly apparent to Hardy), but the desolation and plenty, the poverty and affluence, which Stevens sees as fundamental to experience. Chromatic effects provide a means of representing scales or spectra of difference distinct from the literally black-and-white effects that make up the surface of writing itself, the surface emphasized whenever Stevens isolates single letters on the page and furloughs them from semantic utility. Chromatic effects seem to hold out the promise of a rich descriptive palette.

The difficulty here arises from the fact that color is not an aspect of writing itself (though it can be a feature of typography, calligraphy, or manuscript illumination). This inescapable fact lends to Stevens' use of color its poignance and complexity. Costello indicates this dynamic in her discussion of Stevens' references to painting in his poetry:

> If we take painting itself (as opposed to this painting or that) as a major analogy, we may identify it with an emotion everywhere in Stevens—a yearning for the conditions of immanence, unity, presentness, and the incarnation of imagination in materiality.

[. . . .]

> Stevens saw the figurative as the root of all thought, and embodiment as
> its irreducible condition. The re-imagined first idea, then, must be a fig-
> ure, not its dependent theory or thought. Painting not only suggested a
> path to immanence not available in poetry (at least in the highly discur-
> sive and rhetorical poetry of Wallace Stevens), it also seemed truer as an
> imitation of thought. (69)

Costello's analysis is more attuned to the subtlety and pathos of Stevens'
"yearning" than much of the literature on the poet's relation to the graphic
arts, tending as this literature does to view the issue too concretely, to take
Stevens too much (or too little) at his word.[16] Because her emphasis is on "the
idea of painting" and not its "technique," an ideal "'not to be realized' but always imagined"(67), she foregrounds the fact that the "yearning" will never in
fact be requited. What appears in her argument is a tension present in Stevens
as well, the tension between the two senses of the word "figure" denoting a
presence both within and outside of language. As Costello describes it, the
painterly *figure,* unmediated by language, is the antidote or "cure" (to use the
pivotal term from "The Rock" [446]) for the metaphorical, rhetorical, linguistic *figurative.* The paradox here, on which Costello does not dwell, inheres
in the fact that the figure itself can never be wholly non-figurative. It can
never be wholly free of the "rhetorician's touch" ("Bouquet of Roses in
Sunlight" 370).

    While it is true that Stevens seeks in the language of color an effect of
"immediateness, unity, and presentness" he seeks as well the poignance of the
fact that "immediateness, unity, and presentness" are most heartbreakingly absent precisely at the moment they are most ardently invoked—at the moment,
for instance, when he wants most to describe "A dirty house in a gutted world
/ A tatter of shadows peaked to white / Smeared with the gold of the opulent
sun" ("A Postcard from the Volcano" 128). The opulence of the sun's gold, in
language, must perforce become a part of the written, the "tatter of [represen-
tational] shadows," which is the poverty of the "gutted house." Whatever opulence anoints the world is an "affluence" that necessarily inheres in "the
poverty of [. . .] words" ("The Planet on the Table" 450). What Stevens' language of color indicates, then, beyond any symbolist value assignable to his
blues, reds, greens, and yellows, are those infinitely variable fluctuations in experience that stand, by definition, *outside* of speech, those phenomena, the
"thousand-leaved" red and green, excluded from the "reflections and repeti-
tions" of speech itself ("Farewell without a Guitar" 461). To the extent that
Stevens' poetry aspires toward the condition of painting, then, it does so in the

full knowledge that painting, as Philip Fisher has pointed out, cannot be quoted (49); it can be described, and it can be named, but it cannot be brought into speech in the way that other speech can be, in the way, say, that Stevens brings lines from "The Lake Isle of Innisfree" into "Page from a Tale" (363).

The issue is not merely a byproduct of the fact that writing is representational, not depictive. It pertains to a deeper difference, the difference between the *immediacy* of sensory perception and the representational and therefore *mediating* role of writing on a page. Thus the tension and resistance between the terms "pure figure" and "figuration" is a subset of the relation between the two meanings of another pivotal term in the poems; this term is "sense," which denotes, on the one hand, the unmediated or unexpressed apprehension of the world through the senses, and on the other, intelligible linguistic signification. Even in poems where the word "sense" does not appear, a large measure of Stevens' undertaking is the attempt to bring these two meanings of "sense" as close together as they can be brought. As is the case with "figure," the closer they come, the greater the tension and resistance between them. It is in the nature of Stevens' work to complicate radically what is meant by so unprepossessing a title as "The Plain Sense of Things":

> After the leaves have fallen, we return
> To a plain sense of things. It is as if
> We had come to an end of the imagination,
> Inanimate in an inert savoir.
>
> It is difficult even to choose the adjective
> For this blank cold, this sadness without cause.
> The great structure has become a minor house.
> No turban walks across the lessened floors.
>
> The greenhouse never so badly needed paint.
> The chimney is fifty years old and slants to one side.
> A fantastic effort has failed, a repetition
> In a repetitiousness of men and flies.
>
> Yet the absence of the imagination had
> Itself to be imagined. The great pond,
> The plain sense of it, without reflections, leaves,
> Mud, water like dirty glass, expressing silence
>
> Of a sort, silence of a rat come out to see,
> The great pond and its waste of the lilies, all this
> Had to be imagined as an inevitable knowledge,
> Required, as a necessity requires. (428)

Flat description is one thing: "The greenhouse never so badly needed paint. /
The chimney is fifty years old and slants to one side." But can it be conceived,
this "plain sense" of the pond, "without reflections" and "expressing silence"?
Which sort of sense is in question? Is the plain sense a plain *meaning*, or an
unmediated apprehension of a scene by the senses, senses uninfluenced by
thought or reflection? Is the plain sense the action of this "requirement," a
sight without elaboration, an "inevitable knowledge" that does not take the
form of human thought, the sight of a "a rat come out to see," a spectator as
inhuman as the crow of bright, malicious eye in "No Possum"? Such questions
show that the "plainness" of this sense, then, is not plain at all; it seems, if anything, to resist immediacy and unimpeded reception. Just as "the absence of
the imagination had / Itself to be imagined," the plainness of plain sense has
to be asserted, declared, ascribed. It is a proposition, not an experience, and
manifests itself not as an ease or a transparency but as the difficulty of choosing "the adjective / For this blank cold."

The primary conflict in Stevens, then, is not between sense and nonsense, or between presence and absence as such, but between referential sense-
meaning and the perceptually *sensed*. "Bouquet of Roses in Sunlight"
confronts the tension most directly:

> Say that it is a crude effect, black reds,
> Pink yellows, orange whites, too much as they are
> To be anything else in the sunlight of the room,
>
> Too much as they are to be changed by metaphor,
> Too actual, things that in being real
> Make any imaginings of them lesser things.
>
> And yet this effect is a consequence of the way
> We feel and, therefore, is not real, except
> In our sense of it, our sense of the fertilest red,
>
> Of yellow as first color and of white,
> In which the sense lies still, as a man lies,
> Enormous, in a completing of his truth.
>
> Our sense of these things changes and they change,
> Not as in metaphor, but in our sense
> Of them. So sense exceeds all metaphor.
>
> It exceeds the heavy changes of the light.
> It is like a flow of meanings with no speech
> And of as many meanings as of men.

> We are two that use the roses as we are,
> In seeing them. This is what makes them seem
> So far beyond the rhetorician's touch. (370)

The poem opens with a claim for the privilege of designation over metaphor. Colors can be specified with exquisite precision: a hue of red so dark it recedes to black in the rose's shadowy interior, or a hue you can make by adding one drop of orange to a gallon of titanium white, or a yellow "pinked out pastily" (401) sold by Benjamin Moore as yellow #2170–60. Stevens implies here, in his plain propounding, that metaphor can in fact be circumvented. He suggests that sense can achieve a sort of zero-degree uninflected fidelity. The challenge for the poet is solely to find designations as precise as the perceptions they specify. In this plain sense, one does not interpret the colors of the roses so much as make "use" of them: "We are two that use the roses as we are." The senses are the instruments of the experiences they register, passive recipients of "an inevitable knowledge." Stevens encourages the reader's assent—that through a speech as plain as this, a plain "sense" can in fact be achieved, that the poem can attain a clarity in which we are visible "as we are." Because the poem invites the understanding that such a clarity is within our grasp, on the page, I take the "we" of the antepenultimate line to refer to the coupling of speaker and reader. A poem such as this is a means of making use of the roses, and if such a use is properly made, then the poem engages us, speaker and reader, "as we are." Engaged thus, "as we are," we perceive, through the poem, the roses as they are, disclosed wholly to our senses. It is this basic, uninflecting *as* that mediates the "plain sense of things" as Stevens undertakes to define it here. This basic clarity between speaker and reader is the basic clarity which, for Charles Altieri, the late poems achieve:

> The *as* literally produces resemblances, affords shifts in the level of discourse, and allows us to entertain provisional sympathies with a variety of attitudes. We see our seeing of *x* as *y*. Within such self-consciousness, the abstract *as* refers directly to the way poetry crosses life, because it names the state of equivalence basic to all acts of valuing. Reading becomes a paradigmatic form for such valuing: In the equivalences it provides we take on other identities and observe ourselves as we so dispose our wills. ("Why Stevens Must Be Abstract" 106)

Reading, for Altieri, is the model of a primary relation, a "stubborn literacy, an intelligence" (387), that links plain referential sense with plain perceptual sense.

> The reading motif allows Stevens the plain propoundings of his last poems because it shifts the burden of lyricism from the confections of metaphor to the simple, self-reflexive process of aligning ourselves to the unfoldings of a speech anyone can speak. (111)

Altieri places the greatest store in the possibility of alignment, of a "simple . . . speech anyone can speak." This basic *as* for him does not participate in the "confections of metaphor" but establishes states of "basic equivalence." Certainly this is the rhetorical accomplishment of Stevens in poems such as "Bouquet of Roses in Sunlight" and "The Plain Sense of Things," but that is the problem; the accomplishment is still a rhetorical one, the *sense* of a plain sense of things; the roses only *seem* "so far beyond the rhetorician's touch." What such an account necessarily omits is full consideration of a line such as "a flow of meanings with no speech" or a phrase such as "expressing silence." To say that reading is the paradigmatic relation is to avoid those other relations that are not mediated by the intelligibility required in acts of reading. Although reading remains a central trope through the final poems, its role is shaped by those experiences which do not conform to its logic; it stands in contrast to other acts, acts of looking and listening, in which the clarity of being "as we are," in a state of mutual intelligibility, gives way to a perception of the world "as it is," not as it discloses itself but as it remains enclosed, opaque, and remote.

INTELLIGIBLE TWITTERING AND
UNINTELLIGIBLE THOUGHT: STEVENS' BIRDSONG

The language of color, for Stevens, does not in the long run afford him the best figure for the "primaries" of the world precisely because it foregrounds the mediation of language even as it holds out the promise of an unmediated sensual presence. From the vantage of the late poems, color effects can in fact seem "crude," an exertion simultaneously clumsy and fastidious, an illustration of the obstacles inherent in a "fauvist poetics." It is as though the early poems concealed a frustrated and naïve desire to express themselves in purely visual terms, to meet the reader outside of writing in a realm of an intenser rendezvous. The late poems, however, reveal a desire to achieve a different elemental register, not one of the eye but of the ear, the clarity not of "white, / In which the sense lies still, as a man lies, / Enormous, in a completing of his truth," but the clarity of a cry before it reaches the intelligibility of speech. Such a cry, Stevens comes to feel, is closer to that "flow of meanings with no speech" that he had sought in the visual. Stevens approaches this cry in his treatment of the trope of birdsong.

Keats's nightingale and Shelley's skylark are never very far in the background when Stevens includes birdsong in his poems, and, as I have suggested, the crow in "No Possum" recalls Hardy's thrush as well. However, two other poems of birdsong by post-Romantic writers more directly address Stevens' concerns in his last decade: Frost's "The Oven-bird" and Yeats's "Cuchulain Comforted." In Yeats's poem, a shade bids the dead Cuchulain, a man "violent and famous," to make a shroud, joining the dead in accordance with their "ancient rule." The shade concludes:

> "We thread the needles' eye and all we do
> All must together do." That done, the man
> Took up the nearest and began to sew.
>
> "Now we shall sing and sing the best we can
> But first you must be told our character:
> Convicted cowards all by kindred slain
>
> Or driven from home and left to die in fear."
> They sang but had nor human notes nor words,
> Though all was done in common as before,
>
> They had changed their throats and had the throats of birds. (332)

Yeats asserts the importance of an "ancient rule" in the poem, a fixed, transcendental tradition, adherence to which secures a degree of ease for the dead. Yeats imagines song as persisting beyond the grave, but in the radically impersonal form of the shades' gibbering; the underworld scene permits him to stage in pure, classical terms a drama that plays itself out in violence and disorder in the mortal world, namely the struggle between the interests of the mortal individual and the interests of the non-mortal collective. Participation in the immortal collective requires—"as a necessity requires"—the surrender of the voice of human particularity: what was done in common "as before" survives, but human notes and words do not. Stevens, on the other hand, does not share Yeats's faith in either the aristocratic collective or the transcendental coherence of "ancient rule"; it is precisely this sort of transcendental national mythology that Stevens, in his particular species of Americanness, repudiates. What he does share is an interest in the category of song as it may persist outside of the realm of "human notes and words." He joins Yeats in the effort to place *song* outside of the category of human meanings.

If Yeats employs birdsong in the underworld as a figure for the *elevation* of song to a radically impersonal level, Frost's sonnet of birdsong is equally radical in its anti-transcendentalist, anti-elevationist claims:

There is a singer everyone has heard,
Loud, a mid-summer and a mid-wood bird,
Who makes the solid tree trunks sound again.
He says that leaves are old and that for flowers
Mid-summer is to spring as one to ten.
He says the early petal-fall is past
When pear and cherry bloom went down in showers
On sunny days a moment overcast:
And comes that other fall we name the fall.
He says the highway dust is over all.
The bird would cease and be as other birds
But that he knows in singing not to sing.
The question that he frames in all but words
Is what to make of a diminished thing. (119)

For Frost, the moral imperative is uttered not by a shade in the underworld but by "a singer everyone has heard." The world of the oven-bird is not posthumous but post-lapsarian; he is the native singer of a world exiled from spring's Eden.[17] Insofar as his admonition is a variation of *tempus fugit*, the oven-bird resembles the speaker of "Provide, Provide," but he is most Stevensian in that "he knows in singing not to sing." Such knowledge recalls the knowledge of the shades in Yeats's underworld, as though the oven-bird has "changed his throat" in order to sing in the otherwise silent mid-summer. Stevens and Frost share an interest in a kind of singing—or non-singing—that manages to sustain itself where one would expect "no bird" (as Hardy said) to "thrill the shades" (451). While for Frost, the diminishment in the last line is the diminishment of summer and of the possibilities for desire's fulfillment, Stevens concerns himself with a more radical form of diminishment, the diminishment of the self not only with respect to its expectations or its belief in "blessed Hopes," but with respect to its very presence in the world. It is toward this extremity of diminishment, that point at which the voice has been reduced to a mere cry, that Stevens presses his late poems.

This is not to say that Stevens makes no use of the trope of birdsong until late in his career. On the contrary, as early as "Invective Against Swans" (3), the second poem in *Harmonium*, Stevens is hard at work exploring its figurative capacities, and not only as a figure for full-throated song, as might befit a younger poet, but as a figure for types of diminishment. Moreover, one could even say that his most resplendent birds, such as that "parakeet of parakeets," "The Bird with the Coppery, Keen Claws," (65) or the peacocks in "Domination of Black" (7) are birds of diminishment—to the extent that they represent earthly manifestations of an anti-transcendentalist vigor. In fact, it is this rhetoric of diminishment (and in the early poems, of deflation) that lends these poems their polemical edge. In "Invective Against Swans," to the "bland motions" of the swans he contrasts the irreverent ministrations of the crows, "anointing the statues with their dirt." To the "holy hush" of the Holy Spirit in "Sunday Morning" he opposes "the green freedom of a cocka-too" and the "ambiguous undulations" of the pigeons in "casual flocks" (56). In "Autumn Refrain," to the "measureless measures" of "words about the nightingale" he opposes the song of grackles, whose voices linger in the evening as a "skreaking and skrittering residuum" (129). In this latter poem, when Stevens writes that the night's "stillness is all in the key of that desolate sound," he intends "stillness" in two senses, "stillness" as the serene quiet that descends upon the autumnal American landscape once European Tradition has been devalued to the point of worthlessness, and as a "residuum," some-thing that "still" remains, a kind of graceless cultural reverberation that per-sists even after the grackles are gone. (The sound is "desolate" because it is the sound both of a lingering and an evacuation.)

In Stevens' late period, however, he strives to move away from such relatively strident contentions; he no longer argues from a vantage that looks out over the possible futures of poetry (futures, he hopes, not too glut-ted with imported birds). Rather, the view from the last years is almost en-tirely of the past: "It makes so little difference, at so much more / Than seventy, where one looks, one has been there before" ("Long and Sluggish Lines" 442).

Stevens' concern, then, with finding the appropriate American bird, the grackle or the rooster of Oklahoman twang, gives way to an interest in finding a bird for a different locale, the "here" of present reality—not a "here" defined culturally in contrast to the "there" of European heritage, but as it makes itself known in the more seasonal and universal phenomena of springtime, sexual desire, advancing age, and awareness of mortality. He shifts his focus from birds of stark, rural, primitive vigor and those of flar-ing, splendiferous plumage to backyard birds, birds that sing, it seems, "be-yond the rhetorician's touch." This shift dispatches Stevens down the path of one of the most remarkable asceses in twentieth-century poetry, his at-tempt to strip voice itself down to what he had referred to in "The Comedian as the Letter C" as its "fecund minimum" (29). This ascesis, however, is not one that Stevens pursues without ambivalence. For a poet with such a strong ascetic bent, his stake in scenes of opulence is enormous. Canto VI of "It Must Change" in *Notes Toward a Supreme Fiction* describes the anxiety that a poet of opulence faces as he seeks out terms for the poverty of the local quotidian.

Bethou me, said sparrow, to the crackled blade,
And you, and you, bethou me as you blow,
When in my coppice you behold me be.

Ah, ké! the bloody wren, the felon jay,
Ké-ké, the jug throated robin pouring out,
Bethou, bethou, bethou me in my glade.

There was such idiot minstrelsy in rain,
So many clappers going without bells,
That these bethous compose a heavenly gong.

One voice repeating, one tireless chorister,
The phrases of a single phrase, ké-ké,
A single text, granite monotony,

One sole face, like a photograph of fate,
Glass-blower's destiny, bloodless episcopus,
Eye without lid, mind without any dream—

These are of minstrels lacking minstrelsy,
Of an earth in which the first leaf is the tale
Of leaves, in which the sparrow is a bird

Of stone, that never changes. Bethou him, you
And you, bethou him and bethou. It is
A sound like any other. It will end. (340)

Stevens is suspicious of the sort of satisfaction that the sparrow's voice prof-
fers, (a satisfaction of which he is less skeptical in the first sections of "Certain
Phenomena of Sound" [255] and, momentarily, in "Things of August"
[417]). The "granite monotony" of the sparrow's song becomes a part of what
Stevens most dreads in "The Plain Sense of Things," "a repetition / In a repetitiousness of men and flies" (428). The sparrow solicits intimate address, but
such a solicitation, Stevens argues, entails a threat, a memento mori, hollowing the world's countenance to a bloodless and lidless skull-like stare. [18] As a
memento mori, the sparrow numbers itself among "the tutoyers of tragedy"
("The Beginning" 368). This is the fatal flaw in the myth of total artlessness;
the poet is faced with the challenge of finding a "fecund minimum" that does
not degenerate into the petrifications of monotony.

For this "fecund minimum" Stevens considers other varieties of birdsong. The alternative voice toward which he first turns is the voice of the
dove; its simplicity, it seems, entails song's minimum element, but without
the lifeless insistence of the sparrow's or the wren's bethouing *ké-ké*. The

dove, the bird of Venus, sings "rou-cou" not in "a single phrase" as the sparrow or wren had; instead, its voice is a "copular" or coupling (*cou*-pling?) of the simplest sound and the simplest desire (339). As the minimum articulation of desire, it is prior to desire for any one thing or person,[19] and desire, in turn (constituted in need) is the minimum condition of "sense," the means in which the self apprehends and comes to know the world. (For Stevens the engagement between imagination and reality is never without its erotic inflection: "The employer and employee contend / Combat, compose their droll affair" ["The Man With the Blue Guitar" 149].) The dove's song, because desire is constituted in difference, is therefore the opposite of the sparrow's monotony. However, in its two-dimensional simplicity, it nevertheless manifests a special form of meaninglessness, a sense purely sensual, its *bethou* that of intimate touch not of intimate address. "Song of Fixed Accord," not in itself a successful poem, articulates the uninflected but desirous "ordinariness" of the dove:

> Rou-cou spoke the dove,
> Like the sooth lord of sorrow,
> Of sooth love and sorrow,
> And a hail-bow, hail-bow,
> To this morrow.
>
> She lay upon the roof,
> A little wet of wing and woe,
> And she rou-ed there,
> Softly she piped among the suns,
> And their ordinary glare,
>
> The sun of five, the sun of six,
> Their ordinariness,
> And the ordinariness of seven,
> Which she accepted,
> Like a fixed heaven,
>
> Not subject to change . . .
> Day's invisible beginner,
> The lord of love and of sooth sorrow,
> Lay on the roof
> And made much within her. (441)

The poem locates within the simplicity, damp humility, and invisibility of the dove the capacity to be the mate of "Day's invisible beginner." The claim is interesting in its minor perversity, but the poem fails to the extent that it replaces the hostile repetitiousness of the sparrow with a limp passivity that has little to recommend it as an alternative. The dove, in this respect is not different from Stevens' cock-birds and roosters, birds necessarily constrained to speak what the sun *makes* them speak every day. In all of these birds, song has been reduced to a reflex, an automatic instrument. In saying that the sun, her lord, "made much within her," Stevens fails to convince the reader that it is not in fact Stevens who has made much *of* her.

"The Dove in Spring," however, is a fuller achievement of what Stevens would like the dove to be:

> Brooder, brooder, deep beneath its walls—
> A small howling of the dove
> Makes something of the little there,
>
> The little and the dark, and that
> In which it is and that in which
> It is established. There the dove
>
> Makes this small howling, like a thought
> That howls in the mind or like a man
> Who keeps seeking out his identity
>
> In that which is and is established . . . It howls
> Of the great sizes of an outer bush
> And the great misery of the doubt of it,
>
> Of stripes of silver that are strips
> Like slits across a space, a place
> And state of being large and light.
>
> There is this bubbling before the sun,
> This howling at one's ear, too far
> For daylight and too near for sleep. (461)

In this poem it is the dove's howling that is a form of making; it "Makes something of the little there, / The little and the dark." This making is a revision of the "minimum of making in the mind" in "An Ordinary Evening in New Haven" (403). The minimum of making here is no longer the minimum of figuration or of rhetoricity, in yet another bid for a poetry of absolute clarity; instead, it is the minimum of extreme poverty, a poverty of almost no remaining life. This poverty is that in which poetic making—the "small howling"—"is and is established." Because the bird is a dove, singing in springtime, in the season of the first inklings of new life, "The Dove in

Spring" joins "An Ordinary Evening" and "The Sail of Ulysses" as a poem
about desire's centrality to being. What this poem contributes beyond those
others, however, is the suggestion that *desire itself* is a form of making, not
merely that which impels a poet, or a person, to make. Such a claim amounts
to a decoupling of desire and the self. The desire that this poem describes is
not capable of satisfaction, either in the form of clarity ("too far / For day-
light") or of consolation ("too near for sleep"). It is not in the mind, or in the
heart, but is a "howling at the ear," an irritation, a small torment that comes
from somewhere *outside* of the self. It resembles, but only resembles, "a
thought / That howls in the mind" or "a man / Who keeps seeking out his
identity." It is this state of externality, this state of being "at the ear" and not
in the mind, the belly, or the heart, to which Stevens gives closer and closer
attention in his final poems. What motivates him is his growing sense that
desire, while still peremptory and poignant, seems less and less an inherent
part of the human; it seems to have a life of its own, wholly distinct from,
and wholly outside of, Stevens' life.

IT WOULD HAVE BEEN OUTSIDE:
SONG AT THE END OF THE MIND

"Not Ideas About the Thing But the Thing Itself," the poem that Stevens places
at the end of *The Collected Poems,* confronts this externality most directly[20]:

> At the earliest ending of winter,
> In March, a scrawny cry from outside
> Seemed like a sound in his mind.
>
> He knew that he heard it,
> A bird's cry, at daylight or before,
> In the early March wind.
>
> The sun was rising at six,
> No longer a battered panache above snow . . .
> It would have been outside.
>
> It was not from the vast ventriloquism
> Of sleep's faded papier-mâché . . .
> The sun was coming from outside.
>
> That scrawny cry—it was
> A chorister whose c preceded the choir.
> It was part of the colossal sun,

Surrounded by its choral rings,
Still far away. It was like
A new knowledge of reality. (451)

The key word in the poem is *outside*. The "scrawny cry" and the "sun" are
coming from "outside." As though to force acknowledgment, Stevens repeats
the word three times. This insistence on the outside provenance of the bird's
utterance amounts to a radical reinterpretation of the etymological sense of
utterance as "outer-ance." The cry is not, no definitely not, something "out-
ered" from within Stevens imagination, from within "the vast ventriloquism
/ Of sleep's faded papier-mâché." Instead, it is uttered from an outer world.
As such, the cry presents itself as another figure for pure freshness, a cry that
unruins the autumnal "choirs where late the sweet birds sang." It resembles
the infant inklings of "A Discovery of Thought": "A trinkling in the parentage of the north, / The cricket of summer forming itself out of ice" (459). The
"c that precede[s] the choir" is pure incipience, a tone that—while meaningless in itself—nevertheless ushers in all meaning, echoing outward through
"choir," "colossal," and "choral."

  However, while the poem is a late instance of Stevens' poems of incipience, it involves a greater astringency than his earlier attempts at refresh-
ment of the world, such as "The Man on the Dump" and "God is Good. It
Is a Beautiful Night." Just as the howling of the dove was like, but only like,
a thought or a man, the scrawny cry resembles, but *only* resembles, "a new
knowledge of reality." It can resemble new knowledge; it cannot *be* new
knowledge.[21] Resemblance here, then, manifests a ratio of "heavy difference"
as much as it registers a similarity (234). The difference specifically is that of
a world fundamentally different from and "outside" the mind. This region
outside the mind anticipates "the end of the mind" toward which "Of Mere
Being" will orient itself, a region not only defined topologically—"at the
edge of space"—but temporally as well, "beyond the last thought" (476).
Outside the mind, the cry marks the border of the intelligible. Stevens knows
it to be a cry, an utterance, a call, and so to that extent it is not without phatic
intent, but to the degree that it merely resembles and does not manifest, it
remains only a cry and bleeds or dissipates into unintelligibility. Part of the
effort of the poem, then, is a holding off or a holding out, a keeping of the
cry outside of the mind, which means in part keeping it outside the sphere
of intelligible meanings. In "Not Ideas," then, Stevens postulates a "minimum of making" like that in "Ordinary Evening" and "Dove in Spring," but
this making now has undergone a further limiting; it is not outside the mind
like the "howling at one's ear," but radically outside the human realm itself.
Unlike the dove in "The Dove in Spring" the scrawny cry does not present a

figure for the human speaker; instead, it presents a figure of the voice *re-moved* from the human speaker. The extreme point of this ascesis brings Stevens into a territory which excludes, to the greatest degree possible, the presence of the human, and which converges upon a point of maximum des-iccation. The native creature of such a region is not the "auroral creature musing in the mind" but a crepuscular creature, already vanishing in the twi-light prior to its own extinction. Its scrawniness must exceed that of the scrawniest bird; not a singer, not a flyer, the sibyl of this final self must be a scraper and a rustler.

When in "The Sail of Ulysses" Stevens refers to the self as a "sibyl," his designation manifestly denotes an oracular center, and resonates punningly with the scholar's note in his Segmenta, "The sibilance of phrases is his, / Or partly his" (414), and with the "droning sibilants" in "Two Figures in Dense Violet Night" (69), and perhaps recalls in "Prologues to What Is Possible" the "man lured on by a syllable without any meaning" (437). Extrinsically, it re-calls the Sibyl of Cumae, who spoke the lines T. S. Eliot took for the epigraph of *The Waste Land.* The Sibyl of Cumae, neglecting to request eternal youth along with eternal life, withered to a point of insect-like desiccation, an ex-oskeletal "residuum" suspended in a bottle, her only wish to die. The voice of Stevens at his limit point is the voice of a similarly exoskeletal dryness; such dryness follows upon the dispersal of all internal vitality, and is wholly blood-less and without warmth. The poem that achieves this note of dryness most fully is "The Course of a Particular":

> Today the leaves cry, hanging on branches swept by wind,
> Yet the nothingness of winter becomes a little less.
> It is still full of icy shades and shapen snow.
>
> The leaves cry . . . One holds off and merely hears the cry.
> It is a busy cry, concerning someone else.
> And though one says that one is part of everything,
>
> There is a conflict, there is a resistance involved;
> And being part is an exertion that declines:
> One feels the life of that which gives life as it is.
>
> The leaves cry. It is not a cry of divine attention,
> Nor the smoke-drift of puffed-out heroes, nor human cry.
> It is the cry of leaves that do not transcend themselves,
>
> In the absence of fantasia, without meaning more
> Than they are in the final finding of the ear, in the thing
> Itself, until, at last, the cry concerns no one at all. (460)

While the leaves recall those in "No Possum, No Sop, No Taters" and of course those in Shelley's "Ode to the West Wind," the leaves to which these leaves address themselves most directly are to be found in one of Stevens' most extraordinary—and extraordinarily refractory—accomplishments, "The Hermitage at the Center" (430):

> The leaves on the macadam make a noise—
>   How soft the grass on which the desired
>   Reclines in the temperature of heaven—
>
> Like tales that were told the day before yesterday—
>   Sleek in a natural nakedness,
>   She attends the tininnabula—
>
> And the wind sways like a great thing tottering—
>   Of birds called up by more than the sun,
>   Birds of more wit, that substitute—
>
> Which suddenly is all dissolved and gone—
>   Their intelligible twittering
>   For unintelligible thought.
>
> And yet this end and this beginning are one,
>   And one last look at the ducks is a look
>   At lucent children round her in a ring. (430)

In this poem achieved desire sings "a duet with the undertaker," a broken, contrapuntal duet with the dry leaves scraping across the macadam. The duet takes the form of two converging poems, the poem comprised by the stanzas' first lines ("The leaves on the macadam make a noise /// Like tales that were told the day before yesterday . . .") and the poem comprised of the indented lines ("She attends the tintinnabula /// Of birds called up by more than the sun . . ."). The first poem is a poem of desolation, exhaustion, and lateness; the wind is "a great thing tottering" about to become the failed "fantastic effort" in "The Plain Sense of Things." The counterpoint poem is a poem of embrace, the desired gathered into the ring of "her lucent children," an ambiance in which even twittering has an intelligible wit. The second poem, the poem of embrace, wins out in the end. Because it wins out, "The Hermitage at the Center" attempts an adjustment of desolation to the vernal plenitude of "the desired" reclining on soft grass "in the temperature of heaven." The poem's undertaking is to "bring the world quite round" (135), but it is only, as Helen Vendler writes "by a great effort of will that Stevens can resume two columns into one at the end, by reciting one of the oldest religious gnomic utterances [. . . .] 'And yet this end and this beginning are one'" (*Words* 58). This "great effort" achieves a local, provisional success, if only in the bravura juggling act the poem pulls off with such unapologetic flair, but the adequation of desire and desolation is not, in the long run, the effort that consumes Stevens most in the last poems. His struggle is not to conceive of the sort of consolation that Eliot in "East Coker" had already offered. What the poem cannot imagine, and what Stevens feels that he must imagine, is "The Vacancy in the Park" (434) into which he will vanish after his "last look at the ducks."

In an attempt to conceive of such a vacancy, Stevens writes "The Course of a Particular," a poem which excludes the possibility of embrace, a poem not of enclosure but exclusion, not of a "rounding" ring but of a radically unassimilable *outside*, an outside that cannot be gathered to the bosom of the interior paramour: "And though one says that one is part of everything, / There is a conflict, there is a resistance involved; / And being part is an exertion that declines." The resistance prevents the cry of the leaves from yielding any "meaning more." It is this resistance that preserves the thing itself from elaborations and distortions, that allows "the life of that which gives life" to remain "as it is." This *as* is one of radical self-equivalence, not the *as* of *as I perceive it,* or of *as it is freshened in my perception of it.* Unlike the *as* in "Bouquet of Roses in Sunlight," the *as* here refrains from saying anything about a relation between perceiver and perceived. It is an *as* that converges upon *is,* a form of "mere being" uninflected and unelaborated "in the final finding of the ear."

This "final finding" is not only what the ear hears with the privileged clarity of its last moments, not only the arrival at a "final found" as in "The Rock" (446); the "finding" denotes also the finding of the ear itself, in which "ear" is the object as well as the subject of "finding," as though the ear, or rather its sense, were a separate thing. This separate thing stands for the self viewed from a posthumous vantage; more radically, in the "final finding of the ear" Stevens imagines what it would be like to come upon and to experience a sense *after* the senses that comprise a sensorium—"the blows and buffets of fresh senses / Of the rider that was"—have dissipated in death (461). (His first approach to this conceptual feat is to be found in "A Postcard from the Volcano" [128].) The task is to imagine a mode of sensibility that could walk among the dispersed senses of the self, perceiving each one merely "as it is." The region where such a perception would be possible would not be the "mind of winter" Stevens imagined in "The Snow Man" but a region without mind, which is to say, a sense without an interior region, wholly skeletal—or in keeping with the nature of the sibyl and the leaves, wholly exoskeletal.

This exoskeletal region, however, is not a lifeless region. The cry is "busy." The wind sweeps the branches. A formal vigor animates the "icy shades and shapen snow." Winter is a "nothingness" to Stevens, but in itself, in its own element, it brings to bear a kind of life, even though that life is not Stevens' life, not even a life in which he can be a "part." He explores here a way of characterizing life that is not his own life, speech that is not his own speech, and desire not his own desire, but that nonetheless persists—even if unconsolidated into the life, speech, and desire of a social other. The otherness is not the otherness of a separate person. In the sparagmos of the leaves, then, Stevens finds a term for what could be called impersonal desire.[22] Its reality is not dependent upon the solidity or the cohesion of the self. In "The Course of a Particular" the life of desire, "the life of that which gives life," is itself "a thing apart."

As had been the case in "Not Ideas," a property of this externality is externality from intelligibility. The cry of the leaves is not an "intelligible twittering." When "one holds off and merely hears the cry" one is merely hearing instead of comprehending, attending upon, or interpreting. "Hearing" in this context is to comprehension what looking is to reading. The cry is a cry, but its value as a cry (and not, say, a rustle or a scrape) does not derive, Stevens asserts, from the interpretive, synthetic, or conceptual engagement of the mind. It is a cry not because he has attributed to it "any misery" of his own (8), or even because one recognizes in it an intention to cry. Such an assertion posits a species of intelligibility which is not the intelligibility of phenomena to the observer, not the intelligibility *of* things *to* an onlooker, but rather an intelligibility *among* things, an intelligibility that does not require the engagement of the mortal mind. In this altered definition, (because there is no longer any self, any interior mind, by which phenomena can be conceived and assimilated) intelligibility resembles something like inherent affinity, proclivity, or tropism. Such affinities, proclivities, and tropisms, Stevens implies, animate the world even in the absence of human apprehension. This world is not a transaction between the imagination and reality, or between what we see and what we think, but is instead a transaction between reality and the desire that traverses it—desire not proper to the self, not isomorphic with the will, but traversing it like "a shade that traverses / A dust, a force that traverses a shade." Consciousness in such a world is not the consciousness sustained by "a strong mind in a weak neighborhood" ("An Ordinary Evening" 404) but a presence for which the best model might be a film or fine foil, all outside and no inside, a membrane of extreme thinness available to be touched by a sweeping wind or a busy cry, but which cannot transform these movements from a "final finding" into even the most minimal making.[23]

"The Course of a Particular," however, is nevertheless a poem of immense pathos. Palpable at every turn, in spite of the impassive register of its delivery, is an unmistakable, and unmistakably human, anguish. "Being part" is an exertion that declines, but the other exertion, that of "holding off," of hearing in the leaves only "the cry of leaves that do not transcend themselves," requires a "fantastic effort." In this effort, in spite of his frailty and ghostliness, Stevens is powerfully present. "The Course of a Particular" is Stevens' poem of extremest poverty, but as such, it can say nothing about the fact that any atmosphere of desolation is by definition a scene of pathos, even (or particularly) one so extreme as "the nothingness of winter."

Stevens' final gesture, in "Of Mere Being," is to imagine such a poverty without anguish or desolation, not in the interest of beholding "nothing that is not there and the nothing that is" (which is after all the act of a "strong mind") but of imagining final things *in the complete absence of a beholder:*

> The palm at the end of the mind,
> Beyond the last thought, rises
> In the bronze decor,
>
> A gold-feathered bird
> Sings in the palm, without human meaning,
> Without human feeling, a foreign song.
>
> You know then that it is not the reason
> That makes us happy or unhappy.
> The bird sings. Its feathers shine.
>
> The palm stands on the edge of space.
> The wind moves slowly in the branches.
> The bird's fire-fangled feathers dangle down. (476)

Like the golden bird in Yeats's "Sailing to Byzantium," the "gold-feathered bird" in "Of Mere Being" asserts a fundamental opposition to extinction. Stevens' "artifice of eternity" differs markedly from Yeats's, however, insofar as it is radically without context, not in Byzantium nor any other human culture. The artifice that Stevens imagines is one without the sponsorship of an emperor's will, or a culture of holiness, or even human pleasure. The poem's central act, by contrast, is to designate a realm *beyond* human meaning and feeling, beyond a world where artifice serves any human purpose. As such the poem must distinguish itself from the marmoreal stasis of epitaph and the human memorial purpose epitaph serves. "At the end of the mind, / Beyond the last thought" a suspension of time is achieved to create not a permanent record but a quality of extremest *ritardando,* a vitality without ongoingness, the slowest possible version of Keats's "slow time." The wind that had swept the dry leaves in "The Course of a Particular" here "moves slowly in the branches." In this ambiance, all movement is in fact a combination of movement and fixity. The tree's "rising" is not an ascent but a standing. The bird does not descend "Downward to darkness, on extended wings" (56); rather, its feathers alone "dangle down." Even "fangled" slows down the quick upleaping flame conjured by the feathers' shining until "fire" approaches, without quite reaching, the motionlessness artifice of an embossed metal. While in "The Course of a Particular" the moment where the cry finally "concerns no one at all" is the poem's terminal point, the bird in "Of Mere Being" has never existed anywhere else *but* at this terminal threshold. Its song, in the most literal sense, is about nothing. While the leaves' cry has to be *pushed back* into non-transcendence, from the beginning the bird occupies a radically intransitive position; it could no more sing *about* something than it could shine about it. The bird speaks nobody's idiom; it is a native of no place, or rather, of Nowhere. It is inevitable then that its song would be "without human meaning" and "without human feeling." Like "The Dove in Spring," the bird sings of an outer region, but this "outside" is not merely the "green freedom" of reality or freedom from an inner life, as in "Not Ideas About the Thing," but freedom from human meaning as such. What is most remarkable in this final ambiance, then, is not that the bird says so little, but that its song remains a song. The bird does not cease to shine. This, then, is Stevens' "final construction"—that such a shining and such a song would continue not only "in the absence of fantasia," not only in the absence of anyone at all to see or hear, but in the absence of any term of human intelligibility whatsoever. In such an absence "Even our shadows [. . .] no longer remain. / The lives these lived in the mind are at an end. / They never were" (445). It is in this most radical sense of withoutness that Stevens conceives of his "foreign song."

For all the austerity and bleakness of its late phase, Stevens' poetry is never without a knowledge of its power, even if that power is eventually understood to persist in the absence of human meaning. Mortal exertion declines, but an impersonal vitality remains. For Stevens, this vitality is ultimately the manifestation of the world's inalienable strength. It is in this way that Stevens' world maintains itself in a kind of innocence. What Philip Larkin will confront in his poetry is the possibility that the world itself, not just the individual mortal speaker, is vulnerable to injury and damage. For him, human meaning is not only circumscribed but subject to terrible violence. While Stevens seeks out ways to include in his poems intimations and inflections of the non-human, Larkin will devise a lyric strategy to register acts of destruction as well as acts of making.

Chapter Three
Philip Larkin: Rather Than Words

It is something of an understatement to say that Larkin's is a poetry of conservative attitudes. His political sentiments range from the stolidly right-wing to the vituperatively xenophobic. Although he read broadly, no one could have accused him of eclecticism or catholicism in his literary tastes. Early in his career, he rejected what he took to be the stupendous innovations and affirmations of High Modernism in favor of a muted, Late Victorian pessimism. Formally, many of his poems appear to have ignored the twentieth century altogether. His beliefs about what literature could accomplish were limited to a tendentiously narrowed ambition. To affirm that poetry could legislate for mankind or fashion the soul or sing the body electric or propound a supreme fiction would be to invite his contempt. Because he saw the poet's world as an untransformable world, given not made, he described his avocation as a specific and circumscribed one:

> I write poems to preserve things I have seen/thought/felt (if I may so indicate a composite and complex experience) both for myself and for others, though I feel that my prime responsibility is to the experience itself, which I am trying to keep from oblivion for its own sake. Why I should do this I have no idea, but I think that the impulse to preserve lies at the bottom of all art. (*Required Writing* 79)

As Larkin describes it, experiences of seeing/thinking/feeling place the poet under an obligation. The obligation is to preserve, to keep the experience "from oblivion for its own sake." This is the positive aspect of the obligation, the obligation to *do something*. There is a negative obligation as well, an obligation *not to do something else*. The poet can do *no more* than preserve. He cannot, Larkin implies, elevate, extrapolate, mythologize, etherealize, or transcendentalize. Preserving, then, requires the poet to be faithful to the experience and *only* to the experience (whatever faithfulness and experience might prove to mean in this circumstance).

Many of Larkin's poems dedicate themselves to fulfilling both the negative and positive aspects of this obligation. Even at their most personal, they lean heavily toward a fidelity to external phenomena. His formal verse patterns imply a poetic of enclosing or capturing, as though the poet resembled a naturalist collecting specimens and revealing a natural order more than an artist engaged in the active *creation* of images. Larkin cherished a tenacious suspicion of Whitmanian or Stevensian transforming subjectivity. Inner experience (feeling and thinking) no less than external, perceptual experience (seeing) obliges the writer to record it with accuracy and precision. In statements such as the one cited above, Larkin espouses a kind of poetic positivism, resolving to pass over in silence that whereof he cannot speak with certainty.

This pledge of allegiance to the rhetoric of verisimilitude is Larkin's commitment to his own version of negative capability. As such, it recalls—and rewrites—John Keats's famous letter to George and Thomas Keats:

> . . . at once it struck me, what quality went to form a Man of Achievement especially in Literature & which Shakespeare possessed so enormously—I mean *Negative Capability*, that is when man is capable of being in uncertainties, Mysteries, doubts, without any irritable reaching after fact & reason—Coleridge, for instance, would let go by a fine isolated verisimilitude caught from the Penetralium of mystery, from being incapable of remaining content with half knowledge. This pursued through Volumes would perhaps take us no further than this, that with a great poet the sense of Beauty overcomes every other consideration, or rather obliterates all consideration. (72)

To be possessed of negative capability is to be "capable of being in uncertainties," and the "irritable reaching after fact & reason" is the expression of the inability to remain "content with half knowledge." One reaches for these at the expense of the "fine isolated verisimilitude." The sense of "Beauty," then, must be stronger than the desire for "fact & reason." Contrasting these two considerations, however, implies a distinct difference between them. While the contrastive rhetoric places the "fine isolated verisimilitude" squarely on the side of beauty, it does so by ignoring verisimilitude's predication on considerations of fact and reason. If verisimilitude is the accurate representation of experience, then a "fine isolated verisimilitude" cannot be beautiful unless it is also true.

While Keats was content to leave the relationship between the true and the beautiful concealed in the penetralium of mystery, Larkin describes his own vocation as one that does not afford him this liberty. He dispenses with Penetralia and Mysteries. What is to be "caught" by art is not an inspiration plucked from heaven but an experience rescued from the void. The sense of beauty can overcome other considerations only if it is also accountable to fact and reason.

Such a conservative interpretation of Keats's letter would contradict nothing of what Larkin said about writing poems, but it would ignore a crucial element of the Keats passage, just as it would misrepresent much of what is in fact at work in Larkin's actual poetry. When Keats takes his shortcut around "Volumes" of exegesis, he implies that the last sentence of the paragraph is the continuation and conclusion of what he has just said; had he concluded by saying "the sense of Beauty overcomes all other consideration," this might have been the case. But when he adds, "or rather obliterates all consideration," he raises the stakes of his argument by an order of magnitude. To say that beauty obliterates all consideration is to impute to beauty a destructive force that strikes at the heart of writing itself. To obliterate, Keats would have known, means—*literally*—to write over letters (from the Latin *ob litteras scribere*). The most radical implication in Keats's assertion is that writing involves an obliteration, a writing out.

I argue in this chapter that one of the phenomena that Larkin's poems record is this act of what Keats calls obliteration. Again and again, his poems take on the subjects of ruin, disintegration, and failure, and they do so in a way that places the force of obliteration at the heart of the poetic project itself. Again and again, Larkin approaches a border where the means of poetic representation collapse. More than any of the other poets discussed in this book, his poems seek to make an account of the destruction and destructiveness of speech itself.

It is surprising that this should be true of a poet whose poems are so consummately shaped, so limited to concrete certainties and minimal affirmations, so dedicated to fleeting moments of clarity and coherence. In fact, Larkin's poems seem in no danger whatsoever of being mistaken for High-Modernist, fragmented shorings-up against ruin. But the fact that Larkin *almost* succeeds in perfecting coherent structures in the face of destruction does not mean that he has fallen short of his goal. My claim is that his goal, rather than the establishment of coherence, is the dramatization of the struggle between coherence and disintegration, between "meaning and meaning's rebuttal" (41).

Throughout his career, Larkin faced what I call obliteration in many different contexts, and with responses ranging from the horrified to the welcoming. In this chapter, I will undertake to show Larkin's strategies for representing, resisting, and incorporating obliteration. First, I will consider

Larkin's complex tropes of preservation and examine how Larkin's attempts to recoup, recover, and record result in a deeply troubled awareness of what it means to survive or remain. I will then consider Larkin's strategies of containment, and show how the shaping of his poems, manifestly engaged in holding in coherence and holding out disorder, ends up holding these two opposed states in inseparable proximity to each other. This deepening awareness of the mutual implication of coherence and obliteration repeatedly brings Larkin to a crisis of faith in the means of representation. This crisis causes Larkin to attempt a series of temporary reprieves from obliteration. He flirts with retreats into anonymity and oblivion, but then finds himself recalled to the world of the here and now. He considers the consolations of the social and the sexual, but ends up marveling at the vast distance and difference between separate persons. He faces up to the fact that even beauty, in its simplest, most persistent manifestations, establishes its contour against a margin of ravaging violence. By allowing obliteration to be not only a topic but an event in his poems, he manages to open a place in them for that which would otherwise be, by definition, unrepresentable—those parts of experience that remain "untalkative" and "out of reach" (137).

A HOTHOUSE FLASHED UNIQUELY: PRIVATE, HERMETIC, AND MEANINGLESS MEMORY

A poetry dedicated to the preservation of experience must, it seems, be dedicated to accurate observation. Certainly it is true that Larkin's lines are rich with vivid, pungent descriptions—descriptions that impress the reader simultaneously with their originality and their fidelity to the actual. "The Whitsun Weddings," for example, records a train journey in a series of brief, limpid notations, with the speaker offering up a frank account of all he sees, smells, and feels.

> All afternoon, through the tall heat that slept
> For miles inland,
> A slow and stopping curve southward we kept.
> Wide farms went by, short-shadowed cattle, and
> Canals with floatings of industrial froth;
> A hothouse flashed uniquely: hedges dipped
> And rose: and now and then a smell of grass
> Displaced the reek of buttoned carriage-cloth
> Until the next town, new and nondescript,
> Approached with acres of dismantled cars. (114)

The stanza proceeds in a series of displacements, the quick alternation between the mundane and the surprising, the new and the nondescript. There is nothing special about the landscape. The traveler is not looking because he expects to find something; he looks because the eye is naturally drawn to the flow of scenery past the window. One notes the smell of carriage-cloth merely because one never has reason to think of it in other circumstances. But the experiences are no less particular for being ordinary. For this reason, the line "a hothouse flashed uniquely" stands as an emblem for all the other notations. Each one presses its imprint upon Larkin's senses with a kind of flash, and Larkin is repeatedly and gently startled to a fresh recognition. But we know no more about the hothouse than that it exists, instantaneously, to be remarked; Larkin's notations are less descriptions than indications; he notes *that* the experiences are, not *how* they are. To this degree, each experience is unique in two conflicting senses: unique in that it is particular, revealed with photographic clarity, but also unique in that it is hidden, inaccessible inside of that particularity, obscured by the flash of its idiosyncratic singularity.

The meaning of the "frail, / Travelling coincidence" remains concealed inside the hothouse, as it were, of Larkin's sensibility, until he stakes the poem on the transformation of this concealment into revelation at the end of the poem.[1] This concealment inside of the unique notation, however, is one that troubles Larkin throughout his career. "Lines on a Young Lady's Photograph Album" (71) represents an attempt to isolate clarity as an independent ideal, to assert that what is most beautiful is what is truest.

> But o, photography! as no art is,
> Faithful and disappointing! that records
> Dull days as dull, and hold-it smiles as frauds,
> And will not censor blemishes
> Like washing-lines, and Hall's-Distemper boards,
>
> But shows the cat as disinclined, and shades
> A chin as doubled when it is, what grace
> Your candour thus confers upon her face!
> How overwhelmingly persuades
> That this is a real girl in a real place,
>
> In every sense empirically true!

The conferred grace is the realness of a "real girl in a real place." The girl is lovely to Larkin, no doubt, but he locates her beauty not in her person but in the accuracy of her representation. Even when he concludes the poem—" . . . you lie / Unvariably lovely there, / Smaller and clearer as the years go by"— the adverb "unvariably" evokes the faithfulness and candor of photography itself. Her loveliness inheres in her seeming to be nothing other than what she is. Larkin's desire is present, but—suspicious as always that "when / Desire takes charge, readings will grow erratic" (32)—he attempts to hold the image of his beloved beyond its range.

What the poem says, it says about candor, and argues for the beauty of the particular, unembellished fact. It says very little about love, or the beloved. It expresses a sentiment no more revealing than "a hothouse flashed uniquely." Larkin tells us *that* the girl and the place are real, but does not depict the quality of the reality. Even an excursion into mimesis itself compromises the beauty of the fact, which must remain not only unembellished but undisclosed. The past is one that "no one now can share." If the poem is a preservation, then, it is not the preservation of the beloved's countenance, or even the unique field of intimacy between two individuals. "The gap from eye to page" is too broad, and the speaker remains isolated, mourning "without a chance of consequence." In this way, the poem extends the deictic simplicity of Hardy's claim in "At Castle Boterel" that the rocks record "that we two passed." Instead of immortalizing the record of a passing, as Hardy does, Larkin mortalizes it. The past is irretrievably past. To say more is to say something meaningless.

Why not, then, restrict oneself to what one can speak of with certainty? Or, on the other hand, why not fall silent? Either course might have been more compelling to a poet less fascinated with meaninglessness itself. Larkin is not an empiricist or positivist, in spite of his many attempts to dissemble his position. In "An April Sunday brings the snow," Larkin considers how even a "meaningless" feeling can exact its own bittersweet pang, and allows this meaningless to rest in uneasy relation to the specific and the unique:

> An April Sunday brings the snow
> Making the blossom on the plum trees green,
> Not white. An hour or two, and it will go.
> Strange that I spend that hour moving between
>
> Cupboard and cupboard, shifting the store
> Of jam you made of fruit from these same trees:
> Five loads—a hundred pounds or more—
> More than enough for all next summer's teas,
>
> Which now you will not sit and eat.
> Behind the glass, underneath the cellophane,
> Remains your final summer—sweet
> And meaningless, and not to come again. (21)

The poem opens with an act of distinguishing. The sudden arrival of the late snow in spring reveals that the plum blossoms are not white, as they had seemed, but green instead. Larkin rescues this exquisite subtlety from transience: "an hour or two, and it will go." Transience, itself, however, becomes the subject of the poem. The brief lingering of spring snow becomes a figure for the briefness of Larkin's father's last summer, and by extension, the briefness of human life. [2] The greenness of vitality, in fact, is only visible against the ground of snow's oblivion. Life, like the summer, is sweet because it is "not to come again."

This act of the poem resembles the act of picking a greenish-white plum blossom and pressing it between the pages of a book to preserve the delicate color—but it is not the only act. Larkin proceeds from the delicacy of the first figure to a more complex, if somewhat more awkward, act of preservation. Instead of spending the hour appreciating the ephemeral beauty of snowfall mingling with petal-fall, he carries load after load of jam from cupboard to cupboard. The summer, preserved "Behind the glass, under the cellophane," is not to come again because it has never left. It weighs upon Larkin as a literal burden, an insistent excess, "a hundred pounds or more—/ More than enough for all next summer's teas. . . ." The father's work remains, in a quantity nearly equal to the weight of a human body. This bodily aspect to what remains is reinforced by the word "sweet," which describes both a memory and a taste, a taste that the dead father can no longer experience. The jam, as far as the father is concerned, is surplus. Larkin, thinking that it is "more than enough" implies that when he eats it, he will be eating for two—for himself, and for his absent father as well.

What began as a poem of sharp distinctions has become a poem of uneasy co-mingling. The sweetness that Larkin tastes in the jam is different from mere sweetness because it is a taste infused with the absence of the father. Just as the blossoms shift from white to green against the ground of the snow, the sweetness shifts to a greeny bittersweet against the fact of the father's death. Why does Larkin say this is meaningless? Manifestly, it is meaningless because the father is beyond caring about such things; it is meaningless because the sweetness is powerless in the face of death's oblivion. However, by allowing the verb phrase "remains your final summer" to assume a nominative implication—the remains *of* your final summer, and by extension, *your* remains—Larkin imbues "meaningless" with something more than its superficial, sophisticated, worldly dismissiveness. Meaninglessness becomes an object of awareness in its own right for Larkin, a problem and a challenge that he will return to again and again.

Although "An April Sunday" is a minor poem which Larkin never published, it partakes in its minor way of the great tradition of distillation or tincture poems, together with such disparate poems as Shakespeare's Sonnet

54 ("And so of you, beauteous and lovely youth, / When that shall fade, by
verse distils your truth") and Stevens' *Notes Toward a Supreme Fiction* ("Fat
girl, terrestrial, my summer, my night. . . . I call you by name, my green, my
fluent mundo. / You will have stopped revolving except in crystal.") Its contribution to the genre is small and somewhat clumsily plotted, but it shows
an early attempt to distill the essence of meaninglessness as well as that of
meaning. In this poem, the distillation can only be partial. It will take poems
of greater scope, and in some cases, greater internal conflict, to advance
Larkin's exploration of the meanings that take their shape against the background of time's obliterations.

FROM RUIN TO RUINS: RENOVATING CHURCHES IN "CHURCH GOING" AND "AN ARUNDEL TOMB"

When Larkin writes "sweet / And meaningless" in "An April Sunday" he is in
part inoculating the poem against an accusation of grandiosity. He concedes
that even though a particular summer may be someone's last, that fact alone
does not freight the summer with special significance. To say that it was sweet
is not, by the strictest standard, news. He acknowledges that his loss does not,
in itself, call upon him to speak. Larkin must search for another situation in
which to pursue credibly his inquiry into meaninglessness and memory, a situation broader and deeper than the private particularity of his own recollection. It is in response to this imperative that Larkin fashions himself into a

poet of public space. Trains, churches, streets, beaches, and fairgrounds all
offer him opportunities to record his inner impressions of an outside world of
which he is a part but only a part. If virtue, for Larkin, is social, as he will later
imply, so too is history. The true substance of memory is to be found in collective institutions, not in the private trove of personal *memories*. For all the
uniqueness of his voice on the page, Larkin is, of all the poets considered here,
the one most suspicious of the heart's claim to be heard merely because it has
been moved by emotion.

    In spite of (or because of) Larkin's intense, fascinated iconoclasm and
anticlericalism, churches provide Larkin with a concrete, external, impersonal
subject for his meditations. While one can never be a disinterested tourist in
one's own soul—poking around, fingering the accoutrements, wondering
without really caring what it would mean to take this dread or that passion seriously—a church is different. In a secular age it offers the onlooker a form
shaped around a belief, a belief that has become a memory, not a person's
memory but a culture's. Larkin is free to keep the church in "Church Going"
(97) at arm's length, to "Reflect the place was not worth stopping for."

Someone would know whether the church had been cleaned or restored, but Larkin doesn't. If anything, he is relieved to remain uncontaminated by concern for such things. Breezily he disavows any "idea / What this accoutred frowsty barn is worth." When he pronounces "Here endeth" more loudly than he'd meant to, he has asserted the end of the Word itself. But by dismissing whatever pieties the church would foist upon him, he has freed himself to be surprised by a sense of significance that has survived both the death of dogma and his own contempt: "It pleases me to stand in silence here; // A serious house on serious earth it is. . . ." This seriousness persists even though the beliefs on which it was originally predicated have fallen away. Larkin permanently exempts the church from obsolescence, though it crumble to a mere "cross of ground," because

> . . . someone will forever be surprising
> A hunger in himself to be more serious,
> And gravitating with it to this ground,
> Which he once heard, was proper to grow wise in,
> If only that so many dead lie round.

What might the wisdom be, into which one could grow in this once-hallowed place? Larkin does not say. The wisdom, if that is in fact what Larkin feels he is near when he is in the church, must be a wisdom without content, a sense to be sensed, not a sense to be comprehended. It inheres simply in the church's having lasted, of having "held unspilt / So long and equably what since is found / Only in separation—marriage, and birth, / And death, and thoughts of these." In fact, Larkin prepares the poem to hold something unspilt that the church itself no longer can. The poem acts as a kind of vitalizing, modernity-resistant rootstock onto which the seriousness of the church can be grafted. The resulting hybrid combines that seriousness with the "bored, uninformed" sophistication of the speaker. To this degree, the poem performs its own act of preservation ("that much can never be obsolete"), but it does so through a process akin to smelting. The distinct content of the beliefs and attitudes that distinguish one religion from another, or from separate groups of political or social assumptions, have given way to a mingling, catabolic deliquescence: the air is "blent"; one seeks a "whiff" of the past; the figure of something being "held unspilt" implies an infusion or a tincture—a cistern or catch-basin for "hungers" and "compulsions" rather than a chalice for the True Blood. The disintegration of the church over time, as Larkin imagines it, is an expansion rather than a destruction, the opening of roof or lancet to let in the actual sky. Nothing is lost if weeds push up through the pavements, or brambles take root in the

narthex, or, as Stevens says, "a sumac grows / On the altar" (529); these in-
cursions do not violate because they manifest yet another form of life, which
is to say, another form of hunger or compulsion.[3]

There is a capaciousness to this topic, an at-oneness with a future radically unlike the present. But this willingness to travel to a distant, unremem-
bering time imposes limits on the poet. In order to view the effacement of the
church from the landscape, Larkin is obliged to imagine someone like himself, but not himself, "his representative." This representative is an exigent invention, but the nomination of this proxy permits a crucial moment in time's
drama to occur off-stage, namely, the moment of the speaker's own death.
There is something too easy in imagining himself both there and not there in
future ages, in including himself in the general "we" that "shall keep / A few
cathedrals chronically on show . . . / And let the rest rent-free to rain and
sheep"—a "we" that in fact will not include him at all. It is Larkin's frustration at this ease that impels him to return to the same territory in "An Arundel
Tomb," a poem equally concerned with a lost age, but in this case the loss intimately implicates the speaker himself, a speaker who, when confronted with
the velocity of time, must struggle to establish those terms that will sponsor
his own survival. In considering the single tomb of a medieval earl and countess, Larkin narrows his focus from the entire church to the image of the tomb
itself, still a public artifact, a commemoration on view, but scaled to single
lives and the future of individual loves. After realizing, "with a sharp tender
shock," that the figures carved in stone are holding hands, Larkin explores the
implications of his unanticipated response:

> They would not guess how early in
> Their supine stationary voyage
> The air would change to soundless damage,
> Turn the old tenantry away;
> How soon succeeding eyes begin
> To look, not read. Rigidly they
>
> Persisted, linked, through lengths and breadths
> Of time. Snow fell, undated. Light
> Each summer thronged the glass. A bright
> Litter of birdcalls strewed the same
> Bone-riddled ground. And up the paths
> The endless altered people came,
>
> Washing at their identity.
> Now, helpless in the hollow of
> An unarmorial age, a trough

> Of smoke in slow suspended skeins
> Above their scrap of history,
> Only an attitude remains:
>
> Time has transfigured them into
> Untruth. The stone fidelity
> They hardly meant has come to be
> Their final blazon, and to prove
> Our almost-instinct almost true:
> What will survive of us is love. (110)

Larkin no longer speaks through the persona of his bored, uninformed representative. He has abandoned the first-person narrative of "Church Going" for the indefinite third, and in doing so, achieves, paradoxically, a more intimate tone. The voice, hushed, chastened, and no longer contented with its jaunty irreverencies, undertakes merely to translate the "sharp tender shock" into words. The long, peripatetic stanzas and relaxed pentameter of "Church Going" have been replaced by edgy tetrameter sestets. Thought is not the product of leisure and reflection, but burns directly, fuse-like, from the moment of arrest experienced at the recognition of their embrace. Prior to this moment, however, the sight of the tomb fails to engage the onlooker; whatever seriousness was meant by the fashioning of their stony countenance has receded into the vague, uninvolving flatness of the pre-baroque, a spare remoteness tinged at first only with the absurdity of "dogs under their feet." As in "Church-Going," here also hath ended the reading, as those who come to this place come "to look, not read." The Latin names the sculptor sought to prolong have become opaque, signifying not people but mere antiquity. Everything significant and important about the pair—their rank, their horses and hounds, the status inherent in their inscribed stone monument, the Latin permanence of their names—everything has fallen away except the single gesture, which becomes, it seems, the "final blazon" of something that has endured and persisted, saved from obsolescence and oblivion. Faced with this eroded antiquity, however, Larkin finds himself unable to sneer at "ruin bibber[s], randy for antique." For all the qualifications and subqualifications of the final stanza, the last line asserts itself as an affirmation, a rhetorical posture confirmed by Larkin's placing the poem at the end of *The Whitsun Weddings*. Love gets the last word.

The poem proposes itself as a certain kind of qualified proof, one that "prove[s] / Our almost instinct almost true." Faced with this almost-proof, the reader is forced to negotiate a question. Has something not been proven after all, and are we left with nothing more than the illusion of truth, maybe even a pernicious, lulling, beguiling illusion at that? Or, on the other hand, has something been expressed in a way that formal logic is powerless to prove or refute, a truth underwritten by tenderness and intuitive instinct rather than by ratiocinative faculties? If something is "almost true," is it true enough, or is a near miss "as bad as a mile" (125)—to quote the title of another poem? Placing "An Arundel Tomb" in the context of Larkin's work as a whole does not offer a definitive answer. The part of him capable of unambivalent tenderness, the poet that wrote "The Mower" or "The Explosion," knows that love can survive—if we do what we ought, are kind to each other, take care of the elderly, watch out for the hedgehogs, and so forth. Writing in this key, he adopts something of the non-reformist social meliorism of Jane Austen or Henry James. However, those poems in which his disdain or bitterness is aroused ("Take One Home for the Kiddies," "Myxomatosis") infuse these lines from "An Arundel Tomb" with a tincture of malevolence, a contempt for those (including himself) who would like to believe in the endurance or immortality of love.

Both of these notes together sound a minor but non-dissonant chord in the poem. Were they the only two notes in his work, as implied by much extant criticism, Larkin's poems would not, as he says, involve the eye as they do.[4] What makes this poem particularly notable is the way in which it moves beyond this relatively mechanical opposition to extend and deepen Larkin's meditation on meaninglessness. When he refers to the "stone fidelity / They hardly meant" he appears to be writing in the same slightly amused, slightly appalled tone established by such phrases as "supine stationary voyage" and "helpless in the hollow of / An unarmorial age." And certainly, "They hardly meant" echoes the detachment of "They would not think" in the third stanza and "They would not guess" from the fourth. "They hardly meant," however, distinguishes itself from these earlier instances by vibrating uneasily against the coolness of the tone. Manifestly the phrase asserts that Larkin's reading of the stonework is not a reading they had intended, and the line strikes a note of sadness and mild apology for laying his own reading over whatever they or the sculptor had meant to say. The poem, however, does not merely pit two meanings against one another, (secular versus the sacred, or belief versus skepticism). Instead, the poem takes both readings—the one that Larkin almost-asserts, "What will survive of us is love," and the intended meaning of the tomb, "Here lie the mortal remains of Earl X and Countess Y, who shall be raised in glory at the Last Day"—and places them together in opposition to the absence of any meaning whatsoever.

How does this absence appear in the poem? This absence is indicated in the brief passage where Larkin describes the "lengths and breadths / Of time" through which the figures have persisted. "Snow fell, undated. Light / Each summer thronged the glass. A bright / Litter of birdcalls strewed the same / Bone riddled ground." At first, it seems that Larkin is making note of the only thing he sometimes feels is worth making note of, the "observed // Celestial recurrences" of "Forget What Did." Or perhaps he is reminding us of the religion he would construct if called upon to do so, wherein he would "raise in the east / A glass of water / Where any-angled light / Would congregate endlessly." He seems to be saying that these minimum recurrences—birth, death, the passage of time, the variable fall of light—will eventually efface any eschatological imaginings. In this passage, however, he forges into a territory beyond the final assertion of "Church Going" that wisdom is to be had through the contemplation of mortality. "Dead lie round" here as well, but they have lost their status as The Dead and have disintegrated into a random assortment of parts. When Larkin says that the ground is "bone-riddled," he is indicating a form of persistence and a survival much more troubling than the form he affirms (or almost-affirms) more directly at the poem's conclusion. He points to the way that human meaning falls apart but does not go away, lingering instead as a trash, a strewing, and a riddling—a riddling in the sense both of a permeating and a mystification. We are fated to look and to puzzle, but we are also doomed never to know, never to read or be read with clear comprehension. The almost-affirmations of the last stanza are powerless in the face of this recognition and can only offer a way of turning away, manifestly with optimism, but also "in shock and sorrow" from the radical fear the poem has encountered.[5]

For Stevens, the palm at the end of the mind is the home of a bird, and the bird's ability to sing and to shine is the final absolute, the minimal manifestation of the supreme fiction. Because it is capable of imagination, the bird is always there, signifying a force in the world that transcends individual experience, the form and force of human meaning without its content, a song foreign to the local objects that make up a single person's world. Similarly Hardy, when he considers the absence left by his wife or his father, cannot help but make a resonating instrument from that absence; the father's violin is a hollow silence, but it is still a violin, echoing with the songs that the father played on its strings. For both Stevens and Hardy, ghostly or posthumous music continues even after human ears can no longer hear it. Each of these earlier poets confidently arrogates to poetry the ability to describe or indicate this "silent" or "meaningless" register of meaning. While Larkin is fascinated with meaninglessness, he is less free in trying to make something of it. When he considers bone-riddled ground, he is torn between feeling that such ground is proper to grow wise in and that the knowledge imparted by the bones chokes off the capacity for thought or wisdom altogether. In "An Arundel Tomb" Larkin's birds do not resemble Hardy's full-throated thrush,

Stevens' final singer, or Frost's oven-bird. Nor, even, do they resemble the birds of celestial re-occurrence in "Forget What Did." They do not offer the speaker a way of imagining an escape from mortal meaning. They fall as a *litter* on the ground, a mere wasting, a noisy part of the "soundless damage" that the air has become. As such, they resemble not so much a generative force as they do the bones riddling the ground, or the snow itself, falling "undated." (As the snow is undated, it is also undating, an effacement not only of the historical moment in which the earl and countess lived, but of the whole idea of history itself.[6]) Birdsong persists as the cruel, twitting, residue of the meaninglessness into which the inscribed names have sunk. If one experiences a sense of meaning, standing at the grave, it is not a meaning communicated by the tomb or the surroundings itself. It is a meaning provisionally erected to contain, as the tomb itself does, a riddling of bones.

COLDER PASTORALS:
"HOME IS SO SAD" AND "FORGET WHAT DID"

As a container of this sort, the tomb reveals its kinship with other containers prominent in the history of English poetry, most notably Keats' Grecian urn and Stevens' Tennessean jar. This line of kinship in turn intersects with another vessel in Larkin's poems. When Keats addresses the Grecian urn, saying "Thou, silent form, dost tease us out of thought / As doth eternity: Cold Pastoral!" he claims for the urn's silence a special privilege above poetry: "Thou foster child of silence and slow time, / Sylvan historian, who canst thus express / A flowery tale more sweetly than our rhyme. . . ."(297). Stevens, in turn, asks what the American equivalent of Keats's Grecian urn would be, and imagines a jar placed on the ground in Tennessee, one whose exterior is bare, without history, as Stevens understands America to be.[7] Placed on a hill, however, the jar establishes a pole around which the landscape throws itself together. (The jar does this both in spite of and on account of its bareness). As different as they are, Keats's urn and Stevens' jar resemble each other in that they present to the world a powerful, impenetrable exterior. What they contain, or were meant to contain, is of no significance to the poet.

The Arundel tomb takes its place alongside these other containers, but with an important difference. While the jar and the urn contain nothing of importance, the tomb (and the poem itself) fits itself around a core of obliterating nothingness. It is an exterior whose function is not, like the urn's or the jar's, to stand as a sort of beacon, but to hide what it contains: extinction and the knowledge of extinction. The qualifications of the last stanza allow for the possibility that the exterior cannot hide the core completely, but the constraints of the poem require Larkin to end on a note of edgy disavowal. As

Larkin's career progresses, however, he struggles to find ways to confront and integrate an account of obliteration that does not require such a disavowal. But how can he write a poem about a lost past without turning it into a poem about survival or transformation?

The small poem "Home is so Sad," offers Larkin a new approach to the problem. In it, he sketches a little scene of the "opaque childhood" that will be mentioned later in "Forget What Did."

> Home is so sad. It stays as it was left,
> Shaped to the comfort of the last to go
> As if to win them back. Instead, bereft
> Of anyone to please, it withers so,
> Having no heart to put aside the theft
>
> And turn again to what it started as,
> A joyous shot at how things ought to be,
> Long fallen wide. You can see how it was:
> Look at the pictures and the cutlery.
> The music in the piano stool. That vase. (119)

As he has previously in "Church Going" and in "An Arundel Tomb," Larkin asks the reader to look with him at a scene, and to experience with him the feelings the scene invokes. But unlike the earlier poems where he moves from description to exposition, here he moves from exposition to description, indeed, description of the barest sort, mere pointing out. The objects here—the pictures, cutlery, piano stool, and vase—are particular objects, calling to mind at first the "local objects" to which Stevens paid such attention. They are particular because they are saturated with memory, but otherwise are in every way ordinary and unremarkable. These objects, however, and the vase specifically, cannot hide in mere mereness. Under the auspices of a kind of wit, the vase presides over a cold pastoral of its own. This pastoral is not one that suspends within its silences the permanent intensities of spiritual and erotic thrall as Keats's does. Like the gesture of the figure in John Ashbery's *Self-portrait in a Convex Mirror*, the vase is both an invitation and a warding off. Neither its surface nor what it contains is described. The sentence fragment that denotes it simultaneously says nothing and leaves nothing to be said.[8] While Keats' and Stevens' urns flaunt their exteriors, Larkin's, by contrast, flaunts an opacity, an inaccessibility. Home is so sad because it simultaneously excites the desire to return and insists upon the impossibility of return. The beliefs and relationships on which this home was founded have passed away, leaving only an inventory of possessions, a residuum of nostalgia. They do not contain or even stand for the past; they mark its absence.

The items, then, ultimately are not Stevens' "local objects." Their mereness lacks the elemental primacy of Stevens' "thing itself" or the unvarnished integrity of Frost's "diminished thing." For Larkin, to attribute a special value to the bareness or simplicity of these objects is to render them top-heavy with imposed significance. The phrase "so sad" in the title partakes of this bareness. Its unrevealing simplicity implies that to say more would be to say too much. It is this acknowledgment of the profound limits of speech that sets this poem outside the genre of elegy. The sadness or grief that the poem indicates is not a force to be harnessed for the work of commemoration or mourning, nor can the poem inaugurate the repair of the world torn by loss. Its essential act is the act of witness; confronted by loss, all one can do is face it, and by facing it maintain a minimal distance from its obliterating pull. This distance is instantiated by the word "that" in "That vase;" "that" acts deictically to indicate the objects of the past and to separate them from the present. The separation is at once mournful (that vase I can no longer hold, part of a past which no longer holds me) and releasing (I am not to be numbered among those things now lost in the past).

The vase, a single object not articulated into a complete sentence, anticipates Larkin's later shift toward a more symbolist mode and a deeper reliance on unexplicated objective correlatives for inner experience. It is not true, however, that Larkin manages, by expanding a more symbolist or objectivist register in his capability, to avoid a radical crisis of confidence in the means of representation. Larkin will never stop struggling to evade the conviction that his muse is "asleep or dead" (217)—not only his private muse, but the muse of poetry itself. For a world so radically demystified and scourged as Larkin's, the credible rationale for making poems flutters in and out of view. Perhaps mere notation, the act of mere witnessing, will suffice to preserve what is sweet from what is meaningless. In "Forget What Did," Larkin explores the limits of this possibility.

> Stopping the diary
> Was a stun to memory,
> Was a blank starting,
>
> One no longer cicatrized
> By such words, such actions
> As bleakened waking.
>
> I wanted them over,
> Hurried to burial
> And looked back on

> Like the wars and winters
> Missing behind the windows
> Of an opaque childhood.
>
> And the empty pages?
> Should they ever be filled
> Let it be with observed
>
> Celestial recurrences,
> The day the flowers come,
> And when the birds go. (184)

The poem proceeds as a relatively straightforward request that the bleak report of words and actions, the heavy weight of personal life, might fall away, yielding space for impersonal notations of seasonal change. The several figures for this stoppage abide uneasily with each other, however, and this uneasiness reveals how complex an undertaking this shedding may prove to be.

- Words and actions are to be hurried to burial, but in such a way that they can be looked back on.
- They can be looked back on, but in such a situation where they resemble both the wars and winters of childhood, without saying how wars and winters might, in turn, resemble one another.
- The windows giving access to this childhood are, however, opaque, and even if they weren't, the wars and winters, we are told, would be missing from their places behind the windows.

The act of burial is portrayed with a sequence of metaphors whose illusion of contiguity conceals a substrate of dissonant figures. Instead of putting something away in an appropriate place, burial opens up an absence, the space left by the wars and winters of a lost childhood. This space, however, is obscured by an opacity. Positive figures of sight and presence permeate the negative figures of blindness and absence, as though memory and erasure could exist in the same time and place.[9]

This mutual permeating of the absent and the present is embodied in the word "cicatrized" of the second stanza. The act of writing is compared to an act of scarring and disfiguration.[10] But when Larkin writes "a blank starting, // One no longer cicatrized," he does not answer the question of whether the opposite of a cicatrice is a wound or a woundlessness. By definition, a scar is an alteration to the body that the power of healing cannot completely expunge. It is the sign of the inability of the body to erase perfectly all evidence of a wound. To say "one no longer cicatrized" is to propose a contradiction in terms. Writing itself, like the vase in "Home is so Sad," instantiates both a presence and an absence. The *that* of "that vase" puts the past at a distance. In "Forget What Did," Larkin endeavors to interpose a *that* between his speaking voice and the words and actions of his own life. The birds and the snows offer a pastoral of oblivion, the plowing of personal particularity into the blank fields, the blank pages, of natural events that proceed without regard to individual experience. "Cicatrized" foregrounds the link in Larkin's poetry between writing and damage. "Forget What Did" offers no answer to a reader who would ask why or whether all words and actions bleaken waking, or whether or not it is always better to forget what did or did not happen. But it points to Larkin's convictions about the limits and the consequences of speech.[11] It is a bleaker poem than it seems at first, and the bleakness it confronts is the wintry expanse that threatens to open if the act of writing can no longer infuse and be infused by the world of experience. For Stevens the fictive power is indistinguishable from the power of thought or sentience itself, always there to be contemplated, theorized, and praised. For Larkin this is not so. The task of writing involves the repair of the world, the establishment of the basic conditions under which poetry is able to flourish. "Forget What Did" proposes a species of writerless writing, a poetic of anonymity, but to what degree writerless writing is a possibility at all, the poem cannot say.

DESIRE FOR OBLIVION:
ATTEMPTING A POETIC OF ANONYMITY

Larkin makes several attempts to repair to a natural world that does not include him. As early as 1950, in the poem "Absences," he was imagining the expanses of a shoreless sea and the skies of "a yet more shoreless day" and reveling in "Such attics cleared of me! Such absences!" (49) As late as 1978, in "The Winter Palace" (211), he was still engaged in the project of envisioning a world cleansed not only of self-awareness but of any awareness at all.

> It will be worth it, if in the end I manage
> To blank out whatever it is that is doing the damage.
>
> Then there will be nothing I know.
> My mind will fold into itself, like fields, like snow. (211)

These poems articulate the desire to escape from the toils of selfhood. They pivot, however, on a paradoxical language game: the ability of the "I" to propose a world in which that "I" would not exist. Larkin is experimenting with an assertion akin to "The next thing I say will be true: the last thing I said was false." He does so in order to construct a situation where he seems to occupy his own absence. Not sustained by the titillations of mere conundrum, he seeks out other resources to conceive of his escape from personality. "Modesties" (26), for instance, poses itself the challenge of establishing a diction purged of all eloquence, composed of words worn down to their simplest sense, like MacLeish's "dumb/ . . . medallions to the thumb" (106)—words like coins whose stamped faces have been worn to featurelessness. The description of unwitnessed flowers that concludes the poem stands as an emblem of the poem's own modest unfolding.

> Weeds are not supposed to grow,
> But by degrees
> Some achieve a flower, although
> No one sees. (26)

In "Cut Grass," a much later poem, Larkin describes another flowering inside of invisibility, this one more explicitly posthumous to the speaker, whose own mortal life is implicitly compared to the life of the (classically and biblically) mortal leaves of grass:

> Cut grass lies frail:
> Brief is the breath
> Mown stalks exhale.
> Long, long the death
>
> It dies in the white hours
> Of young-leafed June
> With chestnut flowers,
> With hedges snowlike strewn,
>
> White lilac bowed,
> Lost lanes of Queen Anne's lace,
> And that high-builded cloud
> Moving at summer's pace. (183)
>   [cf. Stevens, "Death of a Soldier"]

Here the snows of oblivion are rendered in "the white hours" of June, the white-flowering hedges and the drooping white lilac. Summer in its natural fullness has pushed human meaning aside, and the world of natural regeneration continues without human presence. The lanes of Queen Anne's lace are "lost,"—no one there to see them, no one there to follow them. Abandoned in this way, they recall the abandoned and overgrowing lane between the two estranged lovers of "No Road," the road slowly effaced by "all time's eroding agents" (47). These lanes, however, do not participate in a social context. They never relied on people for their being in the first place. A poem such as this is itself a kind of lost lane, unpopulated, going nowhere, depicted with a plainness that, though lovely, "hardly involves the eye." Larkin includes this poem in "High Windows" as a kind of break—a weekend pass from the human tragedy—before concluding the book with the deep, fatal disturbance of "The Explosion" (184).

Each of these poems is either a sketch for, or a footnote to, the first of Larkin's major poems, "At Grass," his great pastoral of anonymity. While the poem is an unqualified success, it is a success founded on the assumption that a kind of blessed anonymity can in fact be achieved. In taking as his subject a pair of retired champion race horses, Larkin locates this realm of anonymity at the juncture between the human and nonhuman worlds. These horses would not exist were it not for the human purposes they serve, but in their long life of superannuation they have retreated to the edges and shadows of this purpose. For Larkin, they embody a far limit of the human (capable like us of answering questions and experiencing joy) and the near limit of the non-human (unburdened not only of their function and obligations but of their very names as well).

> The eye can hardly pick them out
> From the cold shade they shelter in,
> Till wind distresses tail and mane;
> Then one crops grass, and moves about
> —The other seeming to look on—
> And stands anonymous again.
>
> Yet fifteen years ago, perhaps
> Two dozen distances sufficed
> To fable them: faint afternoons
> Of Cups and Stakes and Handicaps,
> Whereby their names were artificed
> To inlay faded, classic Junes—
>
> Silks at the start: against the sky
> Numbers and parasols: outside,
> Squadrons of empty cars, and heat,
> And littered grass: then the long cry
> Hanging unhushed till it subside
> To stop-press columns on the street.
>
> Do memories plague their ears like flies?
> They shake their heads. Dusk brims the shadows.

> Summer by summer all stole away,
> The starting-gates, the crowds and cries—
> All but the unmolesting meadows.
> Almanacked, their names live; they
>
> Have slipped their names, and stand at ease,
> Or gallop for what must be joy,
> And not a fieldglass sees them home,
> Or curious stop-watch prophesies:
> Only the groom, and the groom's boy,
> With bridles in the evening come. (29)

The vivid excitement of their race days rises to a crescendo,—"the long cry / Hanging unhushed"—and remains there, in the past, an eternity of artifice that suspends their names in permanent fable. A property of this permanence is that it requires a conversion from lifted voices to printed words. Their legend is a written legend, the inlaying on a plaque, the almanacking of their record times. The clamor of their fame subsides "to stop press columns on the street." But while the immortality of their names is sponsored by writing, the realm of writing is precisely that realm where the horses themselves cannot dwell. They must "slip their names" and recede into a distance of speculation and attribution where "the eye can hardly pick them out" before they stand "anonymous again." Larkin admires and envies their lot, freed from the galling harness of their pasts (splendid though it was), with stop-watch, fieldglass, and riding crop all replaced by "unmolesting shadows" and cropped grass, their only distress the wind's playful dis-tressing of tail and mane in the "cold shadow they shelter in."

The shadow both cold and sheltering indicates that Larkin sees the horses' life as a kind of idyll, but an idyll inflected with darkness as well. If there is something mournful about the arrival, with bridle, of the groom at the end of day, as though the Grim Groom himself has arrived, it is because the life of the horses is already an afterlife. If they reside in cold shade and unmolesting shadow, it is because they too are shades, indistinct and nameless. Larkin stands as though on the near bank of a horse-country Lethe, and the horses he watches have been pastured in the Elysian Fields.[12]

This is the first major poem that Larkin wrote for his first major book, *The Less Deceived.* (Only one earlier poem, "Wedding Wind" made it into the volume.) While it achieves a higher level of accomplishment than anything he had written previously, the world of the horses is too otherworldly to reward the rigors of his sensibility. Beneath the surface of mastery, the pitch-perfect tonal shifts, the tight, assured music of the tetrameter sestets, and the beautiful, contrapuntal slipping free of metrical regularity in the cantering third stanza, a suspicion intrudes, a suspicion of the very surety that lends the poem its air of unfaltering confidence. When Larkin asks, "Do memories plague their ears like flies?" he sets up for himself the clinching reply, "They shake their heads." In the unmolesting world of the poem, nothing about the horses would indicate that shaking their heads means anything other than a denial: "No, no memories plague them." Compared to the ample spaciousness of their liberty, the quibble that horses shake their heads precisely *because* flies plague them seems at first an intrusive pedantry. Nevertheless, the poem makes room for doubt by referring again and again to the inability of the observer to be sure that he is seeing what he believes himself to be seeing: "the other *seeming* to look on," "and gallop for *what must be* joy" (italics added). More and more as his career progresses, Larkin's attention turns to the affliction of memory, to the unshakeable past, and to the fact that even though he would deny these memories (by shaking his head), the gesture of denial is always an act of acknowledgement too. The past persists. The name can never be slipped. The heart is always fastened to a dying animal.

THIS UNIQUE DISTANCE FROM ISOLATION: THE PROBLEM OF OTHER PEOPLE

As hard as Larkin worked to portray himself as the Hermit of Hull, a curmudgeon, a recluse, he is, perhaps more than most of his contemporaries, a social poet. This in part derives from his suspicion of depth, whether in the form of deep historical determinism (Yeats), religious tradition (Eliot), philosophical inquiry (Stevens), or the psychoanalytically inflected lyric (Plath, Berryman, or Lowell). We are stranded on the island of the here and now, an unavoidably human here and now. To attempt to venture beyond its shores is to venture off the edge of the world. Mythologizations of Anglicanism, the Welsh countryside, the Supreme Fiction, transmogrifying passions, or even money itself promise false worlds that cannot truly sustain the spirit. Nevertheless, the need to be with people wars constantly with the desire to be free of that need. In the early poem, "Wants," Larkin asserts that "the wish to be alone" lies beyond any of the social, familial, or sexual impulses, and is in fact a derivative of a greater, darker desire, the desire for oblivion. All well and good, the later Larkin implies, as he returns to these propositions in "*Vers de Société*," but even if these are our deepest desires, their fullest satisfaction would be an accomplishment incompatible with life. And life, which includes the social world, is "where we live," to paraphrase "Days" (67). In "*Vers*" he ponders a colleague's invitation to join a "crowd of craps . . . [to] waste their time and ours" and his impulse to salt his refusal with:

> In a pig's arse, friend.
> Day comes to an end.
> The gas fire breathes, the trees are darkly swayed.
> And so *Dear Warlock-Williams: I'm afraid—*
>
> Funny how hard it is to be alone.
> I could spend half my evenings, if I wanted,
> Holding a glass of washing sherry, canted
> Over to catch the drivel of some bitch
> Who's read nothing but *Which;*
> Just think of all the spare time that has flown
>
> Straight into nothingness by being filled
> With forks and faces, rather than repaid
> Under a lamp, hearing the noise of the wind,
> And looking out to see the moon thinned
> To an air-sharpened blade. . . . (181)

As the poem continues, however, Larkin is forced to acknowledge the flaw in his assertion: time spent "with forks and faces" is not the only kind of time that flies straight into nothingness. By the final stanza, Larkin has realized that it is these very faces that keep the nothingness at bay:

> Only the young can be alone freely.
> The time is shorter now for company,
> And sitting by a lamp more often brings
> Not peace, but other things.
> Beyond the light stand failure and remorse
> Whispering *Dear Warlock-Williams: Why, of course—*

One of Larkin's central endeavors is to figure out how to accept the invitation to the world even if all his inclinations encourage him to reject it. The darkly swayed trees recall the "cold shelter" the grazing horses sheltered in—and elsewhere the woods of oblivion Frost contemplates in "Stopping by Woods on a Snowy Evening" and "The Wood-Pile," as well as the "good night" so seductive to Dylan Thomas. While Larkin feels a temptation to recede from the world, he feels also that this temptation is false; the world is not something from which one can, in fact, recede. The poem then articulates simultaneously a resolution and a quandary. Larkin is resolved to remain a part of the world, but he feels that nothing shows him how to do that successfully, especially how to establish successful relations with other persons. It is one thing to imagine a world both cold and companionable for animals, as he had for the horses[13] or as Yeats did for the wild swans at Coole Park. It is quite another to imagine such a world for actual people.

In "The Whitsun Weddings" Larkin imagines the transformative experience of being held with others in a special hour, an hour united through ritual with the most elemental forces of fertility and regeneration. He comes to realize, however, that "This frail travelling coincidence" teaches him, the solitary subject, nothing about how to bridge the gap between his own specific individual experience and the experience of other individuals. Even the cherishing intimacy of "Lines on a Young Lady's Photograph Album" peers across the wide gap between eye and page, or between the world of the present and the unvariable heaven of the past. Without a heaven or a transforming hour, how is Larkin to understand the conditions of true companionship? A world can be shared, but the terms of sharing he outlines in his later writings approach a threshold of minimum assertion. He suggests that the mere fact of having had something to do with one another at all is a good unto itself.

As unremarkable as this claim may seem, this mere fact is what Larkin celebrates in "Poem about Oxford," an occasional piece he wrote on the flyleaf of a book he gave to his sometimes lover and companion, Monica Jones. If there is nostalgia for his university years, it lies beneath his deprecation of those "blacked-out and butterless days." He looks back at this period of his youth neither through the mists of nostalgia nor through the "windows of an opaque childhood," but with something closer to Robert Lowell's Nietzschean, uninflected "it was."[14] Oxford was not the transformative celestial railroad of "The Whitsun Weddings" but a "City we shared without knowing." Nevertheless, it continues, even after thirty years, to sustain something of who Jones and Larkin were and are: "It holds us, like that *Fleae* we read about / In the depths of the Second World War." The only wedding that the figure contemplates is Donne's non-sacramental, accidental commingling of two people's blood in the body of a flea. They do not share a memory of Oxford. (Larkin knows too well that no memories can be shared.) Nonetheless, their past constitutes a common ground on which they can meet. The act of the poem is the demarcating of this common ground. Unlike Hardy's, Larkin's past landscapes are not haunted. It is not the rocks that record "that we passed," but Larkin himself. In fact, Larkin implies, what really holds them like the flea is not a past "that no one now can share" but the poem itself. The poem itself mediates between two people when other institutions—marriage, nostalgia, romantic idealization—cannot.

The good thing, then, about Oxford is that it held them both, even if being there was no fun, even if Jones and Larkin didn't know each other. Even this appreciation of such a minimal form of togetherness, however, keeps that togetherness safely in the past. Oxford in the early Forties does him the service of being separate and remote enough, like the flea, to foster a tolerable proximity to the lover whom he dreaded living with and would not marry. Another account of Oxford, written fifteen years before the poem for Monica, reveals a more complex account of what it means to exist in relation to other people.

> I don't approve of Oxford and I don't want to go back there. It crushes the spirit in a more subtle way than I had imagined possible. I hardly wrote a line during my stay there, except in vacations, although I acquired a certain first-hand knowledge of people and what it is like to be implicated with them.[15]

It is this deep sense of implication that infuses and complicates the intimate relations described in Larkin's poems. In *"Vers de Société"* Larkin turns from solitude because solitude brings a sense of failure and remorse. What he does not address in this poem is the fact that being with people can bring about the same sense. The experience of intimacy becomes the experience of distance and alienation, exacerbated by the deeper knowledge that to seek anything more is to seek something that does not exist. Irreconcilable differences between persons replicate the irreconcilable differences within the self. "Talking in Bed" demonstrates how a distance between persons is in fact the inevitable extension of an internal psychic division:

> Talking in bed ought to be easiest,
> Lying together there goes back so far,
> An emblem of two people being honest.
>
> Yet more and more time passes silently.
> Outside, the wind's incomplete unrest
> Builds and disperses clouds about the sky,
>
> And dark towns heap up on the horizon.
> None of this cares for us. Nothing shows why
> At this unique distance from isolation
>
> It becomes still more difficult to find
> Words at once true and kind,
> Or not untrue and not unkind. (129)

Elsewhere Larkin is more apt to simplify this distance and cast it in terms of the conflict between self-interest and concern for others (as in "Sympathy in White Major" and "Life with a Hole in It"), but here the conflicting allegiance is not between persons, but between the different interests to which a person must at different times respond. The difficulty of speaking stems ultimately from the difficulty of responding from a position simultaneously of kindness and honesty. Because kindness and honesty cannot exist harmoniously together, neither can we. Closeness, then, appears as a mutual contract to refrain from puncturing our shared illusion of closeness. Stoicism in the face of this realization affords little consolation because to speak this truth would amount to a cruelty. We are forced to avert our eyes from it—and to pay the price of this "costly" aversion, as costly as the "aversion of eyes from death" ("Wants" 42).

The dominant trope of the poem is, one notes with some surprise, pathetic fallacy. When Larkin turns his attention to the expanse of windy space outside the room, he is in fact turning toward the expanse of space between him and his bedmate. The wind, building the clouds, disperses them with the same gesture, an act of dismantling and separation. Other habitation is always a horizon away. The failure of the environment to care for the couple mirrors their failure to find a way of caring for one another. To be together, then, is merely to indicate another distance, the distance from isolation, the isolate center whose gravitational pull increases the farther we are from it. The biggest distance, Larkin asserts, is the distance between our divided inclinations, the desire to speak the truth on the one hand, and on the other, the desire to be kind. Larkin sees the perfect union of the two (expressed in the implied notion of *being true* to one another) as an impossibility.

When Larkin says "Nothing shows why" this should be so, he is asserting that the cause of this inevitable, growing alienation is the only issue that remains in question. In doing so, he excludes the possibility that there might be conditions where kindness and truth can in fact coincide. "Mr. Bleaney" is a poem that relies less heavily on an untestable primary assumption. In the boarding-house room previously occupied by a Mr. Bleaney, Larkin finds an apter emblem of two people at once unignorably together and utterly separate. Mr. Bleaney is not present in the poem; his absence and the room he had rented are. Larkin, setting his bag down in the room, is beset at once by both Mr. Bleaney's presence and absence:

> [. . .] So it happens that I lie
> Where Mr. Bleaney lay, and stub my fags
> On the same saucer-souvenir, and try
>
> Stuffing my ears with cotton-wool, to drown
> The jabbering set he egged her on to buy.
> I know his habits—what time he came down,
> His preference for sauce to gravy, why

He kept on plugging at the four aways—
Likewise their yearly frame: the Frinton folk
Who put him up for summer holidays,
And Christmas at his sister's house in Stoke.

But if he stood and watched the frigid wind
Tousling the clouds, lay on the fusty bed
Telling himself that this was home, and grinned,
And shivered, without shaking off the dread

That how we live measures our own nature,
And at his age having no more to show
Than one hired box should make him pretty sure
He warranted no better, I don't know. (102)

Larkin stuffs his ears because the jabbering set unceasingly insinuates that Larkin too warrants no more than one hired box. Even to stub out a cigarette is to come into contact with a souvenir of Mr. Bleaney's. The irony of the poem inheres in the speaker's dread that his own life is just as limited and bleak as Mr. Bleaney's; this irony encourages the reader to counter the concluding "I don't know" by saying, "Of course you know, with a sickening certainty, what Mr. Bleaney must have felt. And still you are not free from that dread. It seems that even your exalted trade as poet affords you no more than the hired box of the pentameter quatrain. . . ." and so forth. Beneath this irony, and beneath the dread, there is another, still starker assertion—an assertion not of likeness but of unbridgeable distance. Beneath the dreadful sense of identification with Mr. Bleaney lies an awareness of the vast distance between all people. Surely it makes no difference whether they knew one another or not, given that the "hired boxes" of our individual lives (and our individual coffins) admit one occupant only. Although one may seem to communicate across the rift (perhaps by means of a jabbering set or saucer-souvenir), between each of our existential dwellings lies "a strip of building land, / Tussocky, littered" that cannot be crossed. We cannot think that this place admits of any building more permanent than those clouds instantly dispersed by the wind in "Talking in Bed." This littered periphery is an emblem of the periphery of damage and waste that surrounds all moments of coherence in Larkin's world. As such, it recalls the littered car lot around the horse track, and the "bright / litter of birdcalls strewing the bone-riddled ground" in "An Arundel Tomb," and includes in the list of "all time's eroding agents" the damage necessarily caused by our essential separateness. This radical separateness damages in part because it induces a toxic or moribund despair. (It is a pain "like dysentery" in "Love Again," or the "ailment" of isolation in "No Road.").

In "Mr. Bleaney," the emotional manifestation of this damage is dread; in "Talking in Bed" it is alienation. Damage is present in varying degrees. On some occasions Larkin does not allow this damage to blot out all capacity for affirmation. ("Church Going" allows for the possibility of wisdom and equable holding. "An Arundel Tomb" posits the survival of love in the face of the strewing, littering, and riddling.) At other times, news of this damage is the only news a poem seeks to impart. Increasingly, however, Larkin's relation to damage changes, and its presence in the poetry shifts from thematic content to formal element. It becomes something that Larkin can no longer merely deplore or conjure away; he must find a way to integrate its powers into his own voice.

A HAND AND SOME BLUE:
VIOLENCE AT THE HEART OF REPRESENTATION

The poems "Sunny Prestatyn" and "To the Sea" have very little in common. While they both have to do with seaside resorts, the first is an ekphrastic lyric of urban blight, and the other a ruminative, reflective lyric of personal history. Each of them, however, presents the reader with the figure of a hand against the background of an expanse of blue sky. They do so to different effects, but the similarity of the figures indicates, I hope to show, how each poem is engaged in the task of assimilating a kind of damage into the text of the poem itself. "To the Sea" is the later of the two poems, but I will consider it first because it represents a retreat to an earlier poetic of containment, as exemplified by "An Arundel Tomb."

> To step over the low wall that divides
> road from concrete walk above the shore
> Brings sharply back something known long before—
> The miniature gaiety of seasides.
> Everything crowds under the low horizon:
> Steep beach, blue water, towels, red bathing caps,
> The small hushed waves' repeated fresh collapse
> Up the warm yellow sand, and further off
> A white steamer stuck in the afternoon—
>
> Still going on, all of it, still going on!
> To lie, eat, sleep in hearing of the surf
> (Ears to transistors, that sound tame enough
> Under the sky), or gently up and down
> Lead the uncertain children, frilled in white

And grasping at enormous air, or wheel
The rigid old along for them to feel
A final summer, plainly still occurs
As half an annual pleasure, half a rite,

As when, happy at being on my own,
I searched the sand for Famous Cricketers,
Or, farther back, my parents, listeners
To the same seaside quack, first became known.
Strange to it now, I watch the cloudless scene:
The same clear water over smoothed pebbles,
The distant bather's weak protesting trebles
Down at its edge, and then the cheap cigars,
The chocolate-papers, tea-leaves, and, between

The rocks, the rusting soup-tins, till the first
Few families start the trek back to the cars.
The white steamer has gone. Like breathed-on glass
The sunlight has turned milky. If the worst
Of flawless weather is our falling short,
It may be that through habit these do best,
Coming to water clumsily undressed
Yearly; teaching their children by a sort
Of clowning; helping the old, too, as they ought. (173)

In this poem, Larkin employs a disjunction of spatial scales to particularly vivid effect. Like the spatial and temporal vistas of "At Grass," Larkin's depth of field, as it were, varies sharply here. The "miniature gaiety of seasides" is a collection of smallnesses, small bathing caps, towels, "small, hushed waves," and the "white steamer stuck in the afternoon" as though it were a tiny ship glued inside a glass bottle. All this diminution is crowded under the immensity of the vast horizon, the sky arching cavernously over everything. The conjunction of the miniature and the gigantic is shown most vividly by "the uncertain children" viewed closely enough to see not only the whiteness of their bathing costumes but the frills on the little suits as well; as small as the children are, and as minutely depicted, the scale of their exploration is huge as they reach up, "grasping at enormous air." In this figure of grasping, Larkin accomplishes something like a reverse Romare Bearden effect. In one of his collages, Bearden might affix an enlarged hand to a person, indicating the grind of manual labor, the weight of the hand of oppression, and the downtrodden person's deformation by suffering into a single gesture of grasping. Larkin emphasizes the hand of the children as well, but in doing so he manages something that could not be achieved in a visual, pictorial field: he invites the reader to consider the difference between objects of incomparably unlike scale, the smallness of a child's hand and the vastness of the entire sky. Larkin proceeds swiftly from this arresting depiction to describe the old people present as well, his own childhood trips to the shore, and his parents' meeting there before he was born, and then concludes the poem by choosing to interpret the scene as a depiction of human ethics, the adults "teaching the children by a sort / Of clowning; helping the old, too, as they ought." The ethical conclusion, as well as the tranquility and unhurried leisure of the poem, belie the fact that like "An Arundel Tomb," "To the Sea" also is a poem of the abyss. The miniature figures are surrounded by enormous spaces: not only the benign blue sky the children reach for and the vast ocean that shrinks speech to "weak trebles," but the echoing expanses of time as well, stretching backward and forward through generations and dwarfing the span of a single human life. The dismantling of the day (like the dismantling of the fair in "Show Saturday" or the imagined disintegration of the church in "Church Going") portends the dismantling of the world, its breaking down to chocolate-papers, tea-leaves, soup-tins, rocks, and sand.

Ruin has taught Larkin here to ruminate no less seriously upon "outworn buried age" than Shakespeare ruminated in Sonnet 65 ("Since brass, nor stone, nor earth, nor boundless sea"). Against the terror of ruin, he praises habit, the quotidian, unaristocratic version of the "custom" Yeats praised in "Prayer for My Daughter." This praise, however, raises a weakened treble against the various damages and ruinations described elsewhere in his work. The children's hands "grasping enormous air" recalls most directly the savage poem, "Sunny Prestatyn," written seven years earlier and published in *The Whitsun Weddings*. By assigning the hands in "To the Sea" to the children, Larkin creates a miniature myth of progress, hinting that in time the children, having been taught by their clowning parents, will get a grip on the enormousness of the world and learn to do what they ought: take care of their own children, obey the habits of culture, tend to the old. "Sunny Prestatyn" by contrast, erects no bulwark against devastation:

> *Come To Sunny Prestatyn*
> Laughed the girl on the poster,
> Kneeling up on the sand
> In tautened white satin.
> Behind her, a hunk of coast, a
> Hotel with palms
> Seemed to expand from her thighs and
> Spread breast-lifting arms.
>
> She was slapped up one day in March.
> A couple of weeks, and her face

Was snaggle-toothed and boss-eyed;
Huge tits and a fissured crotch
Were scored well in, and the space
Between her legs held scrawls
That set her fairly astride
A tuberous cock and balls

Autographed Titch Thomas, while
Someone had used a knife
Or something to stab right through
The mustached lips of her smile.
She was too good for this life.
Very soon, a great transverse tear
Left only a hand and some blue.
Now *Fight Cancer* is there. (149)

The hand and the blue here do not join in the child's gesture of reaching up-
ward into the spaces of the world, but stand only as a remnant, both dismem-
bered extremity and valedictory wave. Photography's candor in "Lines on a
Young Lady's Photograph Album" has become a different kind of brutal unblinking scrutiny. By concluding with the line "Now *Fight Cancer* is there,"
Larkin indicates that such advertisements, so exploitative of our desires, so co-
ercively sexualized, are themselves a kind of cancer, the excrescence of a cyni-
cal commercialism metastasizing through the culture. If the poem, however,
presents itself with a critique of advertising's empty excitements, it does so
only by disavowing a violence in which the poem is more deeply implicated,
the participation in the gleeful rampage that the poem manifestly deplores.
The vandals are not defacing an advertisement so much as they are defacing
the image of a girl; she would suffer no more merciful a fate if her picture portrayed merely "a real girl in a real place." She is punished not because we can
never achieve a permanent seaside paradise in Prestatyn but because we will
never possess her body. Behind the gesture that lifts her breasts is a gesture of
cruel withholding, for which, Larkin obliquely implies, she is justly dismem-
bered. If cancer by definition represents a ravaging of the body, then it most
properly invokes the ravaging of the girl's body, not the corruption of the culture by enticing ads. In the end, the pen that writes the poem takes its place
alongside those other instruments of violence, the pen that sets her "fairly
astride / A tuberous cock and balls," the knife that stabs her in the mouth, and
the hand that tears her from the wall.

The word misogyny needs no redefinition to denote justly an element
in this violence, the presupposition that the girl, merely by being, represents an
engulfing, seductive force which must be countered with an equal, rending

counterforce. She, Larkin implies, like the "bitch / Who's read nothing but *Which*," deserves our hatred—or at the very least, standing within the purview of her radiance, we cannot help feeling something of this defensive loathing. The force that leaps from us to slap her up or tear her down is a part of the ineluctable force that disperses whatever we build and tramples whatever we sow. It is a part of the destructions for which Time itself, Larkin implies, bears the ultimate responsibility.

This notion pervades Larkin's understanding of desire. What rescues it from classification as sheer hostility or nihilism is the care Larkin takes to show how close this destructiveness is to our most humane impulses. In "The Mower," the third-to-last poem Larkin published, he tells of killing a hedgehog while mowing the lawn:

> Now I had mauled its unobtrusive world
> Unmendably. Burial was no help:
>
> Next morning I got up and it did not.
> The first day after a death, the new absence
> Is always the same; we should be careful
>
> Of each other, we should be kind
> While there is still time. (214)

The strength of this poem pivots on the semicolon in the antepenultimate line. Surely only a sadist would delight in murdering hedgehogs with a lawnmower, mauling not only their unobtrusive world but that aspect of our world that can support and shelter them. And so the reader assents: yes, we must be careful and we must be kind. But the grief and resolve of the conclusion, weakly separated by the semicolon from "the new absence after a death," caves into that absence. The absence is not only the absence of the hedgehog, but the absence of the knowledge of how to be careful or kind. One can stop mowing the grass, or bequeath most of one's wealth to a society for the protection of animals, as Larkin did, but he knows that even the most basic acts of living—such as falling in love or mowing the lawn—can result in the damage and at times, the destruction of other lives. And he is convinced, as "Sunny Prestatyn" indicates, that the desire for other persons, for their love and care, is a desire not only doomed to, but derived from, the experience of violent frustration.

"Love Again," the poem written immediately after "The Mower," also addresses the link between desire and damage. Like "The Mower," it too contains an absence at its center, but an absence presented formally rather than thematically. Feeling the dysenteric pain of "Love again" while "wanking at ten past three," Larkin imagines his beloved in the arms of another man:

> Someone else feeling her breasts and cunt,
> Someone else drowned in that lash-wide stare,
> And me supposed to be ignorant,
> Or find it funny, or not to care,
> Even . . . but why put it into words?
> Isolate rather this element
>
> That spreads through other lives like a tree
> And sways them on in a sort of sense
> And say why it never worked for me.
> Something to do with violence
> A long way back, and wrong rewards,
> And arrogant eternity. (215)

The undetermined "violence / A long way back" is some personal, private harm, an unhealable injury, a damage sustained by the equally undetermined "wrong rewards." To supplement these causes of his "indigestible sterility" (39) Larkin implicates "arrogant eternity" as well. When he says that love "spreads through other lives like a tree" and "sways them on in a kind of sense," he is saying that this "sense" is only a plausibility, a rhetoric of significance, the illusion of sense. Once this "sense" has been rolled over by eternity's arrogant machine, all that remains of it is an isolate element, "a hand and some blue." Faced with the knowledge of this destruction, the purpose of putting the hand to work melts away, be this work the work of writing ("but why put it into words?") or masturbation. But put it into words he does, and in such a way that the poem contains a representation of this melting away, specifically the falling silent after "Even. . . ." Manifestly, what is elided is the possibility of actually enjoying the thought of their lovemaking. On a larger scale, the ellipsis represents an end to thought, and it opens a gap in the poem where not only human connection but meaning itself has been replaced by a "transverse tear." Like a Francis Bacon painting whose figurative surface is obscured by a splash of paint, both "The Mower" and "Love Again" include at their center, as it were, a streak or smear of effacing white. The effect for Bacon, as for Larkin, is simultaneously an effect of destruction and of beauty—sublime beauty indistinguishable from violence. These moments afford Larkin a compromise in response to his question "why put it into words?" They allow him to be both in language and outside it.

Larkin's most explicit, and most successful, thematization of this poetic stance is the poem "High Windows":

When I see a couple of kids
And guess he's fucking her and she's
Taking pills or wearing a diaphragm,
I know this is paradise

Everyone old has dreamed of all their lives—
Bonds and gestures pushed to one side
Like an outdated combine harvester,
And everyone young going down the long slide

To happiness, endlessly. I wonder if
Anyone looked at me, forty years back,
And thought, *That'll be the life;*
No God any more, or sweating in the dark

About hell and that, or having to hide
What you think of the priest. He
And his lot will all go down the long slide
Like free bloody birds. And immediately

Rather than words comes the thought of high windows:
The sun-comprehending glass,
And beyond it, the deep blue air, that shows
Nothing, and is nowhere, and is endless. (165)

The blue here is not the flat, tearable blue of "Sunny Prestatyn" or even the blue of "flawless weather" in "To the Sea." It is the blue of the sky opening beyond the comprehending reflective surface of the windows, surfaces that both reflect the sun and allow the sun to be "looked into." The blue, in one sense, because of its unspecificity, resembles the Stevensian pure blue of the imagination, or Mallarmé's "*azur.*" It is Larkin's attempt to designate the abyss as an "endless" sublime good, a nothingness that is still a "deep, blue air," a part of the breath or afflatus of poetry. By proclaiming this air deep and blue (thereby separating it from the whiteness or colorlessness of effacement), he seeks to put the idea of damage at arm's distance, outside the margin of the poem. He arrives at an emblem for a poetry that might find a medium "other than words," a medium that is "sun-comprehending" but at the same time "shows / Nothing."

One can agree with Larkin that the blue represents an endless good, or one can argue, as Paul Bowles might, that it is a sheltering sky that insulates us from the terror of the void, or one could say, as A. R. Ammons might, that the sky's blue is one of the facts of our earthly condition—not endless because humans are not endless, and therefore not to be transcendentalized. The blue itself refrains from preferring one opinion over another. Larkin knows this, and offers the poem not as a last word, but as the narrative of a transient mood, a flash of coherence no less transient than sunshine in Hull. Larkin's choice to end the poem with "endless" shows the kind of serious, ironic playfulness that allows him to propose a possibility without wholeheartedly avowing it. The poem like glass can comprehend, in its own way, the sun, but the realization— or the comprehension—it proposes is not one at which we can gaze for long.

SWERVING TOWARD WORLD'S END: THE "HERE" OF LARKIN'S POETRY

To conclude, I will consider two poems, "Solar" and "Here." Each of these poems thematizes a relation to the realm of wordlessness indicated in "High Windows." This relation, in turn, characterizes the relation of Larkin's oeuvre as a whole to this realm, which is simultaneously at the center of, and radically outside of, his poetic project. In "Solar," Larkin, turning, flower-like, directly toward the sun, risks the vulnerability of frank praise:

> Suspended lion face
> Spilling at the centre
> Of an unfurnished sky
> How still you stand,
> And how unaided
> Single stalkless flower
> You pour unrecompensed.
>
> The eye sees you
> Simplified by distance
> Into an origin,
> Your petalled head of flames
> Continuously exploding.
> Heat is the echo of your
> Gold.
>
> Coined there among
> Lonely horizontals
> You exist openly.
> Our needs hourly
> Climb and return like angels.
> Unclosing like a hand,
> You give for ever. (159)

The sun is without human need of aid, support, or recompense, a first thing on which all things depend, around which all things gather. It is "simplified by distance / Into an origin," and thus resembles Stevens' first idea of the solar primitive. But this simplification is the simplification of distance, of removal. The human complexities, including language, that sponsor its visibility, stand at a remove from it, and must transform it into something other than an origin—a lion, a spilling vessel, a head, an exploding flower. We perceive it only in its secondary manifestations, in the heat, for instance, which is the palpable echo or secondary manifestation of its primary gold. It is this gold for which the poem endeavors to coin a series of figures; when each one is spent, another one can be readily coined anew. Each figure is neither more nor less apt to describe the sun, hence the poem's circular, appositional, paratactic pattern. The figures arrange themselves around the sun in a ring: spilling, pouring, unclosing—all going on all the time, because the sun exists outside of earthly time. It is only "our needs" that respond "hourly," climbing and returning "like angels";[16] Larkin contrasts our needs (including our need for terms such as "hours" or "angels") with the unneediness of the sun itself. The sun is at once sponsor of and alien to our impulses and desires.

The pleasure of turning the face toward the sun resembles Stevens' "Pleasure of Mere Circulating" (120). The motion does not mirror or body a transcendental truth, but is a pleasure in its own right, a positive version, as it were, of Hardy's compulsion to return, grieving, to the site of his courtship of Emma. The Larkinian first idea (though he would never attempt the gigantism of such a formulation) is not the sun but the approach and return to the sun, the approach and return to the edge of the realm of words.

It is Larkin's great poem "Here" that confronts most directly this swerving to and from the edge of intelligible experience. While "Solar" and "High Windows" offer the reader a theory of a certain form of happiness, they also suggest a theory of poetic success. Each one entails, in the sun or in the endless blue, something that stands outside of words but toward which the words of the poem climb and return. The mode of being they indicate by their direction of approach is always too distant, and the arrow of their vector always falls short. What the poem "Here" documents is the way the traversal itself, while never to arrive at the gold of the sun or the blue of the endless, provides a sustenance of its own:

> Swerving east, from rich industrial shadows
> And traffic all night north; swerving through fields
> Too thin and thistled to be called meadows,
> And now and then a harsh-named halt, that shields
> Workmen at dawn; swerving to solitude
> Of skies and scarecrows, haystacks, hares and pheasants,

And the widening river's slow presence,
The piled gold clouds, the shining gull-marked mud,

Gathers to the surprise of a large town;
Here domes and statues, spires and cranes cluster
Beside grain-scattered streets, barge-crowded water,
And residents from raw estates, brought down
The dead straight miles by stealing flat-faced trolleys,
Push through plate-glass swing doors to their desires—
Cheap suits, red kitchen-wares, sharp shoes, iced lollies,
Electric mixers, toasters, washers, driers—

A cut-price crowd, urban yet simple, dwelling
Where only salesmen and relations come
Within a terminate and fishy-smelling
Pastoral of ships up streets, the slave museum,
Tattoo-shops, consulates, grim head-scarfed wives;
And out beyond its mortgaged half-built edges
Fast-shadowed wheat fields, running high as hedges,
Isolate villages, where removed lives

Loneliness clarifies. Here silence stands
Like heat. Here leaves unnoticed thicken,
Hidden weeds flower, neglected waters quicken,
Luminously-peopled air ascends;
And past the poppies bluish neutral distance
Ends the land suddenly beyond a beach
Of shapes and shingle. Here is unfenced existence:
Facing the sun, untalkative, out of reach. (137)

The poem that "Here" most closely resembles is "The Whitsun Weddings."[17] The visible first-person speaker of the earlier poem, however, is not visible here. In fact, there is something luminously *unpeopled* about the vantage that the poem assumes. The first sentence in the poem swerves through the entire widening, slow progress of the first three stanzas, not to end until the first line of the fourth. "Swerving," the first word, which initially appears to be a present participle, is in fact a gerund, and the subject of this sentence; it is swerving itself that "gathers to the surprise of a small town." While the poem narrates a horizontal journey through different kinds of scenery—the rural, the urban, the suburban, the mercantile, and the coastal—it swerves through vertical, temporal layers as well. "Swerving east," travelling against the direction of the sun in the sky, is in effect a travelling back in time, beginning with the present, actual dawn, the sale-day pilgrimage of the trolley-riding consumers, and moving back to take note of the older, less ephemeral presences, the unchangingness of the harbor-front, the tattoo-shops, consulates, and grim head-scarfed women not different from those who were there centuries before. The haystacks and fields indicate an agricultural past extending even further back, and beyond that, those ancient presences unsponsored by human activity, the river, the land itself, the sky. The poem swerves (rather than drilling or excavating) because these elements exist alongside one another, and no view can include one without including the other. However, beyond the land there is a world wholly other than the land's compound striation of spatial and temporal zones. This world begins with the beach "Of shapes and shingle." The beach is the margin where the land has broken down to unelaborated form (shapes) and matter (shingle), and beyond it there is only the sea, which is Larkin's emblem for "unfenced existence." The sea is a shifting, broken, sun-comprehending glass, not an endless blue but "bluish neutral distance," and what it comprehends it does not share with us. It is "untalkative, out of reach." The poem is a limit poem, a poem of approach and implicit return, in which the *verse* is also this movement of traversal and reversal. It informs us that life is an affair of swerving toward and away from a realm that does not care for us but sustains us nonetheless if we face it, as the untalkative sea faces the sun.

It is not merely a coincidence that Larkin's career itself arrived at an untalkative end some years before his death. Like the individual poems, the oeuvre itself arrives at its own blank space, one for which Larkin, in infirm age, could find no reckoning. The final collapse is in fact prefigured in all the small collapses that the single poems negotiate. But the work as a whole presents the reader with an attempt to chronicle this swerving to and from voicelessness. In spite of and because of the damages to speech that Larkin's poems narrate and sustain, Larkin manages to extend a poetic of negative capability to an austere, untalkative extreme. In this light, one can read George Mackay Brown's "Shroud" as a gloss on Larkin's own practice:

> Seven threads make the shroud,
> The white thread,
> A green corn thread,
> A blue fish thread,
> A red stitch, rut and rieving and wrath,
> A gray thread
> (All winter failing hand falleth on wheel)
> The black thread,
> And a thread too bright for the eye.

Larkin discovered how to weave into his poems a thread too bright (or too dark) for the eye.

What, though, of a poet who does not find herself blessed, or cursed, with the ability to retreat into silence? Sylvia Plath, like Larkin, is a poet of stark sensibility, but what in Larkin's experience had seemed to be an inherent *vulnerability* to destruction, appears to Plath as an outright, dreadful inevitability. It is away from Larkin's fragile, fault-torn world and toward Plath's fated and haunted one that we now turn.

Chapter Four
Sylvia Plath: The Stars' Dark Address

Seamus Heaney refers to "Edge," perhaps the last poem that Sylvia Plath wrote, as "problematically. . . . a suicide note" (165). To do so is to make a link between the intimate address of the suicide and the public address of the poet, and in turn to point out how complexly fraught such a link must be. Whether the poem is a suicide note, depends of course, on the definition of suicide note. Whatever might be at stake in this definition (a relation of art to life, or of person to persona), questions arise concerning not only "Edge" but another document, Sylvia Plath's very last piece of writing, the note that she pinned to the perambulator before she gassed herself: "Please call Dr. Horder" (Stevenson 297). In one sense, as her last words, the note brought her speaking to an end, but as a last request—to have words, to say something to someone else—they marked a beginning. Although she could not have predicted it, the conversation inaugurated by these unfinal words would rage on for decades, a conversation both informing of and informed by the interpretation of her poems.

The influence of this conversation is visible in Dr. Horder's own account of the suicide, his own last word on what had happened in the kitchen of 23 Fitzroy Road that cold morning in February, 1963. His remarks resonate with some of Plath's deepest and most disquieting themes:

> The care with which the kitchen was prepared was only too obvious. My judgment has always been that this was a very determined attempt to end her life[. . . .] She "chose" the one period when no one was free to be with her. The act occurred at the time when suicides are most common, at the end of the night[. . . .] I believe, indeed it was repeatedly obvious to me, that she was deeply depressed, "ill," "out of her mind," and that any explanations of a psychological sort are inadequate[. . . .] I believe [. . .] she was liable to large swings of mood, but so excessive that a doctor inevitably thinks in terms of brain chemistry[. . . .] [T]he

irrational compulsion to end it makes me think that the body was governing the mind. (Stevenson 298)

What Horder offers is a psychiatric, somatic account of suicidal motivation:
the mind, and indeed the person, cannot withstand the onslaught of the
body's malign "chemistry," and the person succumbs to a self-destructive impulse. In the local context of the ensuing disputes about "what Plath really
meant" to accomplish that morning, Horder's contention is directed against
those who would assert that Plath did not intend to do herself in, but had
staged her suicide as the familiar cry for help.[1] He is preferring an account
based on visible facts to one founded on speculation. He resigns himself to the
banality and helplessness of a story constrained to avoid "explanations of a
psychological sort." However, from beneath the surface of these remarks,
from beneath the surface of their apparent superficiality, questions emerge
concerning agency, determination, the contours and definitions of the self,
and the conditions under which a coherent image of the self may be maintained—all questions that lie at the heart of Plath's best work. By setting off
chose in quotation marks, Horder lifts up the concept of autonomy and suspends it in a field of uncertainty. Yes, Plath chose to die; she was *determined*
to do so. But the act of choosing and the state of determination were alienated, at least partially, from her will. Plath's mind was being "governed" by
Plath's body. Not only was Plath unfree to act otherwise than she did; this web
of unfreedom ensnared not only her but others as well: "No one was free to
be with her." Something "makes [Horder] think" the way he does; he thinks
"inevitably" of brain chemistry, of a body governing the mind. Thus, two
kinds of "end" take a central role, the end a person made to her life (brought
about, as usual, at the end of night), and the other intended ends—the purposes and determinations—that shaped the course of her life and continue to
shape her story. The conclusions Horder had no choice but to draw, that the
body was governing the mind, that chemicals were governing the body, implies a chain of agency stretching away from the autonomous *I* through the
governing body, which is in turn governed by chemicals, in turn governed by
other laws (heredity, environment, consequence), a chain with no visible end.
It is this manner in which agency, or agencies, traverse and transcend the self,
the lyric and historical *I*, that I take to be Plath's great topic, and her account
of it Plath's great contribution to poetry in English.

When I say that these are among the deepest concerns of Plath the poet,
by "Plath the poet" I mean that name under whose imprint several hundred
poems, one novel, assorted short stories, letters, journals (incinerated and otherwise) have been gathered. It would be my preference to observe my custom

in preceding chapters of allowing all uncertainties about the isomorphism of author and person to stalk my argument from beyond its periphery. To do so, however, would be to make the assumption that the name "Plath" refers as placidly to a body of work as it does to a historical person (as placidly, at least by comparison, as "Hardy," "Stevens," and "Larkin" do). This would be an evasion of the very questions her work puts so urgently to the reader: who am I, and how do I know? and more radically, what is an "I," and what does "to know" mean?

The "story" about the "facts" to which Horder contributes has been more than forty years in the telling and is not complete. As shrill, maddening, repetitive, and small-minded as it has sometimes seemed, the story is important for several reasons: it establishes the context in which a group of the twentieth century's most arresting poems can be read; it casts some light on the complex relation between the poet in the poem and the poet in the world; it has colored and been colored by certain political and ethical undertakings—feminism perhaps foremost among them—avowedly committed to the dismantling of oppressive institutions, the relief of suffering, and the equitable allocation of power. Much has been written, sometimes for and sometimes against Plath, in the service of these political and ethical projects. And at a further remove, much now has been written on how Plath simultaneously colludes with and subverts any single agenda.[2] What these accounts share is a fundamental conviction that Plath is someone who has a story, and that the story can and should be clarified. A property of these disputes, whatever side one might incline toward, is to suppress the troubling realization that Plath's poetic labor was dedicated in large part to refuting the assumption that there is an integrated self about which the specifics of a story can be established. Of course this assumption is one that all readers must make, at least most of the time, in order to account coherently for poems that merit painstaking contemplation—and in order to preserve sanity. The questions, however, remain. What can be said about a writer for whom the preservation of sanity and a coherent account of the speaking self were in the end impossible? And what may be said of a body of poetry that entails even in its most unique, personal, and self-possessed moments a complication and a critique of what it means to be a unique person, what it means to assume an *I* at all?

AT ONE WITH THE DRIVE:
THE RIDDEN AND RIDERLESS HORSE

My approach to these questions begins with a consideration of a figure as central to Plath as it is to an entire tradition of Western poetic figuration, the figure of the horse and rider, a figure deeply implicated with questions of mastery and power, selfhood and otherness. In an early, awkward poem, "Whiteness I Remember," Plath's describes an experience of clinging to her white horse, Sam, as he gallops out of her control. The poem concludes with Plath "Almost thrown, not / Thrown: fear, wisdom, at one: all colors / Spinning to still in his one whiteness" (102). This conclusion proposes an event of sublime unification; the experience of spinning out of control—all the colors of the landscape blurring—elevates the speaker from the mundane into the transcendent, where the particular, distinct colors of her daily world are spun into a unified, compound whiteness. Plath, however, is reaching toward something she will not be able to grasp until later. The poem is weak because it does not specify why wisdom should necessarily derive from this fear, nor does it say why the horse is capable of subsuming the entire spectrum of experience into "its one whiteness." Although at first Plath thought that "Whiteness I Remember" might be a "book poem" (288n) she did not in fact include it in *The Colossus*. Her decision not to do so implies a recognition that the poem's topic—the role of the self transported by a surge of force—would require a different, deeper treatment. Dismantling the poem for parts, she gave it that deeper treatment in "Ariel" (239).

Like "Whiteness I Remember," "Ariel" brings together horse and rider in one surging movement, absorbing the central phrase "at one" from the earlier poem:

> Stasis in darkness.
> Then the substanceless blue
> Pour of tor and distances.
>
> God's lioness,
> How one we grow,
> Pivot of heels and knees!—The furrow
>
> Splits and passes, sister to
> The brown arc
> Of the neck I cannot catch,
>
> Nigger-eye
> Berries cast dark
> Hooks—
>
> Black sweet blood mouthfuls,
> Shadows.
> Something else

Hauls me through air—
Thighs, hair;
Flakes from my heels.

White
Godiva, I unpeel—
Dead hands, dead stringencies.

And now I
Foam to wheat, a glitter of seas.
The child's cry

Melts in the wall.
And I
Am the arrow,

The dew that flies
Suicidal, at one with the drive
Into the red
Eye, the cauldron of morning.

In "Whiteness I Remember" the different realms of experience remain relatively distinct through the end of the poem. It is the horse that leaps out of Plath's control, and in the course of the wild gallop, Plath is lifted toward and into the blur of his power. Woman and horse remain necessarily distinct, just as the world of the animal-immortal and the world of the human-mortal in Yeats's "Leda and the Swan" remain distinct. After all, a transfer of force cannot occur from one realm of being into another unless the boundary between them remains in place. In "Ariel," however, the question of who is who remains unclear from the beginning. From whose stasis does the poem emerge? Horse's? Woman's? Are horse and rider pouring into the distances, or are the distances pouring into them? Once the rider has "foamed to wheat, a glitter of seas," does she remain separate from them, or does she become a part of them, assumed bodily like the dew into the sunrise? Among these indeterminacies, the juncture of horse and rider takes on a particular importance, even while their separateness breaks down. "God's lioness" appears at first to be Plath's term for the horse, her servant animal, as powerful and enslaved as Prospero's servant spirit, but rider and horse are never separate enough to establish a stable polarity of master and servant, rider and ridden. "God's lioness" refers more properly to the compound beast they form together, woman and horse combined in one kinetic element, a surging fusion of divine, overmastering intelligence and brute power articulated around a shared pivot. The poem hauls the horse/rider, largely undifferentiated, from the dark stasis of its prehistory. The first pronoun is "we" in the fifth line: "how one we grow." The *I* of the poem remains indistinct. When it first appears, it designates less an autonomous individual than a link in a chain, less a single self than a gesture reaching to catch the horse's brown neck, which in turn is less a neck than an "arc" of movement reaching out over the open furrow, which in turn reaches off into the dissolving "pour of tor and distances." The *I* achieves full presence only in the penultimate stanza, blazing into visibility before vanishing into the eye of the sun.

In its second appearance in the middle of the poem, the *I* denotes the "White Godiva" unpeeling from herself the "Dead hands, dead stringencies," encumbrances which recall the hooks cast by the "Nigger-eye" berries. These central stanzas further complicate the fluctuations between self and other by introducing an additional order of otherness. Manifestly, the branches of the nigger-eye berry bushes take their place among the stringencies that impede the horse and rider's flight, among the attachments and obligations that tether them to the world—impediments, once sloughed off, that reveal a pure naked whiteness, Lady Godiva, the body of nakedness itself. In contrast with this white nakedness, the nigger-eye berries would signify total abjection, blackness as ravenous, loathsome, the object of vitriolic, racial hatred. But to the precise degree that these berries represent an abject otherness, they take an opposite position as well, not only subjugated ("nigger") but subjugating ("casting hooks"). Their blackness is not merely the absolute, expendable Other to Godiva's whiteness, but a part of it as well; they are its "shadows," and therefore "sister[s] to / The brown arc" of her movement, with the horse's brownness the median hue between the white of nakedness and the black of the berries. Furthermore, as "black sweet blood mouthfuls" they are no longer wholly different from, or external to, the rider—not even to the extent that her shadow is. Rather, they establish a link with the interior of her body, the intimacy of a taste filling the mouth, the juice of the berry a dark red like the dark red of blood, blood which for Plath is not only the sign of mortality but of womanhood as well (compare "Childless Woman" 259). In this poem, what seems most external is in fact most internal.

The poem, then, describes two different kinds of movement. The first is a linear vector, pure trajectory and pure transformation rhetorically akin to the conclusion of Larkin's "The Whitsun Weddings"—an arrow into dew into the sun. The other movement is a countervailing pull, back toward the dark center of the poem, toward the dark center of the body. The act of flying, suicidal, into the sun is an act of death, and as such, returns the speaker to the realm of the dead hands and dead stringencies; it is an evaporation of clear dew but also a spilling of red blood, the sweet blood mouthful of the nigger-eye berries. This countervailing pull is not merely an arrow pointing in the opposite direction, down instead of up; what it countermands is linearity itself, expressed particularly as a progression from self into otherness in a narrative of self-transcendence. Rather, the arc of transcendence is shadowed by the loop of return.

To the degree that most critical accounts of Plath have based their arguments on the fundamental assumption of selfhood underwriting the work, they have been constrained to ignore or downplay the more radical implications of poems such as "Ariel." In fact, much of Plath criticism is engaged in a concerted effort to incorporate—literally—her poems into a discourse of integrated selfhood. This description of the poems in *Ariel* in Seamus Heaney's forceful article "Sylvia Plath's Indefatigable Hoof-taps"[3] demonstrates the ease with which the virtues of her poems have been understood as congruent with the virtues of selfhood itself:

> There is the pressure of absolute *fiat* behind them: a set of images springs into presence and into motion as at a whimsical but unignorable command. . . . Their metamorphic speed and metaphoric eagerness are boosted by the logic of their own associative power, and they rush towards whatever conclusions are inherent in their elements. These poems are the vehicles of their own impulses. . . . They are, in Lowell's words, events rather than the records of events, and as such represent the triumph of Sylvia Plath's romantic ambition to bring expressive power and fully achieved selfhood into congruence. The tongue proceeds headily into its role as governor; it has located the source where the fixed stars are reflected and from which they transmit their spontaneous and weirdly trustworthy symbols.

The poem from which Heaney takes his last figure, and the title of his essay, is the poem "Words." He reads "Words" as a poem of discovery, a "location of the source where the fixed stars are reflected and from which [the stars] transmit their spontaneously and weirdly trustworthy symbols." He appropriates "Words" to praise Plath's achievements in her period of highest accomplishment. What he praises is the accuracy of a reflection, the clarity of a signal, and the trustworthiness of the symbols it transmits. The passage describes Plath's arrival at the flaring efflorescence of her talent as an arrival at a kind of neo-Platonist enlightenment—all cobwebs cleared, all static squelched, and every instrument fine-tuned to an exquisitely accurate sensitivity. "Words," however, does not make these assertions on its own behalf:

Axes
After whose stroke the wood rings,
And the echoes!
Echoes traveling
Off from the center like horses.

The sap
Wells like tears, like the
Water striving
To re-establish its mirror
Over the rock

That drops and turns,
A white skull,
Eaten by weedy greens.
Years later I
Encounter them on the road—

Words dry and riderless,
The indefatigable hoof-taps.
While
From the bottom of the pool, fixed stars
Govern a life. (270)

Like "Ariel," "Words" is a horse-and-rider poem, but one in which beast and human have not fused together to form a single chimeral creature. The rider is only present as an absence, just as the words themselves have departed from the speaker who uttered them. The utterance that inaugurates the poem is the resounding gesture of division, the axe-stroke that cleaves word from echo. Furthermore, the stroke divides the word from the appositional figures that describe it, that make up the entire poem. What the original words said or meant remains obscure, and so the poem's own originary point is one of disruption and disjunction, a traveling out from a center that is not itself visible. There is no point in the poem where the words themselves are governed by the intelligence that spoke them.[4]

The poem embodies its own act of figuration in a series of expanding, concentric rings. The figures that make up the poem are like echoes ringing outward from a source, or the ringed waves troubling the surface of a pool, each wave or echo simultaneously repeating and revising the one that preceded it. To the extent that this poem describes a trajectory outward from a source, it resembles the flight of "Ariel," and like that earlier poem, "Words" too entails a complicating return. The echo-horses return, but "dry and riderless," saddled with an absence. The absence is not only of the rider but of the blooded vitality that the words once may have had; this is what "dry" means. They have become productions of pure sound, pure repetition, a tireless iteration of taps. A rift has opened between form and content that cannot be closed.

This rift is not wholly an abstract or theoretical proposition. It calls into question the very nature of the speaker who speaks the poem. "Words" is a poem of mourning, mourning for a lost image of the self. (As such, it appropriately recalls, and hybridizes, the myths of Narcissus and Echo.) The tears elicited by this mourning attempt to re-establish a reflective surface that can sustain this image, but something has been irrevocably lost. The image has already been pulled apart, a skull has already sunk in a pool, surrendered to the shadowy, masticating catabolism of its depths. The mirror will never be re-established, just as the horse will never reassume its rider.

The poem then is an elegy for the perfect image, whether the image is conceived as the perfect reflection of a face, or the echo blooded with the voice of the speaker, or the body (perhaps as God's image) perfected by death. In order to appropriate the figure, then, of the stars as trustworthy governors, Heaney must suppress this elegiac strain in the poem. He shares the desire of the "tears" themselves to re-establish the integrity of the water's mirror. And in one sense, he is justified in doing so. The force and coherence of Plath's final work gives credence to Heaney's assertion that the poet has realized her "ambition to bring expressive power and fully achieved selfhood into congruence." Surely some kind of full achievement has been managed, and a fresh, vigorous power of expression has been unleashed. But the powers and the selves that "Words" describes are radically out of congruence. It is not enough to say that Plath found a way to write powerfully coherent poems about experiences of powerful incoherence, lack, and dissociation. The reader is compelled to conceive of the *I* of this poem as standing at an intersection between the authorial, lyric *I* and the *I* that appears in the third stanza, the one that encounters the horse-echoes and is a fragment or an aspect of the larger, dissociated "life" dispersed as the poem's many elements: axes, echoes, tears, disrupted mirrors, riderless horses, cannibalistic depths, wounds, strivings, and so forth.

"Words," in fact, compresses so many different parts into one small space that their relations to one another remain obscure. Frustration awaits any eagerness for specification (what words? what center? whose tears? which is it, rock or skull? what stars? fixed by whom?). It is at this cost that Plath purchases the gnomic intensity of the poem. "Words," however, represents a late fusion of elements treated in greater detail elsewhere. What the poem invokes most pointedly is Plath's preoccupation with the different agencies that govern, or seek to govern, a life, and the nature of the division between them. As an elegy for an *I* that disperses into a group of disparate properties, the poem focuses most closely on a loss, the loss of the image of the self, and to this extent, the shadow of a coherent self falls across the poem. The poem does not show Plath working at her most unhuman register. In fact, it is suffused with human presences lingering after recent departures. After all, horses are to be ridden by human riders, and axes are to be wielded by human hands. It is, therefore, human agency, though departed, that remains in the forefront, present as echoes and taps.

The dispersal occurs largely as an unfolding of natural physical properties, the movement of echoes or animals, the expansion of ripples on a pool. By moving outward and away from the violence of its first gesture (the axe stroke) the poem moves away from the violent and rending forces that bring about the loss. For all the indefatigability of the hoof-taps, there is still a quality of settling, and the self, by breaking into parts, has drawn nearer to an entropic homeostasis. Other poems do not admit so readily the possibility of an easeful death. In these works, when the self appears in its fragmented form, the different components manifest their own insatiable and incompatible appetites.[5]

AN ENGINE, AN ENGINE:
THE AUTONOMY OF THE MACHINE

Juxtaposing a poem such as "Ariel" with one such as "Words" reinforces the impression that a Plath poem tends to take one of two paths, either the path toward apotheosis or the path toward disintegration and death. A corollary to this argument would be that there is a kind of Manichaean division of forces in her world: the powerful, integrative, fusing force (horse and rider blent in one surging motion), and the force of destruction (axes biting into trees, weeds eating into skulls). And as Heaney says, Plath's poems do seem to throw themselves open at times to good spirits, at times to bad (157). Such an account of Plath's work, however, necessarily ignores the promiscuity with which these forces blur into one another in her poems.

The work is full of machines. These machines show how these disparate forces combine, how they may be articulated one with another, and how they stand away from the human body, self-sufficient and subject to their own logic. Plath is drawn toward machines for the simultaneous reasons that they are like people (doing things, accomplishing tasks, effecting transformations, breaking down) and unlike people (manufactured not born, non-mortal, able to be dismantled, assembled from interchangeable parts, mindless). They exert a further fascination to the extent that the components of a life or body, viewed in isolation, resemble machines more than they resemble humans. A consequence of this is that the vitality that animates a person and the sum of particularities that constitute personhood seem, upon closer inspection, to derive from realms of being and ways of doing antithetical to personhood. It is in this sense that the status of Plath's poetry as personal or impersonal must ultimately be assessed. The strain in Plath criticism which has argued for one designation instead of the other has not given sufficient account to the crucial intersection of the personal and non-personal in the poems.[6]

At times this convergence troubles Plath and at times it does not. When she writes, in "Morning Song" (156), "Love set you going like a fat gold watch," the benign fatness of the watch shares the baby's chubby rotundity, plumped and vital. Love finds a point of congruence with the Watchmaker God, procreation and creation articulating a series of springs and gears, a device of intricately interlaced unwinding consequences. In "Tulips" the attitude toward this "setting-going" is more ambivalent. In the liminal stupor of the hospital, the tulips manifest a vitality as intense as it is unwanted:

> The tulips are too red in the first place, they hurt me.
> Even through the gift paper I could hear them breathe
> Lightly, through their white swaddlings, like an awful baby.
> Their redness talks to my wound, it corresponds.
> They are subtle: they seem to float, though they weigh me down,
> Upsetting me with their sudden tongues and their color,
> A dozen red lead sinkers around my neck[. . . .]
>
> The vivid tulips eat my oxygen.
> Before they came the air was calm enough,
> Coming and going, breath by breath, without any fuss.
> Then the tulips filled it up like a loud noise.
> Now the air snags and eddies round them the way a river
> Snags and eddies round a sunken rust-red engine. (160)

At first the tulips seem wholly alien, blooms from a nether-land of pure threat. They signify a death entirely different from the swaddling oblivion the speaker craves. As sinkers, they will drown her, not in the numbness of opiates but in a river of snags and eddies flowing around the heavy, discarded carcass of an engine. Because the engine is sunken, it offers at first an image of her body brought down by the red sinkers, but the engine is also a figure for the tulips themselves. The body and what is alien to it converge in this one defunct, mechanical figure. Like the same engine, polished and rebuilt, the heart creaks into its wonted motion: "I am aware of my heart: it opens and closes / Its bowl of red blooms out of sheer love of me." In an anguished convergence, tulips, wound, and engine come together as the heart, the heart which forces an unrefusable vigor back into the body.

Two years later, as the conviction hardens that health is a country Plath will never in fact reach, the vital machine splits from her body once again and takes the more malignant form, in "Paralytic," of an iron lung:

> My mind a rock,
> No fingers to grip, no tongue,
> My god the iron lung
>
> That loves me, pumps
> My two
> Dust bags in and out,
> Will not
>
> Let me relapse
> While the day outside glides by like ticker tape. (266)

Here it is not the heart that opens and closes but an external apparatus. As in "Morning Song" love sets the body going, but "love" in this context, with a fierce but superficial irony, denotes a dedication closer to sadism or mindless automatism. In "Gigolo" this mechanization of eros takes on more nuance, stripping central figures from "Morning Song" and "Tulips" and re-fitting them with deepened menace. The gigolo speaks, describing the cool, mechanical workings of his anonymous assignations:

> Pocket watch, I tick well[. . . .]
> It is best to meet in a cul-de-sac,
>
> A palace of velvet
> With windows of mirrors.
> There one is safe,
> There are no family photographs,
>
> No rings through the nose, no cries[. . . .]
>
> My mouth sags,
> The mouth of Christ
> When my engine reaches the end of it.
> The tattle of my
> Gold joints, my way of turning
>
> Bitches to ripples of silver
> Rolls out a carpet, a hush.
>
> And there is no end, no end of it[. . . .] (267)

Here the figure of the love-watch represents desire as a frictionless machine, a soulless excellence irresistibly melting away any frigid rebuff. Perfectly lubricated, it brings all of its objects to a state of equally lubricated desire. Perfection, however, is achieved at a cost. When Plath, speaking as the gigolo, writes, "My mouth sags, / The mouth of Christ / When my engine reaches the end of it," Love Incarnate assumes a miniaturized and denatured form as carnal love, a glittering, implacable penis-Christ, raised endlessly not from death but flaccidity, and "there is no end" to this empty repetition. Such a repetition, with dark comedy, blurs the distinction between eros and thanatos. "Gigolo" takes its place in a series of hungry-machine figures in Plath's poetry; in these figures, appetite resembles less the appetite of a body for food or for sexual gratification than the appetite of death for the body itself. The confusion between the site of appetite—of the body, for the body—reveals one of Plath's most enduring topoi, the non-congruence of the self and its desires.

The engine that "gets to the end of it" appears elsewhere as a principle of mortality—death as unstoppable locomotive devouring the distance to its terminal destination. A property of this locomotive is that its motion is also a form of eating, as in the opening passage of "Getting There":

> How far is it?
> How far is it now?
> The gigantic gorilla interiors
> Of the wheels move, they appall me—[. . . .]
> Now is the time for bribery.
> What do wheels eat, these wheels
> Fixed to their arcs like gods,
> The silver leash of the will—
> Inexorable[. . . .](247)

This engine approaches a place of death, a place of no return, and it devours what stands in its way. In "Getting There" Plath hopes that the engine might be placated with some sacrificial food-offering, a substitute for her own body; in "Totem" what the engine eats is the track itself, burning up its trajectory like a fuse: "The engine is killing the track, the track is silver, / It stretches into the distance. It will be eaten nevertheless. // Its running is useless" (264). In "Sheep in Fog," the engine is a machine for the expenditure of oxygen, and it appears as death's horse, its harness bells tolling an imminent end: "The train leaves a line of breath. / O slow / Horse the color of rust, / Hooves, dolorous bells—." Shadowing each of these locomotive figures is the image of the trains transporting prisoners to concentration camps during the Second World War. This topic is treated most explicitly, and most infamously, in "Daddy":

> [. . .] I never could talk to you.
> The tongue stuck in my jaw.
>
> It stuck in a barb wire snare.
> Ich, ich, ich, ich,
> I could hardly speak.
> I thought every German was you.
> And the language obscene
>
> An engine, an engine
> Chuffing me off like a Jew.
> A Jew to Dachau, Auschwitz, Belsen. (222)

The engine is as inexorable as the ones in "Getting There" and in "Totem," but in this poem, a special, additional association has been made. The engine is not merely the engine of mortality, or even the ineluctable engine of historical destruction. The engine here is the engine of speech itself. The claim that speech is an engine, a vehicle that both holds and consumes the self, is the claim toward which all other claims in her poetry concerning will, personhood, and fate ultimately point.

MY FACE A FEATURELESS, FINE JEW LINEN: SURFACE OF THE BODY, SURFACE OF THE TEXT

By equating speech and the engine in "Daddy" the speaker locates the site of enunciation both inside and outside of herself. The German language embodies linguistically a cultural and ethnic heritage that the speaker can neither escape nor avow. On the one hand, it signifies a foreign tongue, the index of difference between German Nazi and Polish Jew, or between German and American. On the other, it represents an innate identification, as inalienable as ethnic or racial identity—mother tongue, speech of the fatherland (literally, because Otto Plath was German). Stuck in the jaw, "native" speech finds itself snared on a contested border ("barb wire") between the inside and outside of the speaker's body; she can't take the language in, she can't get a word out. This contested border traverses the speaker as well as her world. When she says *I* she is also *not* saying *"Ich"* and vice versa; the subject of the poem is not so much an *I* as an *"I-Ich"*—or more precisely, a *"neither-wholly-I-nor-Ich."* By staging the poem in this way, Plath makes the point that voice itself—the constitutive, inalienable instrument of the lyric speaker—has as one of its properties a foreignness, something both familiar and unfamiliar, a set of sounds neither wholly inside nor wholly outside the self that it appears to predicate.

Jacqueline Rose, in her acute and illuminating account of the poem, assigns special privilege here to the infantile or regressive status of speech. She sees the speaker as struggling to find a place for utterance on a gradient whose downward pull threatens meaninglessness or silence:

> If this poem is in some sense about the death of the father, a death both willed and premature, it is no less about the death of language. Returning to the roots of language, it discovers a personal political history (the one as indistinguishable from the other) which once again fails to enter words[. . . .] Twice over, the origins of the father, physically and in language, are lost—through the wars which scrape flat German tongue and Polish town, and then through the name of the town itself, which is so common that it fails in its function to identify, fails in fact to name[. . . .] Wars wipe out names, the father cannot be spoken to, and the child cannot talk, except to repeat endlessly, in a destroyed, obscene language, the most basic or minimal unit of self-identity in speech; "ich, ich, ich, ich" (the first draft has "incestuous" for "obscene"). The notorious difficulty of the first-person pronoun in relation to identity—its status as shifter, the division or splitting of the subject which it both carries and denies—is merely compounded by its repetition here[. . . .] The effect, of course [. . . .] is not one of assertion but [. . . .] of the word sticking in the throat. (225–7)

Rose sees the speaker as having been exiled from language and driven to a point of primitive utterance. There is, however, nothing particularly primitive about Plath's *I-ich*. The problem is not that the speaker has been forced out of speech, but that she finds herself too much in it, too aware of its costs and consequences. Encountering the "root of language" does not necessarily entail a "failure to enter words."[7] The stark, burlesque violence of the scenario (the outsized boot, the fat black heart), together with the cooing rhyme and insistent, loose-jointed trimeters and tetrameters, serve to emphasize the most basic contrasts (good/bad, Nazi/Jew) and sound patterns (*I, I, I, oo, oo, oo,*) in a gesture of "scraping flat" into a partially abstracted, cartoon flatness. The effect is not, however, a Roethkean submersion into the prelinguistic. The basis toward which the poem pushes the speaker is not infancy but a primary, peremptory fascination with the terms of selfhood and difference. This obsessional focus serves to illuminate and dramatize the conflicts and costs inherent in any speech whatsoever. To have entered into language *at all*, she implies, is to have assumed a condition no less fraught with political and ontological risk than the specific cultural predicament of her speaker. That the terms of this assertion are by definition outrageous does not disqualify them

from compelling internal consistency with the nature of Plath's poetic practice. "Given the way Plath stages this as a problem in the poem, presenting it
as part of a crisis of language and identity," Rose writes, "the argument that
she simply uses the Holocaust to aggrandize her personal difficulties seems
completely beside the point. Who can say that these were not difficulties
which she experienced in her very person?" (228). Or, rather, who can say that
these were not difficulties which she experienced in the very act of speaking,
of assuming a persona?

This account emphasizes the inherent distinction between the speech of
the speaker (the poet's medium) and the speech of ethnicity (speech of the
group, the mother tongue). Speech in the first sense, the sense of the poet's
medium, is as much a way of relating to the world as it is a set of words governed by grammatical rules. It is (in a particularly Heideggerean-Stevensian
way of thinking) that in which the world has its being, a world which is, by
definition, the set of everything that is the case, and which is, therefore, indivisible. On the other hand, speech in its second sense, the language of the
group, is the manifestation of a divided world, a world shot through with distinctions between us and them, self and other, native and foreign. The first is
the voice of the speaker who assumes in the very act of speaking that she can
"talk to you." The second is the voice that requires a translator (a "Polack
friend") and implies distinctions of mortal import ("the language obscene //
An engine, an engine / Chuffing me off like a Jew"). Rather than opening
communities of comprehension, it is the figure of incomprehension and untranslatable difference.

The fractiousness in the critical debates concerning "Daddy" reflects
this internal struggle between the two different roles of language. The questions with which the speaker struggles resemble those questions put to the
poem and the poet: to what degree can a language be appropriated ("I used
to pray to recover you")? what are the constraints that limit poetic speech ("I
could never talk to you")? what are the alternatives to speech (the telephone
"off at the root," the stake in the "fat black heart")? what does it mean to
make a model ("A man in black with a Meinkampf look") or to attribute resemblances ("talk like a Jew," "no less a devil for that," "the vampire who said
he was you")? Prior to these questions are the questions of the basis on which
subjectivity is founded: when I consider myself, or when you consider me,
am I an *I* (a participant in a conversation conducted by an unlimited number of *I*'s) or am I a *Jew* (a member in a fixed system composed of one sadist-
subject, the Father-Nazi, and one victim-object, the Daughter-Jew)? For
Plath, this is not only, or chiefly, a question of cultural identity but a question of the linguistic basis of subjectivity. Rose points out that the first line

of the poem, "You do not do, you do not do," "allows us to read it both as English and German: 'You du not du,' 'You you not you'" (226–7). Once we see that Plath has authorized us to read the poem as a kind of macaronic composite, we recognize not only the you-not-you that Rose points out but also an I-not-I in the word *Jew* itself. On the one hand, *Jew* repeats the *oo* sound, already consecrated to the second person by the tenacious rhyme, recalling *you* and stressing its homophony with the first syllable of the German *jude*. When Plath writes "I may be a bit of a Jew," she is also saying, "*I* may be a bit of a *you*." On the other hand, *Jew,* capitalized like the English *I,* and containing in its first two letters the French *je,* exerts a counterpressure away from objecthood back toward subjectivity. To be a Jew, as she employs the term, is to be by definition a subject lodged athwart the throat of speech, both local and alien, the voice occupied, like Poland or France by another, *I* and *you, je* and *du* together.

Critical emphasis on "Daddy" has distracted from the localized, transient role of the holocaust trope in Plath's work. She turns away from this topos into a world ravaged by the conflicts enacted by the Second World War but no longer engaged in those struggles. Whereas "Daddy" narrates a desperate struggle to defend against or compensate for a terrible loss or wound, the poems that follow increasingly presume a world where the loss or wound has been irremediably sustained. In "Mary's Song" Poland is a "cicatrix." In "The Munich Mannequins," Munich is a "morgue between Paris and Rome." The pitiless action of fate carries on, unsponsored by a single antagonist. The engine of death, and the engine of language, do not operate at the behest of a malign but human agent but of their own accord. Whereas the world of "Daddy" is premised on a belief in justice, the world that follows is impervious to redress.

If "Daddy" originates in a presumption about how certain persons deserve to be treated, it leaves Plath, and the reader, with a radical doubt as to the nature of personhood. In "Lady Lazarus" Plath pursues her inquiry into this doubt by questioning what it means to have a surface, and where such a surface might be located:

> [. . . .]
> A sort of walking miracle, my skin
> Bright as a Nazi lampshade,
> My right foot
>
> A paperweight,
> My face a featureless, fine
> Jew linen

Peel off the napkin
O my enemy.
Do I terrify?—[. . . .]

What a trash
To annihilate each decade.

What a million filaments.
The peanut-crunching crowd
Shoves in to see

Them unwrap me hand and foot—
The big strip tease.
Gentlemen, ladies

These are my hands
My knees.
I may be skin and bone,

Nevertheless I am the same, identical woman. (244)

Where is the surface of a body that retreats endlessly into the recesses of its wrappings, the grave clothes which seem to take the place of the body itself? The unveiling is a "strip tease," but as in "Gigolo," "there is no end, no end to it."

Ash, ash—
You poke and stir.
Flesh, bone, there is nothing there.

The face "is a featureless, fine / Jew linen," not a recognizably human countenance, but a "valuable," a negotiable object whose value is established in an economy of other values. The face underlying (or underwriting) this valuable is composed of absences and remnants, "eye-pits" and "ash, ash" (recalling the *Ich, ich* of "Daddy"). In this way the poem's textiles, the linen face-shroud and the winding-sheets, take on a particularly textual quality. They are woven surfaces, surfaces of value and of art, that assume the place of the "actual self" that has vanished beneath them, eaten by the "grave cave" or incinerated away in a holy (or unholy) fire. The body is a composition of veils, and each veil is a composition of filaments. And just as the body has led Plath to consider veils, veils lead her to consider these filaments.

Like Plath's engines and machines, and like the personae of Nazi and Jew, these filaments are reductions, partial abstractions. The gigolo machine is the reduction of a person with desires and appetites into the mechanism of those appetites alone. The locomotive eating the track is the inexorable action of death represented as nothing more than an unstoppable force and the interval of track yet to be consumed. Machines reveal themselves as consortia of component implements, the hooks, wheels, screws, and blades to be found throughout Plath's work. If there is any limit to this reduction, Plath suggests, it does not appear until all recognizable aspects of the world have broken down. To this degree, there is a pointillist surface to her world: the face reduced to woven veil, linen unraveled to filaments, and filaments reduced to particles. Plath responds to this disintegrative phenomenon at times with dismay, at times with sublime awe; it is what she thinks of when she writes, in "A Birthday Present" (206), "Sweetly, sweetly, I breathe in, / Filling my veins with invisibles, with the million / Probable motes that tick the years off my life." In "Purdah," another veil poem, she is impressed with the disregard these particles show for human concerns; they are the "million ignorants" that make up the "chandelier / Of air" (243). In "Gulliver," Plath describes her newborn's fall into this web of myriad, mindless influences:

> The spider-men have caught you,
>
> Winding and twining their petty fetters,
> Their bribes—
> So many silks.
>
> How they hate you. (251)

These fetters recall the "stringencies" and "hooks" in "Ariel," but their web cannot be so easily shaken off; Plath comes to see this web as the medium of form, not form's hindrance.

Ultimately what the fragmentation and separateness of these influences represent for Plath is death itself. Death as it is elaborated in her poems, however, is not merely the end or the extermination of the mortal individual, nor is it a state that is by definition the opposite of life. It is everything that the temporary, illusory coherence of the subject is not. This is the news that the conclusion of "Totem" means to impart:

> Shall the hood of the cobra appall me—
> The loneliness of its eye, the eye of the mountains
>
> Through which the sky eternally threads itself?
> The world is blood-hot and personal
>
> Dawn says, with its blood-flush.
> There is no terminus, only suitcases

Out of which the same self unfolds like a suit
Bald and shiny, with pockets of wishes,

Notions and tickets, short circuits and folding mirrors.
I am mad, calls the spider, waving its many arms.

And in truth it is terrible,
Multiplied in the eyes of the flies.

They buzz like blue children
In nets of the infinite

Roped in at the end by the one
Death with its many sticks.

When Dawn says that "the world is blood-hot and personal" the adjectival form
of "personal" marks the great distance between the category of the "personal"
and the category of the "person." The implication is that the personal does not
in fact depend upon a person. In fact, the "personal" may be as close as we ever
get to the person as such. Life is present in a hot suffusion of blood, but the
blood is uncontained; it is the heat of the dawn that might "congeal and stiffen
to history" ("A Birthday Present"). In place of a single *I*, there is an "eye" through
which a string of associated perceptions threads itself.[8] The self in "Totem" as in
"Lady Lazarus" is a composition of surfaces and disruptions, of suits and folding mirrors, abortive notions and faulty connections. Death, the spider, appears
in its refracted, multitudinous form, reflected in the flies' eyes.[9]

What gives these webs their central place in Plath's accomplishment,
however, is the link they establish between, on the one hand, the fragmentation and disintegration of death, and on the other, a process that seems to be
its complete opposite, the creation of images. It is not enough, Plath's poems
say, to view the filaments cast by the spider men in "Gulliver" as merely those
forces which will eventually rope the body in, the million probable motes that
tick the years off a life, or the million ignorant influences that shape it. Each of
these poems is as much about reflection as it is about disintegration. They say
that the creation of an image and the disintegration of the self are related acts.

MIRRORS UTTERING NOTHING BUT BLOOD: DISTILLATION AS EFFACEMENT

The link between the filament and the mirror is one that concerns Plath even
in the relatively early "Private Ground," a poem about the draining of the
ponds at Yaddo before the arrival of winter.

All morning, with smoking breath, the handyman
Has been draining the goldfish ponds.
They collapse like lungs, the escaped water
Threading back, filament by filament, to the pure
Platonic table where it lives. The baby carp
Litter the mud like orangepeel[. . . .]
The woods creak and ache, and the day forgets itself.
I bend over this drained basin where the small fish
Flex as the mud freezes.
They glitter like eyes, and I collect them all.
Morgue of old logs and old images, the lake
Opens and shuts, accepting them among its reflections. (130)

The pools are described first as surfaces composed of filaments that can thread back to their origin, which is a Platonic realm of forms preceding and sponsoring the images that the pools reflect. In the last stanza, however, this Platonic realm has yielded its position to a mere lake, not a Platonic point of origin, but a "morgue of old logs and old images." The poem is a poem of saving (the small lives of the fish preserved by their transfer to the lake, or at the very least, commemorated), but already visible is the connection between this act of saving and an act of death; the fish are saved but in the lake's morgue of images.[10]

The connection that Plath indicates here exists only on an intuitive level; it is not until the later poems that she turns her attention more directly toward its implications. By the time she writes "Gulliver," she has already begun to move in this direction. In this later poem, before shifting to the central figure of a newborn already fettered by consequence, she describes the comparative freedom of the clouds:

Over your body the clouds go
High, high and icily
And a little flat, as if they

Floated on a glass that was invisible.
Unlike swans,
Having no reflections;

Unlike you,
With no strings attached.
All cool, all blue. Unlike you—

The clouds are different from the child not merely because they have not been born into the web of human obligations; they are different from swans and children because they have no reflections. An implication of this assertion is that to have a reflection is to be caught in that web of obligations. The clouds are unlike the children precisely because they have not been mortgaged to a world of representation. Plath is proposing a new account of Adam's curse: to be mortal is to be doomed, not to the necessity of work, as in Yeats's poem, but to representation itself.

Plath in this poem sets up a specular structure, clouds above, invisible glass in the middle, and child below. The relation between the clouds and the child resembles the relation between a body and its reflection in a mirror, a mirror not of likeness but of unlikeness. "Gulliver" then provides a commentary on the moment of most striking invention in "Morning Song": "I'm no more your mother / Than the cloud that distills a mirror to reflect its own slow / Effacement at the wind's hand." These mirrors reflect not a person but an act of effacement. Another way of putting this is to say that the mirror, rather than containing an image, contains a narrative, the story of a person's dissolving.

Pointing backward toward "Morning Song," "Gulliver" points forward as well to "Childless Woman," where the filaments of fate take a form similar to the "featureless, fine / Jew linen" of "Lady Lazarus," but the triumphalism of the death-artist in the earlier poem has given way to more reflexive, un-willed forms of making: the rattling of a pod, the moon passively discharged from a tree, images spun out like spiders' webs, arterial or menstrual blood shed from the body:

> The womb
> Rattles its pod, the moon
> Discharges itself from the tree with nowhere to go.
>
> My landscape is a hand with no lines,
> The roads bunczhed to a knot,
> The knot myself,
>
> Myself the rose you achieve—
> This body,
> This ivory
>
> Ungodly as a child's shriek.
> Spiderlike, I spin mirrors,
> Loyal to my image,
>
> Uttering nothing but blood—
> Taste it, dark red!
> And my forest

> My funeral,
> And this hill and this
> Gleaming with the mouths of corpses. (259)

In a vivid anticipation of "Edge," the body has been cut free from a world of others. It is its own sarcophagus, the repository of the children it can never have. Whereas in "Edge" it is the children who are folded back into the body, in "Childless Woman" it is the images themselves that cannot detach themselves. The body's every utterance is blood, "blood-hot and personal" but unarticulated into human form. This spinning of images and reflections, this replication of "the identical, same woman" as in "Lady Lazarus" is a deathly replication. Where there is only sameness, the poem implies, there is in fact "nothing there," only endlessly reduplicated "ash, ash." By this account, representation is to be purchased at the cost of one's life.[11]

A DISTURBANCE IN MIRRORS: ART AS PERFECTING MIRROR AND DEVOURING POOL

As I indicated above, Plath's interest in representational surfaces (looking glasses, pools, and ultimately, poems themselves) derives in part from the way that these surfaces present the looker with a likeness that is also a terrible unlikeness. In "Mirror" (173) the speaker, a looking glass, announces itself to be "silver and exact," faithful to the image of whatever stands before its surface, displaying it "just as it is, unmisted by love or dislike." But for all its faithfulness, the mirror is a slave to its own appetite: "Whatever I see, I swallow immediately." Like the "morgue of old images" in "Private Ground," it contains an archive, not only of a fixed past but of a surging, uncreated future as well: "In me she has drowned a young girl, and in me an old woman / Rises toward her day after day, like a terrible fish." The mirror, exact, also "exacts," requiring of the viewer the payment of her body.[12]

Even in her earliest poems in this vein, Plath's concern with the faithful image is never very far from her concern with the constraints and obligations of the artist. In "Mussel Hunter at Rock Harbor," Plath stumbles onto a colony of fiddler-crabs while searching for mussels. She had not expected to find this particular world; what she had expected to find was a natural landscape indistinguishable from the artistic representations it has inspired:

> I came before the water
> Colorists came to get the
> Good of the Cape light that scours
> Sand grit to sided crystal
> And buffs and sleeks the blunt hulls

> Of the three fishing smacks beached
> On the bank of the river's
>
> Backtracking tail. (95)

Both the watercolorists and the wind follow an artist's calling, the conversion of the world from something found into something made. Away from the watery, tellurian world of the "mass-motived hordes" doomed to welter and rot in the shallows, she finds "High on the airy thatching / Of the dense grasses"

> The husk of a fiddler-crab,
> Intact, strangely strayed above
>
> His world of mud—green color
> And innards bleached and blown off
> Somewhere by much sun and wind;
> There was no telling if he'd
> Died recluse or suicide
> Or headstrong Columbus crab.
> The crab-face, etched and set there,
>
> Grimaced as skulls grimace: it
> Had an Oriental look,
> A samurai death mask done
> On a tiger tooth, less for
> Art's sake than God's [. . . .]

The crab, obeying its obscure impulse, has ventured off to turn his body into an etched, sanctified relic, his face etched into a death mask. It is this accomplishment that Plath praises, but she does so by placing this act of etching in a special context. She compares it not only to the action of the watercolorists and the action of the scouring wind, but distinguishes it also from the catabolic action of the wet death that awaits all of the other crabs. The hero crab dies

> Far from the sea—
> Where red-freckled crab-backs, claws
> And whole crabs, dead, their soggy
>
> Bellies pallid and upturned,
> Perform their shambling waltzes
> On the wave's dissolving turn
> And return, losing themselves
> Bit by bit to their friendly
> Element [. . . .]

This is the fate that the one crab managed to escape, charting a course from the world of the masses into the world of art and from there into the presence of the solar god. [13] It seems at first that the world of art is synonymous with the scouring, etching, airy world of the high grasses, but the crabs succumbing to aquatic death practice an art of their own. Death is a "perform[ance]," a "shambling waltz" in the "wave's dissolving turn / And return." This latter action of the waves, the turn and return, invokes the turn and return of verse itself. The distinction between the two ways a crab can die is not between art and its opposite, between the triumph of form and the triumph of formlessness, but between two different kinds or conceptions of art. Encountering the suspicion that art is not the establishment of an annealed permanence, Plath is terrified. When she writes "less for / Art's sake than for God's" the attempt is to limit or restrict this sense of what art might do to the self. Ultimately, "Mussel Hunter" is less concerned with the purification and annealing of the physical body than it is with the purification and annealing of art itself. On this level, the poem is an attempt to separate permanently one of art's properties, that of distillation and preservation, from its more troubling aspect, that aspect in which the self and the body can be pulled apart and rendered unrecognizable. [14]

It is this definitive discrimination that Plath is never able to secure. Although greatly to be desired, perfection is too "terrible," either sterile ("The Munich Mannequins") or lethal ("Edge"). Unconsoled, she returns repeatedly to a version of the pool in "Mussel Hunter" to pose her questions, in slightly different form, to art's mirror. (In this regard the mirror resembles less Narcissus's pool of self-enchantment than the Queen's mirror in *Snow White*, a source both of reassurance and of dread.) Each return to the pool is a further step into a radical, troubling understanding of art's relation to the world.

It would be tempting to say that "Mussel Hunter" was a culmination of interests first explored, with less vigor and assurance, in "Watercolor of Grantchester Meadows" and "Magnolia Shoals"—if it weren't for the fact that these two poems were written *after* "Mussel Hunter." The relative awkwardness of these later poems I take to be symptomatic of the problem that Plath had addressed but not solved in "Mussel Hunter." In these poems she once again struggles to define the relation between the permanence that art vouchsafes and the violence that it threatens. In "Watercolor," employing the verbal equivalent of dilute, translucent washes, she sketches an idyll populated by small birds, lovers, cows, cygnets, owls, and a vegetarian water rat—only to strip away this surface of pale benignities to reveal a shrieking underworld of predation and death: "The owl shall stoop from his turret, the rat cry out" (111). As before, the divide between these two worlds is water's reflective surface: "Cloudwrack and owl-hollowed willows slanting over / The bland

Granta double their white and green / World under the sheer water / And ride at anchor, upside down." In "Magnolia Shoals" the separation between the world of permanence and the world of destruction is mediated by water as well. The scene recalls "Mussel Hunter," but the realms of preservation and destruction are transposed; the water world is now the custodian of the imperishable image, while the upland is marked by fragmentation and collapse:

> Up here among the gull cries
>   we stroll through a maze of pale
> red-mottled relics, shells, claws
>
> as if it were summer still.
>   That season has turned its back.
> Though the green sea gardens stall,
>
> bow, and recover their look
>   of the imperishable
> gardens in an antique book
>
> or tapestries on a wall,
>   leaves behind us warp and lapse [. . . .] (121)

Perhaps the world of reflections, of filaments woven into a tapestry, is the true world of the permanent, and by going down into that world the self can partake of that permanence. ("Lorelei" and "Lyonesse" suggest this possibility as well.) This poem, however, fails to clarify which path the artist should take. While it ends with a note of incipience, what the poem ushers in remains unspecified:

> The watercolorist grips
>   his brush in the stringent air.
> The horizon's bare of ships,
>
> the beach and the rocks are bare.
>   He paints a blizzard of gulls,
> wings drumming in the winter.

In the image of the blizzard of gulls, Plath reaches for a Stevensian figure of bareness and wintry astringency, but rather than evoking a vital ascesis, the poem ends in an uncertain stasis, a failure to clarify what the winter will bring or what the artist is to make of it.

It is at this point that Plath recognizes that these dyadic, oppositional formulations are too static for her purposes. She is not drawn toward Stevens' dialectical formulations, and her most compelling vocal register, she comes to discover, is not one invested in what Glück will call "immaculate distinctions" (*The Seven Ages* 52) but in a voice given over more fully to a tormenting medium. In "The Manor Garden," a poem written before the birth of Plath's daughter, the central tropes of this given-over voice "converge / With their gifts to a difficult borning." The poem, addressed to the child, anticipates not only the child's birth but the advent of a new relation to the poetic instrument. Because so many of the major late themes are present here in germinal form—death flowers, a death bird, bees, suicides, and fixed stars—I quote the poem in full:

> The fountains are dry and the roses over.
> Incense of death. Your day approaches.
> The pears fatten like little buddhas.
> A blue mist is dragging the lake.
>
> You move through the era of fishes,
> The smug centuries of the pig—
> Head, toe and finger
> Come clear of the shadow. History
>
> Nourishes these broken flutings,
> These crowns of acanthus,
> And the crow settles her garments.
> You inherit white heather, a bee's wing,
>
> Two suicides, the family wolves,
> Hours of blankness. Some hard stars
> Already yellow the heavens.
> The spider on its own string
>
> Crosses the lake. The worms
> Quit their usual habitations.
> The small birds converge, converge
> With their gifts to a difficult borning. (125)

The poem is sponsored by clear delineations—between the *I* and the *you*, between the present and the future, between here and there, between future child and expectant mother. Over the next three years, these distinctions will break down and the world of boundaries will manifest increasingly grave ruptures and effacements. The lake will become the pool that eats the skull-stone in "Words," and the "spider on its own string" will become the spinner of mirrors in "Childless Woman." Children will appear again ("For a Fatherless

Child," "Nick and the Candlestick," and "Child"), but their fate will be to lose all difference from the mother as they are folded back into her body.

The chief rupture that these intermediate poems enact is the broaching of the boundary which had separated poet from the poem. She ceases to portray herself as a watercolorist because the figure of painter-plus-landscape detaches her too absolutely from the subject matter, turns her into a Sunday painter, a mere connoisseur of good light or scenic bleakness. In "The Colossus" artist and landscape and artwork are thrown together in a jumble; the speaker finds herself engaged in the endless undertaking of reassembling the ruin of her dead father. In the seventh section of "A Poem for a Birthday" (entitled *The Stones),* this disassembled person is now the poet herself—or more properly, the voice behind the poem:

> This is the city where men are mended.
> I lie on a great anvil.
> The flat blue sky-circle
>
> Flew off like the hat of a doll
> When I fell out of the light. I entered
> The stomach of indifference, the wordless cupboard.
>
> The mother of pestles diminished me.
> I became a still pebble.
> The stones of the belly were peaceable,
>
> The head-stone quiet, jostled by nothing.
> Only the mouth-hole piped out,
> Importunate cricket
>
> In a quarry of silences [. . . .] (136)

The body is no longer a speaking subject, but a distribution of stones and a mouth-hole, an integration into a landscape, no longer separate from it as the mussel hunter or the watercolorists, or even the daughter and the colossus, had been. "The stomach of indifference" which has broken her down into these parts is most properly a stomach of un-differentiation. The poet, both speaking the poem and narrating the reassembly, has undergone a particular kind of fragmentation. Self and scene have merged with the effect that the self is no longer a site, no longer a point of enunciation, but a landscape of hollows and absences, region of the "mouth-hole" and the "quarry of silences." Plath's attempt here is to imagine a world from which a speaker has yet to be distinguished, and to this extent the poem attempts to construct a negative myth of origin. This construction, however, is provisional at best, and one whose integrity Plath does not seek to maintain. The idea of an originary self, even one whose origin is to be found in absence or silence, grows increasingly foreign.

After these intermediate poems, the sense of doom in Plath's work gathers its strength, and the forces that draw her toward her end rise to their full unappeasable stature, figured in the unstoppable locomotive, the inescapable web. The preoccupation with an end, a determined, inevitable end, rises to the forefront, and the sense of trajectory is strongest in these final poems. It is this doom to which her poetry gives such precise and troubling definitions. It is a bitter destiny, in her account, to be identified with an image, a reflection, that always stands outside and away from the self that appears to sponsor it. In fact, it is the property of this reflection to call into question the very reality of the self to which it refers.

Even the stars, those signs of fate's fixity, have no being outside the world of representation. In "Nick and the Candlestick," Plath writes, "Let the stars plummet to their dark address" (240). There is never any doubt for her that the stars will fall, and so to this degree she is resigning herself to the fate of the world and to her own fate. It is not, however, the stars that are sending her to her own dark address. The stars themselves are falling from their courses, falling from their grooves of determined and determining destiny. The "fixed stars" in "Words" have established their fixity only after falling into the pool. They are not fixed in the heavens but in the dark address of the pool itself. Address here, then, is not only the destination, the end of the stars, the terminus of the skull-stone, but the dark address of speech itself, a means of utterance as well as an end. Just as the "fine Jew linen" covered a face of absences in "Lady Lazarus," the speech of a speaker in this world is perceived as these fixed stars are perceived—the reflection of an object that cannot be found at its origin. The reflection is a presence in its own right, but it points toward something that cannot in fact be found. In this negative light, "Morning Song" emerges as Plath's address not only to her daughter but to her poems as well. She is no more their speaker "Than the cloud that distills a mirror to reflect its own slow / Effacement at the wind's hand."

Many poets writing after Plath's death adopted or attempted to adopt something of the bald intensity of her rhetoric; very few poets, on the other hand, took it upon themselves to investigate and extend the account of subjectivity so powerfully at work in her best poems. In the final chapter of this book, I argue that Louise Glück, like Plath, writes a poetry preoccupied with the dislocations and displacements inherent in lyric speech. The challenge Glück faces is to acknowledge her radically unsettled position without succumbing to the destruction or silence it threatens.

Chapter Five
Louise Glück: I Was Here

Plath's suicide, Larkin's silence, and the stillness and hush of Stevens' late poems demonstrate the difficulty of continuing to speak once the edge of the intelligible has consumed the attention of a poet. (Hardy could continue to write because he found it easier to turn away from those preoccupations which increasingly preoccupied Stevens, Larkin, and Plath.) Moreover, in the case of each of the poets I have discussed so far, the limits of speech have now converged with the absence opened by the poet's actual death. (This is one of the ways in which history suffuses the fictive space of the lyric; it is impossible now to read Lowell's poem "Obit" [*Collected Poems 642*] as one might have before he died.) Because these historical circumstances have so far imposed this artificial limit on my argument, I have chosen in my last chapter to consider a living poet, Louise Glück, who has engaged with questions of the unintelligible throughout a varied and prolific career. Her work demonstrates how interest in that category continues to shape contemporary poetic practice, even for a poet whose style conforms to a relatively conservative definition of lyric utterance. Her poems offer what I take to be one of the most probing, supple, and radical inquiries into the nature of lyric subjectivity, particularly its deep complicity with states of absence, loss, and (to quote the title of one of her essays) "disruption, hesitation, [and] silence." In fact, as I will argue, subjectivity as mediated by Glück's lyrics is not a state *at the border* of human meaning so much as it is a condition infused with, sustained by, and constituted within a matrix of antithetical, incompatible, or unassimilable relations. It is through the discovery of its essential *foreignness* that her lyric voice arrives at its most complex and lasting achievement.

In her essay "The Education of the Poet" Glück addresses this issue with specific reference to the role of "intention" or "will" in art. She begins by discussing the issue of gender in writing, and ends by articulating, in miniature form, an entire aesthetic theory:

> My sister and I were . . . never given to believe that [glorious] achieve-
> ment was impossible, either to our sex or our historical period. I'm puz-
> zled, not emotionally but logically, by the contemporary determination
> of women to write as women. Puzzled because this seems an ambition
> limited by the existing conception of what, exactly, differentiates the
> sexes. If there are such differences, it seems to me reasonable to suppose
> that literature reveals them, and that it will do so more interestingly,
> more subtly, in the absence of intention. In a similar way, all art is his-
> torical: in both its confrontations and evasions, it speaks of its period.
> The dream of art is not to assert what is already known but to illumi-
> nate what has been hidden, and the path to the hidden world is not in-
> scribed by will. (*Proofs* 7)

If the sexes are in fact significantly different, then the literature that reveals
these differences will do so best "in the absence of intention." In saying this,
Glück is arguing against the critique implied, for instance, by the poems of
Adrienne Rich, poems which take on, explicitly and with forceful intent, issues of gender, sexuality, race, and class. [1] But what would it mean to write "in
the absence of intention"? If "the path to the hidden world is not inscribed by
will," how does one set out upon it? What does such a formulation say about
inscription itself, that (willed, intentional) act which brings poems into being?
It remains for her poems, not her essays, to address themselves to these questions. What can be said, however, is that the tradition which her poems extend is the tradition of poetry most concerned with the limits of the will.
Consequently, in distancing herself from specific contemporaries, she is implicitly aligning herself with others:

> Each book I've written has culminated in a conscious diagnostic act, a
> swearing off. After *Firstborn*, the task was to make latinate suspended
> sentences, and to figure out a way to end a poem without sealing it shut.
> Since the last poems of *The House on Marshland* were written concur-
> rently with the earliest poems in *Descending Figure*, the latter seems more
> difficult to speak of independently. I wanted to learn a longer breath.
> And to write without the nouns central to that second book; I had done
> about as much as I could with moon and pond. (*Proofs* 17)

When Glück mentions the nouns "moon and pond," she is of course naming two terms central to the work of Sylvia Plath. For Plath, the mutable,
cold, illuminated, and obscure surface of her moon and the shifting, reflective surface of her pools were the surfaces to which she could pose her questions about fate, determination, intention, image, and the terms of
representation. Glück, then, positions herself at the edge not only of her own

prior accomplishments but of Plath's as well, and in doing so, identifies her own desire specifically to pick up where Plath left off. Perhaps "moon" and "pond" are now exhausted terms, but they illuminate a path of inquiry into the nature of lyric subjectivity that Glück undertakes to extend, an inquiry that Plath began but could not complete.

THE "UNMUSICAL" IN THE EARLY WORK: SITUATING WRITING BETWEEN THE CRY AND THE LETTER

Because *intention* is not the same as *act* or *will* or *outcome,* the word necessarily implies a slippage between what one wants the world to be (or become) and what it is. To express the problem in more Stevensian terms, the slippage is the rift between desire and fact. For Glück, this experience is the root of torment:

> The fundamental experience of the writer is helplessness. This does not mean to distinguish writing from being alive: it means to correct the fantasy that creative work is an ongoing record of the triumph of volition, that the writer is someone who has the good luck to be able to do what he or she wishes to do: to confidently and regularly imprint his being on a sheet of paper. But writing is not decanting of personality. And most writers spend much of their time in various kinds of torment: wanting to write, being unable to write; wanting to write differently, being unable to write differently. In a whole lifetime, years are spent waiting to be claimed by an idea. The only real exercise of will is negative: we have toward what we write the power of veto. (*Proofs* 3)

One does not claim authority; one is claimed by an idea. An implication of Glück's acerbity is that there is no originary, undivided impulse to write. There are impulses and there is writing, but the minute the poet feels the impulse-to-write, she finds herself pulled between two different claims, the claim made by the impulse seeking expression and the claim of writing as it imposes upon that impulse all the constraints of representation. While the initial impulse seeks to express itself with utmost sincerity and artlessness, such artlessness in the lyric is in fact the achievement of highly constrained artifice, no matter how "free" the verse. (Nothing gets said that has not been *put into* words; this putting is by definition a constraint.) To this degree, each lyric poem locates itself on the continuum between reflexive cry and purely abstract pattern. (A corollary of this assertion is that each poem can be seen as inclining toward one end of this continuum or the other. A lyric by Allen Ginsberg, for instance, might yearn toward a pre-verbal, guttural howl or caw, whereas a lyric by James Merrill might betray a secret desire to be a Fabergé egg.) Plath, writing as a "pure gold baby / that melts to a shriek," most often yearns toward the cry, but it is only formally and not thematically that her poems seek to embody it. "Elm," "Purdah," and "Lady Lazarus" do not seek to impersonate or transcribe a cry of pain or distress so much as they seek to establish, through their rapid breaking from one figure to another, a formal correlative within lyric for the cry's lean clarity and the force with which it breaks through silence or complacence. In "Morning Song" when Plath describes the newborn's "bald cry" as it "takes its place among the elements" (*Collected Poems*, 156), she combines the act of the cry with an act of situating, of taking place. She seeks out the terms in which a cry can take its place among the elements of the lyric tradition, a taking-place that ensures the stability of such ephemeral utterances; the question she sought to solve (to paraphrase "Lady Lazarus") was how to make an opus from a shriek. Glück begins her career striving for such effects, writing poems overwrought with respect to both formal elaboration and the rhetoric of distress. "My Life Before Dawn," in *Firstborn* shows Glück awkwardly taking up Plath's shriek and trying it on for size.[2] The speaker is male, a woman's spiteful ex-lover:

> Sometimes at night I think of how we did
> It, me nailed in her like steel, her
> Over-eager on the striped contour
> Sheet (I later burned it) and it makes me glad
> I told her—in the kitchen cutting homemade bread—
> She always did too much—I told her Sorry baby you have had
> Your share. (I found her stain had dried into my hair.)
> She cried. Which still does not explain my nightmares:
> How she surges like her yeast dough through the door-
> way shrieking It is I, love, back in living color
> After all these years. (*Firstborn* 28)

Over the course of the next two books, Glück will move away from experiments such as this, seeking to avoid Plath's cruder legacies, the jacked-up, flattened-out cartoon-clashes unleashed upon the world by "Daddy" and "Purdah."[3] What comes to trouble Glück about this shrieking revenant is not only its resemblance to Plath's "Lady Lazarus" (the "pure gold baby that melts to a shriek"), but the impassioned unity of the woman—at least as she is imagined by the man—bound by her rage into a single, univocal, tormenting purpose. In the end, the poem leverages against emotional intensity an unsupportable claim—that the vengeful soul knows what it is and what it wants. Glück loses interest in the shriek of revenge because it takes too much for granted, reducing its object to a two-dimensional evil, be it jackbooted fascist or nightmare misogynist.

Glück discovers that the cry at the horizon of her poems is not so much a vengeful cry as a sexual one (a cry notably absent from Plath's work). Whereas the cry of vengeance polarizes the world into starkly differentiated subjects and objects, the sexual cry breaks down this distinction. Moreover, such a cry situates her work in a broader poetic context, one that includes, most immediately, Stevens' poems of desolate, erotic birdsong. "Aubade," a poem in *Descending Figure*, Glück's third book, includes the cries of birds and lovers both:

> Today above the gull's call
> I heard you waking me again
> to see that bird, flying
> so strangely over the city,
> not wanting to stop, wanting
> the blue waste of the sea—
>
> Now it skirts the suburb,
> the noon light violent against it;
> I feel its hunger
> as your hand inside me,
>
> a cry
> so common, unmusical—
>
> Ours were not
> different. They rose
> from the unexhausted
> need of the body
>
> fixing a wish to return:
> the ashen dawn, our clothes
> not sorted for departure. (140)

The sexual cry captures Glück's interest because it oscillates across the boundary that distinguishes body from world. On the one hand, it represents the voice as reflex, spontaneously lifted by ecstasy from the body. But ecstasy, Glück knows, is the state of being outside or beside oneself. The cry is the sign of the self blurring its contour into the trajectory of a single desire not wholly contiguous with the self. Rather than confirming a site of personhood, the cry ruptures or penetrates it, like someone *else's* "hand inside." In the "Nocturne" section of "Lamentations," a sequence poem that takes place in an Eden abandoned by God, Glück renders the world in a palette of pure appetite. Even the color of the trees is a plangent cry:

> Together they were beasts.
> They lay in the fixed
> dusk of his negligence;

> from the hills, wolves came, mechanically
> drawn to their human warmth,
> their panic.
>
> Then the angels saw
> how He divided them:
> the man, the woman, and the woman's body.
>
> Above the churned reeds, the leaves let go
> a slow moan of silver. (*Descending Figure* 148)

Whether the moan is a moan of ecstasy or pain, it evokes a world of automatic tropisms, man drawn toward woman, wolf drawn toward humans, trees (silver-leaved birch or aspen) releasing a silver note of longing. Desire, as pleasure or anguish, forces the speaker to "let go" a cry, spontaneously, "in the absence of intentions" properly her own. Coercive force is also at work in "Mock Orange." The speaker deplores

> the cry that always escapes,
> the low, humiliating
> premise of union—
>
> In my mind tonight
> I hear the question and pursuing answer
> fused into one sound
> that mounts and mounts and then
> is split into the old selves
> the tired antagonisms. (*Triumph* 155)

In the cry of sexual union the lovers merge and lose distinction, splitting afterward not only into their opposing roles, but back into the state of having selves at all, selves surrendered in the throes of passion. In *The Wild Iris*, the speaking flower in "Trillium" wonders whether voice is the vehicle of reasoned discourse at all: "I did not know my voice / . . . would be so full of grief, my sentences / like cries strung together" (*The Wild Iris* 4).

The cry, for Glück, takes its place at the outer limit of speech. [4] It marks the place where intelligibility breaks down into pure phatic presence *vis à vis* its narrated action. In "Aubade," however, the cry throws into stark negative relief the poem's essential writtenness; to write, "a cry, / so common, so unmusical" is to designate a cry without in any sense embodying it. At an even farther remove from the written is "the slow moan of silver." The poem is constrained to articulate itself in the black ink of the printed word, and not in the releasing of a moan or in the application of silver leaf to the page. [5] What

Glück's work does not attempt is the mimesis of moaning or of silveriness. It does not strive to abstract "pure emotion" into "pure music" or "pure verbal color." Nor is her work, in the strictest sense, songlike; it rarely conforms to recognizable musical patterning. Her poems, then, are unmusical not only as the raw cry is, but as writing itself is, residing on the page and not in the voice.

It stands to reason, then, that one of Glück's most characteristic tonal modes is the tone of the letter—the voice of the epistle, a distant or absent voice established on the written page. This is the tone she perfects earliest in her career, in the cool, detached *reportage* of "Letter from Our Man in Blossomtime," and "Letter from Provence" (*Firstborn* 33 and 36); certain kinds of communication, these poems imply, can be mediated only by the written page itself. A later poem, "The Letters," renders this fact in the most concrete terms.

> It is night for the last time.
> For the last time your hands
> gather on my body.
>
> Tomorrow it will be autumn.
> We will sit together on the balcony
> watching the dry leaves drift over the village
> like the letters we will burn,
> one by one, in our separate houses.
>
> [. . . .]
>
> Look how the leaves drift in the darkness.
> We have burned away
> all that was written on them. (*House on Marshland* 97)

The leaves of the trees, soon to fall away, stand as an emblem of the "vegetable love" of the lovers, but they are also the leaves of the letters, the letters that have recorded the lovers' feeling for one another. The bond—like the words, the pages, or the leaves themselves—can be burnt away. These letters establish a distance between the persons concerned, a distance bridgeable only through writing. What Glück tempers by these means is the rhetoric of the love poem that seeks to establish the maximum presence between the lover and the beloved—Shakespeare's declaration, for instance, that his love will live in his lines, or Whitman's assertion that to hold *Leaves of Grass* is to hold his very body. Both the cry and the letter have a quality of *aftermath*. Each marks a site of departure. For Glück, the *written* emphasizes that the writer is no longer here; the *cry* rises up at that moment when the person surrenders her will. So one can say further, then, that the phatic presence denoted by the cry and the written is not the presence of a speaking *person* as such, but more radically, the presence of a *site* of utterance, a voice that comes into being precisely where speaker or writer has ceased, if only temporarily, to exist. What Glück arrives at in these early books is an understanding of the lyric as a means uniquely suited to mark where the intelligibility *of the self to the self* breaks down. The form of intelligibility surrendered here is the intelligibility that mediates self-recognition, the knowability of the subject to itself. To put it differently, for Glück the lyric—situated between the cry and the written—can speak at those moments when the speaker can no longer say with confidence *who* or *what* is speaking.

THE DIALOGUE WITH THE DEAD: FORMS OF ABSENCE IN *DESCENDING FIGURE*

Glück's first major poem, the three-part sequence "Descending Figure," adds a crucial new dimension to this understanding, the dimension of absence. The figure indicated in the title is the poet's older sister, who died in infancy; this figure, not quite a person, not quite a shade, not quite at peace in the past, is never *not* descending, never quite arriving in the underworld. It is in this deferral of arrival that the manifest topographical denotation of the title converges with its musical sense as well; the poem searches, like a descending phrase in music, for a point of rest, the secure resolution of the tonic. This resolution, however, is denied, and the poem ends in a suspension, the speaker still searching for the lullaby that could sing the dead sister to sleep. The poem suggests in concrete terms that for this speaker at least, lyric is an utterance at the frontier with what cannot be uttered. The words of the poem, directed toward a voiceless interlocutor, simultaneously open and cover up the absence in which this speaker resides.

This relationship between absence and presence is first experienced as a violent conflict. In the second section of the sequence, entitled "The Sick Child," in which a mother holds her dying child, the conflict plays itself out as the tension between the mother's inconsolable grief and her other children's struggle to survive in their own right:

> A small child
> is ill, has wakened.
> It is winter, past midnight
> in Antwerp. Above a wooden chest,
> the stars shine.
> And the child relaxes in her mother's arms.
> The mother does not sleep;

> she stares
> fixedly into the bright museum.
> By spring the child will die.
> Then it is wrong, wrong
> to hold her—
> Let her be alone,
> without memory, as the others wake
> terrified, scraping the dark
> paint from their faces. (*Descending Figure* 114)

The stars and the mother's fixed stare recall the "fixed stars" of Plath's "Words," and in doing so, they indicate that the poem will comment, as Plath's had, on the relation of art to fate. These stars, however, are not reflected in a pool, as they had been in Plath's poem, but in a painting hung in a museum. The fixity of the image embodies the fixity of the past and the fixed fate of the infant. The mother stares at two fates, the fate of the daughter (that she will die) and the fate implied by the bright museum itself (that we all take our place in the archive of the past). But just as it is "wrong, wrong" to continue to hold the child after she is dead, it is wrong never to tear one's gaze from these facts. The appropriate response can be grief, but it can also be terror; this is the response that falls to the other children. Their struggle will always be to tear themselves out of the fixed picture; they must find a new form of visibility in the world, now that their mother's gaze has been claimed forever by the countenance of their dead sibling.

This struggle places art in a divided position. Art and the past present the viewer with established forms: tradition, codifiable pattern, rules of interpretation, implied syntax, and so forth. But they also fill the viewer, particularly the viewer-as-artist, with the desperate desire to make something new from what has already been established. The essay "The Education of the Poet" addresses this divided position in a passage that makes implicit but vivid reference to "Descending Figure":

> It is very strange what cannot be achieved in life. The high jumper knows, at the instant after performance, how high he has been; his achievement can be measured both immediately and with precision. But for those of us attempting dialogue with the great dead, it isn't a matter of waiting: the judgment we wait for is made by the unborn; we can never in our lifetimes know it. (*Proofs* 4)

Manifestly, Glück is speaking about the literary ambition to establish a voice among the voices of her predecessors. In "The Sick Child," however, Glück adds an additional register of resonance to the phrase "dialogue with the dead." The challenge facing the writer in the poem is not so much to secure a place on Parnassus; instead, it is to record a dialogue with what is not, or what is no longer, or what can never be. The deepest question, then, that the sequence poses concerns this dialogue: what is poetic speech, and what does it mean to use poetic speech, if to speak poetically is to engage in dialogue with negative presences?

For Glück, the sister's death illuminates the uncertainties that underpin any identity. Would the speaker have been conceived at all had her sister not died? In "Descending Figure's" first section, "The Wanderer," Glück poses this question with specific regard to naming: would she have made rendezvous with her own name if her sister had survived? Are there parts of the self that remain nameless? And if so, what claims do they make upon the speaker? We see the poet as a child playing with the ghost of her dead elder sister:

> At twilight I went into the street.
> The sun hung low in the iron sky,
> ringed with cold plumage.
> If I could write to you
> about this emptiness—
> Along the curb, groups of children
> were playing in the dry leaves.
> Long ago, at this hour, my mother stood
> at the lawn's edge, holding my little sister.
> Everyone was gone; I was playing
> in the dark street with my older sister,
> whom death had made so lonely.
> Night after night we watched the screened porch
> filling with a gold, magnetic light.
> Why was she never called?
> Often I would let my own name glide past me
> though I craved its protection. (*Descending Figure*, 113)

The game in the poem is a game played by the living with the dead. The scene is autumnal, crepuscular, liminal, the leaves both fallen and persisting, the sun sinking. The sun, however, is not wreathed in clouds but "ringed with *cold* plumage." The "iron sky" it hangs in resembles Yeats's "cold and rook-delighting heaven" (125) a place of flight, an elevation, but one deeply incompatible with human concerns. It is this cold solitude in which the sister must stay, like the ghost in Yeats's poem, a solitude the living sister can only partly share. This poem is the attempt to find words for the lost sister, a language viable in both the cold world of extinction and the "warm, magnetic light" of the screened porch. The attempt, like the ambition of attempting dialogue with the "great dead," always remains provisional, incipient, never quite success or failure. "If

I could write to you / about this emptiness—" begins a sentence that cannot be completed.

The last poem in "Descending Figure," "For My Sister," refines further the terms of engagement with the dead sister, formulating the relationship as one of nurturing, of responsiveness to infant hunger[6]:

> Far away my sister is moving in her crib.
> The dead ones are like that,
> always the last to quiet.
>
> Because, however long they lie in the earth,
> they will not learn to speak
> but remain uncertainly pressing against the wooden bars,
> so small the leaves hold them down.
>
> Now, if she had a voice,
> the cries of hunger would be beginning.
> I should go to her;
> perhaps if I sang very softly,
> her skin so white,
> her head covered with black feathers. . . . (115)

The cold plumage has become the damp wisps clinging to a baby's head. The dry leaves, as light as they are, now hold the child under the earth. The infant self is confined in speechlessness but does not consent to be quiet. Because Glück conceives of her own identity, her name, as partially fused with the identity of her sister, the poet-speaker represents only a part of the self; the other part is caught beneath the dry leaves, obscured behind the black feathers. This last poem, then, is a self-portrait as speaker *and* infant, in which the speaker responds as a mother would to the imagined hunger-cries. In "The Sick Child" the struggle was to find some compromise between form and formlessness, between fixed fate and the children's need to tear free of the mother's grief. "For My Sister" recasts the struggle so that it takes place between speech and speechlessness, or between the world and nothingness. It is at this juncture that the poet receives her vocation: "if I sang very softly. . . ." She is called to find a mode of utterance that soothes the infant, a way of singing that links this world with the world of restless shades, "those that will not learn to speak."

CHOOSING SOUVENIRS: FACT OF HISTORY AND FACT OF DESIRE IN *THE TRIUMPH OF ACHILLES*

Plath's self-portrait in "Ariel" was a self-portrait as woman-and-horse, the suicidal arrow flying into another world. Glück recognizes in herself a similar tropism; her heart, like her mother's, is drawn downward toward the world of the dead as though by "a tiny pendant of iron" (*Ararat* 27). This pull, however, stimulates the reflex to struggle against it, to scrape the dark paint from the face. To speak schematically, if Plath's poems strive to take the (manifest) form of an arrow, Glück's take the form of oscillation toward and away from the world of speechlessness. This oscillation plays itself out in her work as a constant cycling or cavitation between a group of opposing poles: the mythic and the personal, the abstract and the concrete, the general and the specific, the permanent and the transient, the cry and the written. What Glück discovers in "Descending Figure" is that this struggle is best elucidated as a tension, an exchange, between immiscible states of being (represented by the speaking poet and the dead infant). Moreover, she discovers that this tension must establish itself within the formal structures of the poem, specifically between different sections of the same poem. This is why it is difficult to say decisively whether a poem such as "Descending Figure" is one poem composed of parts, or several poems arranged in a group. This grouping technique is different from that which organized "The Garden" or "Lamentations," where the sections arrange themselves according to a more episodic logic. "Descending Figure" undertakes instead to make three distinct cuts through an original solid, letting the variants adjoin one another as might three separate facets of a single object.

This is not to say, however, that Glück has turned away from narrative. This faceting, aspectual approach establishes, in its own right, a tension with linear narrative itself. It is this tension specifically that determines the progression from *Descending Figure* toward *The Triumph of Achilles*. Encountering in the table of contents such abstract titles as "Metamorphosis," "Brooding Likeness," "Seated Figure," "Mythic Fragment," "A Parable," and "Legend," one might not expect *Triumph* to focus more closely on the fine grain of the quotidian than had the earlier volumes, but where the book breaks new ground, it does so by bringing together the narrative and the emblematic, the abstract and the particular, in surprising ways.[7]

The longest and most adventurous poem in the volume is the sequence "Marathon" (176–185), the subject of which is a recently concluded love affair. The poem is as much about time (which takes all loves away) as about love (which can, seemingly, stop or retard time). The fourth poem in the series, "Song of Obstacles," describes love as the abandonment of self to erotic force; in the grip of this force even time itself appears suspended:

> When my lover touches me, what I feel in my body
> is like the first movement of a glacier over the earth,
> as the ice shifts, dislodging great boulders, hills

> of solemn rock; so, in the forests, the uprooted trees
> become a sea of disconnected limbs—[. . . .]

> Then for us, in its path, time doesn't pass,
> not even an hour. (179)

"Marathon," however, does not begin in this state of innocence. The endless present of "Song of Obstacles" is a condition perceived in retrospect. "Song of the River" specifies that this happiness derives chiefly from a state of delusional amnesia:

> Once we were happy, we had no memories.
> For all the repetition, nothing happened twice.
> We were always walking parallel to a river
> with no sense of progression.

This river is both the river of history, the Heraclitean river into which one cannot step twice, and the river outside of history, the Lethean river of forgetfulness, the Stevensian River of Rivers "that flows nowhere, like a sea" (*Stevens,* 451). To be a lover is to ignore the river's one-way flow and what it carries: "While, in the river, things were going by—/ a few leaves, a child's boat painted red and white / its sail stained by the water—." The river's flotsam is simultaneously insignificant and portentous; a handful of leaves floats randomly but signifies the passage of the seasons; the boat is a child's toy, painted in Venus's "damask'd" colors, but with a sail ominously stained. In love's collusive narcissism, however, the two lovers see only their own reflections:

> As they passed, on the surface we could see ourselves;
> we seemed to drift
> apart and together, as the river
> linked us forever, though up ahead
> were other couples, choosing souvenirs. (177)

Memory intrudes as the souvenir; even the timeless moment beside the eternal river is composed of bits and pieces that will become the souvenirs of lost time and lost love.

Once one has experienced this love, however, one cannot step cleanly out of passion back onto the shore of illusionless truth; this is because the opposition between passion and truth is in fact another illusion. Passion, Glück writes in the third section, "The Encounter," "will run its course, the course of fire." This fire will burn itself out but will leave a mark, "setting a cold coin on the forehead, between the eyes." The body, touched by passion, remains subjugated to passion's purpose: "you must have known, then, how I wanted you. / We will always know that, you and I. / The proof will be my body" (178). The body, proved by fire, remains a testament to passion's power, the power to undermine the individual's claim on a dispassionate, objective point of view. This is a momentous recognition for a poet so deeply pledged to the virtues of clarity, discrimination, unflinching scrutiny, and sincerity. "Last Letter," the first poem in "Marathon," describes how this realization accompanies the realization that the affair is over for good:

> I got up finally; I walked down to the pond.
> I stood there, brushing the grass from my skirt, watching myself,
> like a girl after her first lover
> turning slowly at the bathroom mirror, naked, looking for a sign.
> But nakedness in women is always a pose.
> I was not transfigured. I would never be free. (176)

The disappointment is that grief and disappointment do not change the body enough; they fail to cleanse it of the attachment to what is lost. As intense as passion and grief might be, they do not transform the self completely, but leave it compromised. Even true nakedness can never be achieved. A woman can never be naked because the nakedness is always posed, rhetorical; the barest sincerity is its own form of artifice, and the body can never purge itself of the desire to have—or to be—something different.

Extending this awareness, the fifth and central section of "Marathon," "Night Song," asserts that there is no eros purified of psyche, no psyche purified of eros:

> I need to wake you, to remind you that there isn't a future.
> That's why we're free. And now some weakness in me
> has been cured forever, so I'm not compelled
> to close my eyes, to go back, to rectify—[. . . .]
>
> You're tired; I can see that.
> We're both tired, we have acted a great drama.
> Even our hands are cold, that were like kindling.
> Our clothes are scattered on the sand; strangely enough,
> they never turned to ashes.
>
> I have to tell you what I've learned, that I know now
> what happens to the dreamers.
> They don't feel it when they change. One day
> they wake, they dress, they are old.

> Tonight I'm not afraid
> to feel the revolutions. How can you want sleep
> when passion gives you that peace?
> You're like me tonight, one of the lucky ones.
> You'll get what you want. You'll get your oblivion.

In her commentary on this poem, "The Dreamer and the Watcher" (*Proofs*, 102), Glück writes that "the figures suggested, as well, the dilemma of sexuality: the single body split apart again, an old subject; the exhausting obligation to recognize the other as other, as not part of the self." The self is divided between the aspect of the dreamer (Eros) and the aspect of the watcher (Psyche). An implication of this is that one must recognize otherness not only in the other but in the self as well. The voice is only one voice of many. And each voice contains an element of dream and an element of scrutiny. One can never in fact be free of the other. To phrase this multiplicity in the way I have, however, is to phrase it too schematically; the problem is not merely that any one voice is one of many, capable of ever-higher levels of integration, but that these voices, like the voice of the speaker and the voice of the infant in "Descending Figure," can never be integrated.

To address this difficulty in Glück's work, one must address her complex use of the term *dream*. Glück does not provide an explication of the term in "The Dreamer and the Watcher," although she does imply that dreaming is not necessarily something to be desired: "The worst this poem can imagine is 'what happens to the dreamers.' The worst is to sleep through a life" (*Proofs*, 103). Glück, writing about her poem from the perspective of the watcher, equates dreaming with sleeping, an evasion of life. If to be in love is to be abducted by a dream, then love in some way must be the opposite of reality, the enemy of watchfulness. It would be easy for Glück—constitutionally inclined as she is toward wariness and ever suspicious of the intoxicated, the enthusiastic, and the false—to assume a univocal position in opposition to all that is dreamy. And it is true that at times she falls back into a rhetorical posture of empty stringency. But the conclusion of the sequence "Marathon" points toward a more complex account of the dream's unsettled status in the psyche (an account that will require several books to flesh out).

> I was not meant to hear
> the two of them talking.
> But I could feel the light of the torch
> stop trembling, as though it had been
> set on a table. I was not to hear
> the one say to the other
> how best to arouse me,

with what words, what gestures,
nor to hear the description of my body,
how it responded, what
it would not do. My back was turned.
I studied the voices, soon distinguishing
the first, which was deeper, closer,
from that of the replacement.
For all I know, this happens
every night: somebody waking me, then
the first teaching the second.
What happens afterward
occurs far from the world, at a depth
where only the dream matters
and the bond with any one soul
is meaningless; you throw it away.

Love is unvarying, absolute; lovers are many. Specific love for a specific person is not important, but the dream of love is. To put this in the language of myth, eros is transcendent and immortal, while psyche is local, specific, and mortal—fit in the end only to be thrown away. The appropriate response to this recognition is a hybrid of resignation and distress. If the bond with any one soul is meaningless, one can be consoled that there is meaning in the dream, even if the dream cares nothing for the preservation of specific bonds, or even, for that matter, the integrity of the self. On the other hand, if only the dream matters, then how is the mere mortal to live, constrained within a world of the specific and particular? Glück as pragmatist might rephrase Larkin's question "Where can we live but days?" by asking, "With whom can we live but other souls?" This poem, then, articulates one of Glück's deepest dilemmas, how to exist between the world of the watcher (detached, theoretical) and the world of the dreamer (released, for a time, from temporal bonds).

This conflict is her version of the Stevensian war/romance between reality and the imagination. And like Stevens, she suggests a theory of Eros, which "traverses" and disrupts—rather than constituting or emanating from—the "integral" self. Glück's sensibility, however, does not spur her toward a Stevensian, idiosyncratically single-minded assault on the problem. For her, the argument between dreaming and watching, Eros and Psyche, is less a heroic conflict, as it had been for Stevens, and more an ironic one. It is in this way that she finds herself aligned with Larkin, a poet whom she otherwise resembles not at all. What she shares with Larkin, and with Hardy too, is a soft spot for the hard truth, and like Larkin's and Hardy's, her poems can betray a sadistic pleasure in pointing out cruel ironies or meaninglessness. Like Larkin's, her poems, particularly in the middle books, are heavily end-loaded, as though their sole determination is to corner and pin an inevitable, difficult truth, a truth from which those of less rigorous temperament might shrink. Glück recognizes this impulse and its limitations: "My own work begins [. . . .] at the end, literally, at illumination, which has then to be traced back to some source in the world. This method, when it succeeds, makes a thing that seems irrefutable. Its failure is felt as portentousness" (*Proofs* 101). Ultimately, however, as had been the case in Larkin, what her work dramatizes is the arrival not at a point of certainty but at a point of unassimilable conflict. Subjectivity can be defined in the terms of Eros or of Psyche, but to attempt to account for both is to introduce unassimilable incompatibilities. Eros and Psyche (which constitute only one set of terms for this oppositional condition) stand in a relation to one another analogous to that between the named, living speaker and the unnamed, dead infant in "Descending Figure." The world of living and of speech, of "human meaning," is not compatible with the world of the mute shades, even though each realm points toward and depends upon the other.

At the end of *The Triumph of Achilles,* Glück stands at a crossroads. Her choice appears to be between the low road of the particular, the historical, the specific, and the biographical, and the high road of the general, the mythic, the abstract, and the transcendent. She will discover, in *The Wild Iris* and *Meadowlands,* that rather than choose between these roads, she must find a way to bring the low and the high together. In the meantime, however, she begins by choosing the particular and historical and exploring them in *Ararat,* a book that—in failing—prepares the way for her most successful work.

IF THE SOUL SPEAKS AT ALL: QUESTIONS OF CLOSURE IN *ARARAT.*

Ararat fails because it retreats from the territory verged upon by the best poems in *The Triumph of Achilles* and *Descending Figure.* In the conclusions of "Marathon" and "The Encounter" ("The proof will be my body") Glück asserts forcefully that knowledge is never distinct from the experience of desire, and that the nature of our desires determines the nature of our world. We come to know the world (which is to say, we come to have a psyche) through our body and its desires. There is no way to be in the world without being in a body. Proof of fact, then, is also always proof of desire—hence the richness of "proof" in this context. A proof is an act of logic, inevitable, irrefutable, but in "The Encounter," the body and the mind both are proved more by fire than by ratiocination, and achieve their temper in desire's flames. The rhetorical mode of most of *Ararat,* however, is the mode of the mathematical or syllogistic proof, the abstract ordering of events or experiences that do not on their surface reveal an inherent logic. The first poem in the book, "*Parodos*," concludes by restricting "proof" to this narrower sense:

> I was born to a vocation:
> to bear witness
> to the great mysteries.
> Now that I've seen both
> birth and death, I know
> to the dark nature these
> are proofs, not
> mysteries—(*Ararat* 15)

The book unfolds as though Glück had set herself the specific task to write in the persona of a univocal *I*, an *I* not significantly distinct from, or alien to, the poet herself. While this strategy strives to establish an unimpeachable credibility of voice, it results instead in a flattening; the speaker all watcher and no dreamer, or rather, taken over wholly by the dream of being a watcher. The dream, more specifically, is that a person can step back and bear witness to the great mysteries embodied in unremarkable experience. (In this case, the worldly subject is a suburban family, its internal workings thrown into harsh relief by the death of the father.) The book on the whole presumes a single nature—a dark nature, but a single one. What is lost is a sense of the turbulence and conflict inherent in subjectivity as Glück has earlier defined it. Instead subjectivity is now defined with reference to a single story; the index of the story's truth is merely the degree of bluntness with which it reveals itself. To this extent, *Ararat* seems at times motivated by the naïvely psychoanalytic or puritan belief that the soul can be healed merely by telling "how it happened." More than anything, what this single self desires is closure, the resolution of narrative tension. And Glück explores this desire in "Celestial Music," a poem about watching, with a friend, the death of a caterpillar:

> I have a friend who still believes in heaven.
> Not a stupid person, yet with all she knows, she literally talks
>   to God,
> she thinks someone listens in heaven.
> On earth, she's unusually competent.
> Brave, too, able to face unpleasantness.
>
> We found a caterpillar dying in the dirt, greedy ants crawling
>   over it.
> I'm always moved by weakness, by disaster, always eager to
>   oppose vitality.
> But timid, also, quick to shut my eyes[. . . .]

In reality, we sit by the side of the road, watching the sun set;
from time to time, the silence pierced by a birdcall.
It's this moment we're both trying to explain, the fact
that we're at ease with death, with solitude.
My friend draws a circle in the dirt; inside, the caterpillar
    doesn't move.
She's always trying to make something whole, something
    beautiful, an image
capable of life apart from her.
We're very quiet. It's peaceful sitting here, not speaking, the
    composition
fixed, the road turning suddenly dark, the air
going cool, here and there the rocks shining and glittering—
it's this silence that we both love.
The love of form is a love of endings. (*Ararat* 66)

Like "Night Song," "Celestial Music" hovers between identification and disavowal. The friend stands simultaneously for the poet and what the poet would
rather not be. The poem, however, is not a colloquy or debate but a leveling.
To love form is to face many risks, especially the risk of being taken in by an illusion, the illusion of symmetry or celestial order where in fact no symmetry
or order exists. What if writing poetry about loss is always an empty gesture,
merely a circle drawn around a dead or dying thing? This question is a deep
one (and recalls Hardy's search for closure in the *Vestigia* poems), but the conclusion of the poem evades it, even while appearing to isolate it for consideration. The conclusion, rhetorically, draws its own circle by asserting an
equation, a circular reciprocity, between the love of forms and the love of endings. What remains unaccounted for is the terrible violence at the center and
the possibility it implies: that the world might in fact be Stevens' "mangled,
smutted semi-world hacked out/ Of dirt. . . ." The only composition that the
poem can contemplate is a fixed one, an arbitrary equilibration. To successfully
negotiate grief, to grow "at ease with death, with solitude" is to achieve a state
of resignation indistinguishable from denial. The poem has set itself the task of
discriminating between those whole and beautiful images capable of life apart
from the maker, images that reveal a hidden or inherent order, from those that
impose an enforced order from without. However, within the restricted *donnée*
of *Ararat*, it is not possible for Glück to meet this challenge.

    This restricted position resembles the one Stevens struggled with in *The
Man with the Blue Guitar*. Eventually Stevens found that this form of inquiry
into poverty and sparseness hobbled his resources. Scoring a lyric oratorio for
a single guitar excluded too many possibilities. This narrowing, however, was
a necessary step toward the broader vocal registers of "Notes Toward a

Supreme Fiction" and the more elegiac austerities perfected in the late lyrics. In her later books, Glück too will seek out more supple and expansive forms, but even in *Ararat* there are indications of discomfort with the book's restricted domain. "Celestial Music," for instance, employs a longer line than Glück uses elsewhere. While this variation does not embody an essentially new approach to the material, it does invite the question whether Glück, during this period, is concerned with notable formal innovation.

The answer must be negative if form is understood here in its most conservative sense, as Frost's famous "net," for instance, or as the tight contour that distinguishes, say, Larkin's "An Arundel Tomb" from Plath's "Tulips." Glück's poems seem relatively unformed compared not only to most formal verse, but much free verse as well, particularly, for example, Eliot's and Pound's scrupulously shaped *vers libre,* so palpably haunted by the invoked music of its converging traditions. She does not seek to imitate their sonorities; neither does she adopt Plath's alliterative croonings or jaunty, mechanized, crank-organ syncopations. What Glück does reveal, formally, is a devotion to the shape of the sentence itself. It is the sentence that emerges as the dominant formal unit, not the foot, the line, or the stanza. This preoccupation is visible from the minute she abandons, early in her career, her assault on more traditional forms. In "The Education of the Poet," she describes how from the beginning syntax has exerted the strongest influence on her ear:

> Plainly, I loved the sentence as a unit: the beginning of a preoccupation with syntax. Those who love syntax less find in it the stultifying air of the academy: it is, after all, a language of rules, of order. Its opposite is music, that quality of language which is felt to persist in the absence of rule. One possible idea behind such preferences is the fantasy of the poet as renegade, as the lawless outsider. It seems to me that the idea of lawlessness is a romance, and romance is what I most struggle to be free of. (*Proofs* 8)

If music were in fact "that quality of language which is felt to persist in the absence of rule" then syntax would be its opposite, but this is not an opposition that Glück's poems bear out. Glück's ear is most highly attuned to what could be called the music of rhetoric itself, the "unmusical" music of sense and rule in their least adorned aspects. A more overtly musical poet would invoke the different kinds of authority that musical pattern can confer upon a line. (Music, here, is another form of the "irrefutable.") Glück, however, is interested in registers of authority that persist in the absence of musical form's implicit confirmation. Larkin's "At Grass," for instance, establishes at the outset its tonal "key." He then departs from and elaborates this musical basis by shifting into the contrapuntal, cantering variation in the middle stanzas, resolving the tension in the last stanza by calling the horses home with the quiescent tonic assonance of the final *home/come* rhyme. For Glück the idea of "home" or "quiescence" is too fraught to permit such an effect. Such a chord inevitably seems too lulling, too seductive. Instead of working to achieve abstract coherence through musical or metrical pattern, she strives for logical and rhetorical cohesion. The containment she most often finds is not one that establishes itself in the interplay between abstract form and specific content, but between question and answer, or between assertion and specification. If Emily Dickinson is the poet of the dash, Glück then is the poet of the colon: the exemplum, the qualification, the claim with supporting evidence, the proposition seeking out its conditions of possibility. But ideal cohesion, Glück learns, can only be desired; it can never be achieved.

In "Lullaby" Glück confronts the problem of musical seduction by writing an anti-lullaby:

> [. . . .]
> It's the same thing, really, preparing a person
> for sleep, for death. The lullabies—they all say
> *don't be afraid*, that's how they paraphrase
> the heartbeat of the mother.
> So the living slowly grow calm; it's only
> the dying who can't, who refuse.
>
> The dying are like tops, like gyroscopes—
> they spin so rapidly they seem to be still.
> Then they fly apart: in my mother's arms,
> my sister was a cloud of atoms, of particles—that's the difference.
> When a child's asleep, it's still whole.
>
> My mother's seen death; she doesn't talk about the soul's integrity.
> She's held an infant, an old man, as by comparison the dark grew
> solid around them, finally changing to earth.
>
> The soul's like all matter:
> why would it stay intact, stay faithful to its one form,
> when it could be free? (*Ararat* 28)

What the body and the soul yearn for is a release from coherent, unitary form. This release cannot be achieved in this world. To have a body means to be called back constantly to singleness, to a single name, a single set of historical and cultural coordinates. The desires that perennially yearn for the "paraphrase of the mother's heartbeat" war with those that reject the paraphrase, that do not want to be lulled. "Lullaby" is a lullaby pulled apart by the forces of inquiry. The poem strives to achieve an authority on the other side of song, desirous not to be soothed but braced, craving the satisfaction of having resisted all seduction. *Ararat,* however, stops short of pursuing the possibility that the austerity of the unmusical can be as great a seduction as the lullaby itself. The foreclosure of optimism by grimness is still a form of closure, an enforced faithfulness. In this book Glück has yet to find a formal correlative for the tendency toward unfaithfulness—a formal fidelity, that is, to the soul's infidelity to form.

The best poem in the volume, "Child Crying Out," reorients Glück to a more open field of inquiry, and looks out over the territory that she will explore in the three books that follow. It alloys "Night Song," the address of a waking lover to her sleeping companion, with "Descending Figure," where the speaker addresses an infant, a creature that speaks only in cries. The poem succeeds because the note of certainty on which it ends is in fact the revocation of certainty:

> You're asleep now,
> your eyelids quiver.
> What son of mine
> could be expected
> to rest quietly, to live
> even one moment
> free of wariness?
>
> The night's cold:
> you've pushed the covers away.
> As for your thoughts, your dreams—
>
> I'll never understand
> the claim of a mother
> on a child's soul.
>
> So many times
> I made that mistake
> in love, taking
> some wild sound to be
> the soul exposing itself—
>
> But not with you,
> even when I held you constantly.
> You were born, you were far away.
>
> Whatever those cries meant,
> they came and went
> whether I held you or not,
> whether I was there or not.

> The soul is silent.
> If it speaks at all
> it speaks in dreams. (*Ararat* 56)

Contemplating a mother's relationship to a child causes Glück to question the fundamental nature of lyric itself, how it is that lyric claims to speak for the soul. The cry here is not the elemental vowel of Plath's "Morning Song," the soul's voice in its most naked, present, and distilled form. Instead, it is a testament to the distance the soul keeps from even the rawest utterances. The soul, like the woman in "Last Letter," can never expose itself fully. Even nakedness "is always a pose." This is not to say that the cries do not have meaning. The meaning, however, is one that cannot be achieved in intelligible speech.

This is a momentous claim. What would it mean for there to be a language *outside* of speech? What would it mean for the soul to have a way of speaking fundamentally silent, separate, or severed from waking language? How then must a lyric poet speak, if she is not to give up her ambition to apprehend the language of the soul? To approach these questions, Glück must leave *Ararat* and conceive anew what a poem, or a book of poems, can do.

NOT SELF, BUT WE, WE . . . WAVES: REFRACTING VOICE IN *THE WILD IRIS*

Ararat brings the poet to a point of crisis. Although Glück never describes this crisis directly, the poems that make up her next book, *The Wild Iris,* are poems of survival. The survival that the book negotiates is not so much of an individual person as it is of a way of speaking. Having confronted the radical uncertainty expressed in "Child Crying Out" ("If [the soul] speaks at all / it speaks in dreams"), the lyric voice must suffer a radical transformation. This new voice, in the opening poem of the volume, enunciates itself from a place *outside* the poet, and the poet in turn assumes the role of listener or scribe. Although a Glück-like *I* will speak in the "Matins" and "Vespers" poems, the primary lyric self, the autobiographical *I,* has undergone a fundamental decentralization.[8] It can no longer wield a superior authority over perspectives that see the poet as a *you*. Like a plant that spends part of the year as bulb and part of the year as an leaf and flower, the poems' unifying consciousness takes different forms—sometimes object, sometimes subject, at times dormant and buried, at other times, verdant and blossoming. In "The Wild Iris" the speaker is such a plant; it addresses the poet:

> At the end of my suffering
> there was a door.

Hear me out: that which you call death
I remember.

Overhead, noises, branches of the pine shifting.
Then nothing. The weak sun
flickered over the dry surface.

It is terrible to survive as consciousness
buried in the dark earth.

Then it was over; that which you fear, being
a soul and unable
to speak, ending abruptly, the stiff earth
bending a little. And what I took to be
birds darting in low shrubs.

You who do not remember
passage from the other world
I tell you I could speak again: whatever
returns from oblivion returns
to find a voice:
from the center of my life came
a great fountain, deep blue
shadows on azure seawater. (*The Wild Iris* 1)

The wild iris is the herald of good news for the poet. The state she fears most,
"being a soul and unable to speak," will not last forever. This last assertion,
however, takes a specific, ambiguous form: "whatever / returns from oblivion
returns / to find a voice." One the one hand, these lines invoke the dynamic
of the unconscious as Freud at first conceived it, where thoughts and memories exiled from consciousness press back forcefully, erupting as symptom,
dream, recollection, or abreaction. The line, however, allows for a less hy-
draulic, more subtle possibility—that the only rescue from oblivion is *the conscious act* of finding a voice. The difference here is between a reflexive or driven
process (the repressed impulse driven toward satisfaction, the revenant driven
to exact revenge) and an act of powerfully intentional self-fashioning. In
Ararat, Glück was writing a kind of family history as a "woman in a state of
fact" (to paraphrase Stevens in "Montrachet-le-Jardin"). "The Wild Iris"
makes a claim instead for the imagination and places Glück face to face not
with fact but with those supreme fictions (Transcendent Being, Nature, the
Self) on which all definitions of fact are premised. In this sense the poem
marks a recovered faith in the imagination, a renewed faith that a voice is
something which can be found and put to use, that having a soul and having

a voice are the same thing. The voice springs up as though of its own separate volition: "from the center of my life came / a great fountain, deep blue / shadows on azure seawater." These two lines encompass a tiny genealogy of the humanist tradition, from the Hellenic-Judeo-Christian homology of the life and the soul, to the Romantic belief in the soul's depth and its capacity for spontaneous, overflowing voice, to the Mallarméan, Stevensian, Symbolist *azur* of the fictive imagination.

Even as the poem realigns Glück with this dominant tradition, however, it forms a more troubling alliance with a more immediate precursor, namely Elizabeth Bishop's early poem, "The Weed."[9] Glück's entire book can be seen as an investigation and extension of the assertions of this poem, in which a dead speaker discovers a weed pushing up through the apparently sterile soil of her "cold heart," splitting it apart and loosing two rushing rivers:

> I dreamed that dead, and meditating,
> I lay upon a grave, or bed,
> (at least, some cold and close-built bower).
> In the cold heart, its final thought
> stood frozen, drawn immense and clear,
> stiff and idle as I was there;
> and we remained unchanged together
> for a year, a minute, an hour.
> Suddenly there was a motion,
> as startling, there, to every sense
> as an explosion. Then it dropped
> to insistent, cautious creeping
> in the region of the heart,
> prodding me from a desperate sleep.
> I raised my head. A slight young weed
> had pushed up through the heart and its
> green head was nodding on the breast.
> (All this was in the dark.)
> It grew an inch like a blade of grass;
> next, one leaf shot out of its side
> a twisting, waving flag, and then
> two leaves moved like a semaphore.
> The stem grew thick. The nervous roots
> reached to each side; the graceful head
> changed its position mysteriously,
> since there was neither sun nor moon
> to catch its young attention.
> The rooted heart began to change
> (not beat) and then it split apart
> and from it broke a flood of water.
> Two rivers glanced off from the sides,

one to the right, one to the left,
two rushing, half-clear streams,
(the ribs made of them two cascades)
which assuredly, smooth as glass,
went off through the fine black grains of earth.

Although the rivers almost destroy the weed, they give it reflective power, and
enable its assertion of continuing life:

The weed was almost swept away;
it struggled with its leaves,
lifting them fringed with heavy drops.
A few drops fell upon my face
and in my eyes, so I could see
(or, in that black place, thought I saw)
that each drop contained a light,
a small, illuminated scene;
the weed-deflected stream was made
itself of racing images.
(As if a river should carry all
the scenes that it had once reflected
shut in its waters, and not floating
on momentary surfaces.)
The weed stood in the severed heart.
"What are you doing there?" I asked.
It lifted its head all dripping wet
(with my own thoughts?)
and answered then: "I grow," it said,
"but to divide your heart again." (20)

The poem offers an elaborate visual explication of the terms " broken heart"
and "spontaneous overflow of emotion." Bishop does not exclude the possibility of sincerity from her definition; the heart, opened by the weed, releases
a racing torrent of images, an unlimited outpouring of "illuminated scenes."
However, the stream (of grief, of consciousness) is only one of two things that
issues from the heart. The other is the weed itself, more foreign, more mysterious, at once native to and parasitic upon the heart, living only to divide it
again. Its emergence has inaugurated a struggle, not only the weed's struggle
to keep from being swept away, but the speaker's struggle to understand the
weed's purpose. In fact, the poem narrates a pure conflict; we know nothing
of the conflict's content or context. The ninth-line "Suddenly" startles the
poem from the early stasis of the grave-like bed; the cause of the germination,
however, remains obscure. The weed may be what the heart's final thought
turns into, but this is only "half-clear," and we know nothing of what the final

thought was, nor what each illuminated scene depicts, nor what images the river has stored. What is important about the grief, however, is not what was lost but the aftermath of loss, the heart's radical division. Having been killed or stunned, the speaker can return to consciousness, but consciousness now has several parts, the part that identifies with *I* and the parts that are foreign, the weed, the stream, even *the* heart and *the* breast (not *my* heart or *my* breast). Each of these foreign elements is comprehended in that mysterious, recollected, foreign body, the dream that occasions the poem.

Glück's wild iris, the fountain springing from the center of the life, is a version of Bishop's weed. It informs the poet that there is life after great suffering, but what springs from suffering's wound will not be the utterance of the *I* but something alien, outside, strange. Unlike Bishop, however, Glück does not make a personal appearance in her poem; instead, the poem is uttered entirely in the voice of the flower. Glück manages in this way to occupy two positions at once, the unified position of the fountain-like iris, overflowing with the exuberance of its message, and the divided position of the poet, who must now come to know herself not as she speaks but as she is spoken to—not only by the iris, but by all the other flowers in the book, as well as by God, and by herself.

The voice that Glück has found is both a voice and *voices,* and to this degree, she resembles, surprisingly, John Berryman, whom she discusses in her essay "Against Sincerity."

> It can be said of Berryman that when he found his voice he found his voices. By voice I mean natural distinction, and by distinction I mean to refer to thought. Which is to say, you do not find your voice by inserting a single adjective into twenty poems. Distinctive voice is inseparable from distinctive substance; it cannot be grafted on. (*Proofs* 43)

The distinctive substance of *The Wild Iris* is the enactment of this breaking apart into selves. For Berryman, the refraction of the consciousness behind *The Dream Songs* into Henry, the first-person speaker, and the unnamed interlocutor is the enactment of a pathology, the representation of a self always struggling toward—and failing to achieve—a self-integration enjoyed by more fortunate, less brilliantly accursed persons. Glück places her book at a remove from this diagnostic self-awareness, replacing idiosyncratic symptomatology with impersonal contemplation. The instant, however, she finds her attention drawn from the soul to the Soul, she discovers that what she is really concerned with are *souls* in the plural, fragments of the self constantly in conflict with one another. The flower "Scilla" tartly describes this condition, reproaching the poet as plural reproaches singular:

> Not I, you idiot, not self, but we, we—waves
> of sky blue like
> a critique of heaven: why
> do you treasure your voice
> when to be one thing
> is to be next to nothing?
> Why do you look up? To hear
> an echo like the voice
> of God? You are all the same to us,
> solitary, standing above us, planning
> your silly lives: you go
> where you are sent, like all things,
> where the wind plants you,
> one or another of you forever
> looking down and seeing some image
> of water, and hearing what? Waves,
> and over waves, birds singing. (*The Wild Iris* 14)

The scilla urges the poet to question the fundamental assumptions on which her craft is based, particularly the belief in single voice. One problem with this narcissism is that it projects images of itself everywhere. As a result, human beings are too often seeking out their image in the nonhuman features of the world. To see, for the scilla, is to impose a pattern. When the poet looks down she *sees* an image, an image of water, the mirroring pool or the fountain of the self. If she were to *listen* instead, she would hear that the water is not a pool of images but a series of waves—not static form but cycle, pulse, interval, and kinesis. What is voice, the scilla implies, but the supplanting of sounds by other sounds? Song is not the treasured voice striving toward God, but waves, and over the waves, birds singing. This is the scilla's "critique of heaven."[10] Here the scilla has reversed the formulation of Frost's "Never Again Would Birdsong Be the Same" (338) where birdsong takes on an "oversound" from Eve's singing, thus becoming more a part of art and less a part of nature. In "Scilla" it is Eve who should become more like the birds, her song more aleatory, less abstract, less exalted.

Paradoxically, it is in taking the scilla's anti-transcendentalist advice that Glück is able to write in the voice of God. Glück heeds the flower's rebuke in a manner different from that in which the scilla itself would have liked—after all, even a relativist such as the scilla likes to have the last word. If one wave displaces another, Glück reasons, then heaven in turn must be allowed to submit its own counter-critique. Thus, God, embodied in certain temporal moments or processes of nature ("The End of Winter," "Clear Morning," "Retreating Wind"), addresses the poet in a manner the scilla never could. In

"The End of Winter" God points out that it is of no importance what the poet thinks the creator is; what matters is the fact of the distance between them:

> Over the still world, a bird calls
> walking solitary among black boughs.
>
> You wanted to be born; I let you be born.
> When has my grief ever gotten
> in the way of your pleasure?
>
> Plunging ahead
> into the dark and light at the same time
> eager for sensation
>
> as though you were some new thing, wanting
> to express yourselves
>
> all brilliance, all vivacity
> never thinking
> this would cost you anything,
> never imagining the sound of my voice
> as anything but part of you—
>
> you won't
> hear it in the other world,
> not clearly again,
> not in birdcall or human cry,
>
> not the clear sound, only
> persistent echoing
> in all sound that means good-bye, good-bye—
>
> the one continuous line
> that binds us to each other. (*The Wild Iris* 10)

Sometimes, God says, it is impossible to hear the voice of a bird as mere singing. Sometimes, the solitary voice is a "call," a summoning, or in Stevens' terms, a "c [that] precede[s] the choir." It is impossible to have been cold long enough to see the black boughs as something other than an emblem of desolation, a sign of human suffering.[11] There may be a cost in believing that the echo of one's voice is the voice of God, but it is also costly to believe that the voice of God is never "anything but a part of you[rself]." When the soul enters the world, the voice of God will persist as an echo, but it will not be, as the scilla claims, an echo of the self. It will be an echo of something that can be apprehended only in negative form, in the experience of loss, of valediction. You may never know God again, but you will never be able to forget him completely. This is Glück's version of Larkin's question, "what remains when disbelief has gone?" ("Church Going" [97]). The God of "The End of Winter" answers with the assertion that it can never be gone; too much of the human experience is tied up in the sense of having been cut free from an originary source.

This poem articulates the terms of an important discovery for the book, not the discovery of a certain aspect of God, but of a certain relationship to absence. To say good-bye to God is a difficult task. On the one hand, it is difficult for the straightforward, Larkinian reason that "we will always be surprising / a hunger in us to be more serious" (97). On the other, it is difficult for the more paradoxical reason that to say farewell with the specified term "good-bye," derived as it is from "God-be-with-you," is to invoke the protection of the very Presence you are trying to consign to absence. (Bidding adieu to God, one would encounter the same problem.) Of course this ignores the inert colloquial sense of "good-bye," but in the colloquial Glück can always hear the resonance of grander themes. What she establishes in this poem is a different kind of wave or cycle between the sense of presence and the sense of absence. That it is God who hovers between *here* and *there* is not, in the long run, of crucial importance to Glück. The more important point is that hovering or oscillation is a fundamental property of the lyric. Lyric, after all, is "the one continuous *line* / that binds" the poet to an absent interlocutor (and, of course, to her reader as well). It is in this way that Glück sees the medium of the lyric, the medium of the line, as essentially elegiac.

The contrastive method that Glück perfects in *The Wild Iris* enables an extended exploration of a single topos that recurs throughout her work, the topos of the relation of figure to ground. "The End of Winter" invokes this topos implicitly, in the suggestion that God can be either a positive presence or a God-shaped hole cut in the world. A poem which treats this issue more directly is "The White Rose," where the flower, addressing God and the poet alike, asks whether its yearning is directed toward light or the darkness from which the light emerges:

> [. . . .]
> I am not like you, I have only
> my body for a voice; I can't
> disappear into silence—
>
> And in the cold morning
> over the dark surface of the earth

echoes of my voice drift,
whiteness steadily absorbed into darkness

as though you were making a sign after all
to convince me you too couldn't survive here

or to show me you are not the light I called to
but the blackness behind it. (*The Wild Iris* 47)

This poem, in its insistence on light's relation to darkness, immediately recalls
the conclusions to several poems from Glück's earlier books. "Pietà"
(*Descending Figure* 112) depicts the magi kneeling like "figures in a painting
/ whom the star lights, shining / steadily in its dark context." Glück investi-
gates this image further in the concluding section of "Day Without Night"
(*The Triumph of Achilles* 197), asserting "The context of truth is darkness
[. . . .]/ Are you taken in / by lights, by illusions? / Here is your path to God,
/ who has no name, whose hand / is invisible: a trick / of moonlight on the
dark water." In "Portrait," Glück describes a mother helping her young
daughter with a drawing:

> A child draws the outline of a body.
> She draws what she can, but it is white all through,
> she cannot fill in what she knows is there.
> Within the unsupported line, she knows
> that life is missing; she has cut
> one background from another. Like a child,
> she turns to her mother.
>
> And you draw the heart
> against the emptiness she has created. (*Descending Figure* 122)

In the drawn line, Glück sees an version of the written line. The implication
is that the lyric line, like the visual line, is in fact a play between backgrounds,
or rather between foregrounds, where shade and highlight collude to create an
illusion of presence. The line in such an account is not a contour, the reliable
map of a specific topography, but a ratio of difference and distance, a gradient that shades—to use the language of "Descending Figure"—into the non-
speech or infancy of the shades.

This is a radical claim about the nature of lyric poetry, indeed about the
nature of representation itself, but one that skirts the border of *The Wild Iris,*
engaging the poems obliquely. *The Wild Iris* is not, after all, a radical book. On
the contrary, it makes an argument for the lyric's traditional modes: the ardent
address of God or the beloved, or meditative reflection upon experience. While

The Wild Iris portrays the soul as a thing of parts, its disparateness is comprehended within a unified tone. Glück takes the experiences of a single person,
her varying moods and orientations toward the world, and separates them,
casting each one as a single vocal part, and then arranging them in the larger
polyvocal unity. The qualities of voice vary, but the unity of tone is never broken; the balance of proclamation to stern interrogation, of lament to resignation, remains consistent from one poem to another, as though certain
assumptions about what a poem should look and sound like are shared by all
parties. What, however, if these assumptions were not shared? What if the divisions between different parts of experience did not converge at a point of
higher unity? In *Meadowlands*, Glück pursues the implications of this question, seeking out a formal correlative for deeper disharmonies, disharmonies
that *The Wild Iris* can describe but not enact.

BICKERING INTO SONG:
THE POETRY OF DISCORD IN *MEADOWLANDS*

The Wild Iris, in spite of its tragic inflections, is a comedy, a *commedia;* the
soul is never an integrated thing, but its proper allegorical form is nonetheless
a garden, a figure of enclosure where the non-human, the human, and the divine come together. *Meadowlands*, on the other hand, though infused with
comic elements, is a tragedy, tracing the course of a marriage's disintegration.
The story is at once ironic and epic; the family is both a contemporary
American family and the royal family of Homer's Ithaca. This overlaying of
the contemporary and the classical, the quotidian and the mythic, allows for
abrupt, arresting shifts in tone. "Penelope's Song," the first poem, swerves pre-
cipitously between the ancient topos of a woman awaiting a seafarer's return,
and anti-heroic, domestic questions—how to greet an errant husband, what
to cook for dinner:

> Little soul, little perpetually undressed one,
> do now as I bid you, climb
> the shelf-like branches of the spruce tree;
> wait at the top, attentive, like
> a sentry or look-out. He will be home soon;
> it behooves you to be
> generous. You have not been completely
> perfect either; with your troublesome body
> you have done things you shouldn't
> discuss in poems. Therefore
> call out to him over the open water, over the bright water
> with your dark song, with your grasping,
> unnatural song—passionate,

like Maria Callas. Who
wouldn't want you? Whose most demonic appetite
could you possibly fail to answer? Soon
he will return from wherever he goes in the meantime,
suntanned from his time away, wanting
his grilled chicken. Ah, you must greet him,
you must shake the boughs of the tree
to get his attention,
but carefully, carefully, lest
his beautiful face be marred
by too many falling needles. (*Meadowlands* 3)

The contrast with *The Wild Iris* is stark and arresting. The content is different (grilled chicken), as is the tone (blunt critique replaced by veiled and veiling irony). Beyond these changes, however, "Penelope's Song" manifests a profound change in the poet's conception of her own voice. Her characterization of her "dark . . . grasping, / unnatural song," while recognizably detached, is ultimately despairing. The book will prove that it is not possible, however dark or passionate the voice, to summon a lover home. Whatever divisions there might have been in *The Wild Iris,* everyone was always listening to everyone else. In *Meadowlands,* this mutual attention cannot be assumed. The other is most often absent, and the voice seems either impotent (what if all he wants satisfied is not his "most demonic appetite" but his craving for chicken?) or destructively strident (what if you mar his face?). It is only with this deeply shaken, disconcerted voice, Glück implies, that one can reliably speak of what goes on in a house— not a garden, but what Frost called in "Directive" "a house in earnest" (377).

"Cana," the poem that follows "Penelope's Song," bids a formal farewell to *The Wild Iris* and alludes to Frost more directly, as well as to the torch which illuminates, for Psyche, the sleeping Eros:

What can I tell you that you don't know
that will make you tremble again?
Forsythia
by the roadside, by
wet rocks, on the embankments
underplanted with hyacinth—

For ten years I was happy.
You were there; in a sense,
you were always with me, the house, the garden
constantly lit,
not with light as we have in the sky
but with those emblems of light
which are more powerful, being

implicitly some earthly
thing transformed—

And all of it vanished,
reabsorbed into impassive process. Then
what will we see by,
now that the yellow torches have become
green branches? (*Meadowlands* 4)

Glück rephrases the question posed by Frost's oven-bird, the question of
"what to make of a diminished thing" (119).[12] The ten years of happiness, the
brilliance of spring, the incandescence of the garden (and of *The Wild Iris* itself) are now past. The poem's title invokes the wedding at Cana where Christ
performed the first of his miracles, the transformation of water into wine.
And indeed, the former world was one of magical transformations: Hyacinth's
body transformed into a flower,[13] love sanctified by marriage into a transcendental union, flowers turned into speaking voices, resinous trees into
torches.[14] But what if a reverse transformation has taken place, the wine
changed back into water, all the world's intoxicating wonder resorbed back
into "impassive process"? If this has happened, the poet wonders whether
there is anything she can say, anything "that you don't know / that will make
you tremble again." The poem does not provide a ready answer. (The green
branches might signify the departure of wonder, or alternately the possibility
of a less transient, more evergreen form of reality.[15]) In fact, the most accurate response to the question may be to say that answers are not to be had.
This recognition is what separates *The Wild Iris* from *Meadowlands*. *The Wild
Iris* was the book of questions and answering voices, answers leading to new
question in cyclical interchange. Even God, intermittently extinct, responded
nonetheless, eager to furnish clarifications (as in "Clear Morning" [8]). The
soul seeking clarification in *Meadowlands* meets with no such response. If
there is a light in the world, "Moonless Night" implies, it is not the light of
the moon, but of a streetlight and fading stars, along with the sound of the
neighbors, the Lights, who are "practicing klezmer music":

A lady weeps at a dark window.
Must we say what it is? Can't we simply say
a personal matter? It's early summer;
next door the Lights are practicing klezmer music.
A good night: the clarinet is in tune.

As for the lady—she's going to wait forever;
there's no point in watching longer.
After awhile, the streetlight goes out.

> But is waiting forever
> always the answer? Nothing
> is always the answer; the answer
> depends on the story.
>
> Such a mistake to want
> clarity above all things. What's
> a single night, especially
> one like this, now so close to ending?
> On the other side, there could be anything,
> all the joy in the world, the stars fading,
> the streetlight becoming a bus stop. (*Meadowlands* 9)

One finds illumination not in the yellow torch of the heavenly light, but in the green branch of humanity (the neighbors), in contingency and irony (they're called the Lights, how do you like that?), and in the charm of fallible mortality (the clarinet only intermittently in tune).

Pondering this descent into the quotidian, Glück arrives at a deeply uncharacteristic conclusion: "Nothing / is always the answer; the answer / depends on the story." It depends upon the story? It doesn't depend on the dark nature pursuing the hardest and most precisely phrased question? A profound shift has taken place. Even the knowledge of death elicits an unusual response. In *The Wild Iris* the impending end filled each voice with a compressed urgency. In *Meadowlands,* while night is also "close to ending," the consequence is that a single night, a single life, appears insignificant, just a part of "impassive process." The englobed egotism of the street-lamp's glow will turn into the common, day-lit, municipal bus stop—not a place to linger, but a place of departing and alighting, of passing through. "Moonless Night," then, revises the final lines of "Cana"; here, the specific results of transformation are less important than the underlying fact of change in the first place.

Such a shift calls for a change in the formal and narrative correlatives employed in the poetry. A mode of subjectivity suspended in change no longer adapts itself to the closed biblical narratives of "The Garden" and "Lamentations." What if the Fall is not from innocence into experience but from identity into mutability? Because change is potentially endless, does one who falls in this way ever reach the ground? "Parable of the Dove" narrates this different sort of descent, a fall with formal as well as existential ramifications for the poet, represented here by a dove, a singing bird:

> A dove lived in a village.
> When it opened its mouth

sweetness came out, sound
like a silver light around
the cherry bough. But
the dove wasn't satisfied.

It saw the villagers
gathered to listen under the blossoming tree.
It didn't think: I
am higher than they are.
It wanted to walk among them,
to experience the violence of human feeling,
in part for its song's sake.

So it became human.
It found passion, it found violence,
first conflated, then
as separate emotions
and these were not
contained by music. Thus
its song changed,
the sweet notes of its longing to be human
soured and flattened. Then

the world drew back; the mutant
fell from love
as from the cherry branch,
it fell stained with the bloody
fruit of the tree.

So it is true after all, not merely
a rule of art:
change your form and you change your nature.
And time does this to us. (*Meadowlands* 31)

If Glück's previous books have documented her interest in form and forma-
tion, in *Meadowlands* the focus has shifted to deformation or malformation.
Change here is not the vector toward perfection, as Plath might have hoped,
but toward a state of mutation. At first this seems monstrous; the word "mutant" leaps from the page with a jarring strangeness. Glück, however, is asking the reader to hear the word in its most literal sense. The dove is a mutant
to the extent that it lives in change; it has no form properly its own to cling
to. If our natures are contingent upon form, then form is what time relent-
lessly alters. "Time does this to us" and never stops doing it.

The implications for song itself are momentous. What had been sweet,
like a silver light, and seemed to represent an innocence, must perforce "sour

and flatten." For the dove of untarnished silver voice perched on a virginal cherry branch, to recognize this is to suffer a deflowering, a wound, an expulsion: "it fell stained with the bloody / fruit of the tree." The themes are still quasi-biblical, but just as the dove finds that the passion and violence of its new feeling are "not / contained by music," the Genesis narrative does not contain the dove. To the extent that there is any principle of justice at work in its world, the dove is sentenced to a kind of sentencelessness. Its punishment is not death, or labor, or worldly suffering—as meted out to Adam and Eve—but an expulsion from the enclosures, causalities, and resolutions of narrative itself. The dove has assumed not only a new form but an entirely new relation to form, in which form is never wholly distinct from formlessness. As Bonnie Costello points out, Glück herself has experienced a kind of fall, from the romanticism of *The Wild Iris* to the comparatively "soured and flattened" registers of *Meadowlands:*

> [. . . .] *Meadowlands* is Glück's most mimetic, and least romantic book. This mirror of life involves sacrifices that will disappoint some readers, attached to the stirring meditations of *Triumph of Achilles* and *The Wild Iris,* with their figurative power and their sense of mystery[. . . .] Louise Glück's plain style has never been so plain, the understatement so strong a check against emotional excess. But desire does have a place to go in its search for harmony—it moves into music with its temporal transformations. ("Trustworthy Speakers" 16)

The search for form does persist, as does the search for apt mimetic correlatives, but the belief in harmony, I suggest, has been shaken. The temporal transformation that the dove discovers is not a refuge as such. Passion and violence eventually decouple and become distinct emotions, but their struggle with one another, and with the world, remains unresolved and uncontained by the music. The challenge that Glück faces is to find a form that can in fact indicate, without seeking to enclose, these uncontained quantities. The form that can do this, as "Parable of the Swans" implies, is not harmonic but discordant. In the poem, two swans, having found each other, are happy enough for a while, but "after ten years, they hit / slimy water. . . ."

> Sooner or later in a long
> life together, every couple encounters
> some emergency like this, some
> drama which results
> in harm. This
> occurs for a reason: to test
> love and to demand

fresh articulation of its complex terms[. . . .]
              But this is not
a little story about the male's
inherent corruption, using as evidence the swan's
sleazy definition of purity. It is
a story of guile and innocence. For ten years
the female studied the male; she dallied
when he slept or when he was
conveniently absorbed in the water,
while the spontaneous male
acted casually, on
the whim of the moment. On the muddy water
they bickered awhile, in the fading light,
until the bickering grew
slowly abstract, becoming
part of their song
after a little longer. (*Meadowlands* 51)

The formal invention that Glück devises in *Meadowlands* is the abstraction of
bickering into song. The parable poems, however, while they comment upon
this development, cannot take the form of conflicts themselves. The poems
that do so are those that enact the arguments between the spouses: "The
Ceremony" (6), "Anniversary" (21), the three "Meadowlands" poems (22, 29,
34), "The Dream" (56), "The Wish" (58) and "Heart's Desire" (60). They
show a marriage no less ceremonial than the one that Yeats wishes for in
"Prayer for My Daughter," but the ceremony enacted is an art of conflict.
"The Dream" is an example of the method that shapes each of these poems,
the voice shifting back and forth between the parties in a quarrel, a quarrel
sometimes cruel, sometimes affectionate, sometimes funny, but one that
never resolves itself into concession agreement. The wife begins, speaking the
indented lines:

I had the weirdest dream. I dreamed we were married again.
You talked a lot. You kept saying things like *this is realistic.*
When I woke up, I started reading all my old diaries.

          I thought you hated diaries.

I keep them when I'm miserable. Anyway,
all those years I thought we were so happy
I had a lot of diaries.

Do you ever think about it? Do you ever wonder
if the whole thing was a mistake? Actually,
half the guests said that at the wedding.

I'll tell you something I never told you:
I took a valium that night.

I keep thinking of how we used to watch television,
how I would put my feet in your lap. The cat would sit
on top of them. Doesn't that still seem
an image of contentment, of well being? So
why couldn't it go on longer?

Because it was a dream. (*Meadowlands* 56)

These poems directly or indirectly pick up threads from earlier fights, in this instance recalling the opening salvos of "Anniversary." Here, the husband begins:

I said you could snuggle. That doesn't mean
your cold feet all over my dick.

Someone should teach you how to act in bed.
What I think is you should
keep your extremities to yourself.

Look what you did—
you made the cat move[. . . .] (*Meadowlands* 21)

The unity of the book, then, is defined not by the enclosed walls of the garden, but by the arena of recurrent conflict; the title denotes not only a pastoral expanse but a football stadium in New Jersey. The conflict in *Meadowlands* never stops, and it determines not only the relationship between the husband and the wife, but between all the different local coherences that make up the book. It is for this reason that *Meadowlands* does not achieve the unity of *The Wild Iris*, which by comparison seems a "woven, budded aureole" (to paraphrase Stevens' "A Postcard from the Volcano"). The books together, however, enter into an unending debate of their own, a debate in which neither comedy nor tragedy ever gains the upper hand. And together, they represent the peak of Glück's accomplishment so far.

FOUND MATERIAL: NEW WORLDLINESS IN *VITA NOVA*.

The ongoingness of conflict and mutability has the effect in *Meadowlands* of breaching or spilling over the narrative structures that had furnished Glück's earlier books with their tightly plotted contours. The fables and meta-narratives tend to describe processes rather than outcomes. In her two most recent books, *Vita Nova* and *The Seven Ages*, Glück explores the thematic and formal possibilities of a world less scripted by fate, or rather, the possibilities of a world whose fate it is to frustrate or undermine the desire for a visible plot. The shaping structure is not that of the epic, with its insistence on an end (no matter how resisted or deferred) but of a fundamentally interminable process of skeptical reflection, at times resembling the asymmetrical dialogue between psychoanalyst and patient, at others the equally asymmetrical exchange between confessor and penitent. While marriages can end, neither analysis nor confession can ever be said to reach a conclusion. To the extent then that master narratives are invoked in the books—Dante's Christian eschatology, the myths of Dido and Aeneas, and of Orpheus and Eurydice—they are intended as stories of arrival at new worlds. These worlds are not only undiscovered worlds, but worlds of *essential* newness, endlessly renewable, which is to say, not only worlds newly discovered, but worlds of discovery. The model for such a progression is not a narrative arc but a fractal expansion, as Glück indicates in "Formaggio":

> The world
> was whole because
> it shattered. When it shattered,
> then we knew what it was.
>
> It never healed itself.
> But in the deep fissures, smaller worlds appeared
> [. . . .] (*Vita Nova,* 13)

The shattered world cannot be mended, but the shattering inevitably creates new worlds. These worlds are branching and provisional, rather than spherical and contained, but in their provisional nature, they provide and nourish in their own way:

> Tributaries
> feeding into a large river: I had
> many lives. In the provisional world,
> I stood where the fruit was,
> flats of cherries, clementines,
> under Hallies's flowers.
> [. . . .]

Identity is not the site of awareness or consciousness but of necessary and arbitrary insistence on cohesion:

> I had lives before this, stems
> of a spray of flowers: they became

one thing, held by a ribbon at the center, a ribbon
visible under the hand. Above the hand,
the branching future, stems
ending in flowers. And the gripped fist—
that would be the self in the present.

The self grips, but the grasp is as provisional as the world itself. Such a world,
then, solicits discovery rather than comprehension. In "Roman Study," to describe this renewal and revision of vocation, Glück adopts the persona of
Aeneas, acutely aware of his belatedness in coming "after the Greeks":

He felt at first
he should have been born
to Aphrodite, not Venus,
that too little was left to do,
to accomplish after the Greeks[. . . .]

And then it occurred to him
to examine these responses
in which, finally, he recognized
a new species of thought entirely,
more worldly, more ambitious
and politic, in what we now call
human terms.

And the longer he thought
the more he experienced
faint contempt for the Greeks,
for their austerity, the eerie
balance of even the great tragedies—
thrilling at first, then
faintly predictable, routine.

And the longer he thought
the more plain to him how much
still remained to be experienced,
and written down, a material world heretofore
hardly dignified.

And he recognized in exactly this reasoning
the scope and trajectory of his own
watchful nature. (*Vita Nova* 10)

The shift is from the world of Plath's "illusion of a Greek necessity" to a
Roman, civic, politic, *worldly* world of the provisional and the possible. No
longer is the real world opposed to an unreal or transcendental counterpart;

the world in *Vita Nova* is a merely material world. Glück makes less appeal to its opposite, the immaterial or transcendent, because she discovers within its "human terms" much that stands away from, and remains other to, the grasp of the "self in the present." Before, in "Descending Figure," the world was the extent of what the self perceived; in order to conceive of something beyond its ken, it had to imagine an anti-world or underworld. In *Vita Nova*, the self has diminished to a single point, tiny in an outer world vast enough to be almost entirely foreign, almost entirely new and unknown.

Such a focus on the material, as distinct from the real, enables Glück to consider certain parts of the world unburdened by the obligation to divide the true from the false. Specifically what this shift sponsors is a renewed and intensified attention to the dream; and it is the question of what a dream is, its nature and place in the world, that is the central question of *Vita Nova*. Like *The Wild Iris, Vita Nova* begins with a poem of waking, a waking not from the dead, as before, but from a dream. Whether the dream is fiction or memory, or a hybrid of both, is less important than its fundamental strangeness, its readiness to be contemplated as an unexpected and surprising discovery— a foreign body found in the mind. Visible immediately in the title poem of *Vita Nova* is a looser, more fragmentary progression of ideas, more notational, more exploratory:

> You saved me, you should remember me.
>
> The spring of the year; young men buying tickets for the ferryboats.
> Laughter, because the air is full of apple blossoms.
>
> When I woke up, I realized I was capable of the same feeling.
> I remember sounds like that from my childhood,
> laughter for no cause, simply because the world is beautiful,
> something like that.
>
> Lugano. Tables under the apple trees.
> Deckhands raising and lowering the colored flags.
> And by the lake's edge, a young man throws his hat into the water;
> perhaps his sweetheart has accepted him.
>
> Crucial
> sounds or gestures like
> a track laid down before the larger themes
>
> and then unused, buried.
>
> Islands in the distance. My mother
> holding out a plate of little cakes—

as far as I remember, changed
in no detail, the moment
vivid, intact, having never been
exposed to light, so that I woke elated, at my age
hungry for life, utterly confident—

By the tables, patches of new grass, the pale green
pieced into the dark existing ground.

Surely spring has been returned to me, this time
not as a lover but as a messenger of death, yet
it is still spring, it is still meant tenderly. (*Vita Nova* 1)

When Glück describes the grass, she is also describing her method: a piecing together, patches of memory and dream fitted and stitched into the existing ground of experience. The preference here is for the found over the made, in the way that a dream, though a production of consciousness, is found rather than made through any conscious agency, and in the way that a memory too is "made" but not willed, and subject to unexpected appearances. This kind of finding, or unwilled making, is Glück's version of the "minimal making" that Stevens explored with greater and greater interest as his life drew to an end. Like Stevens, Glück has turned her attention to the most basic units of coherence that make up the world, and to the processes, largely unbidden, by which these coherences come into being. And as Stevens had, she finds in this light that birds interest her especially. She focuses, however, not on what they sing, but on what they *build*, because the bird-as-builder resembles a human being in a different way than does the bird-as-singer. Song, for Glück's purposes, too readily implies that the self is the *source* of what it makes, the wellspring of feeling and emotion. Building, on the other hand, is that act which requires, by definition, a *material*, in a way that song, in seeming to be made out of thin air, does not. The great bird poem in *Vita Nova* is "Nest." In it the poet declares that she is "trying to be / a witness not a theorist," but her act of witness entails a theory of "base material":

A bird was making its nest.
In the dream, I watched it closely:
In my life, I was trying to be
a witness not a theorist.

The place you begin doesn't determine
the place you end: the bird

took what it found in the yard,
its base materials, nervously

scanning the bare yard in early spring;
in debris by the south wall pushing
a few twigs with its beak.

Image
of loneliness: the small creature
coming up with nothing. Then
dry twigs. Carrying, one by one,
the twigs to the hideout.
Which is all it was then.

It took what there was:
the available material. Spirit
wasn't enough.

And then it wove like the first Penelope
but toward a different end.
How did it weave? It weaved,
carefully but hopelessly, the few twigs
with any suppleness, any flexibility,
choosing these over the brittle, the recalcitrant.

Early spring, late desolation.
The bird circled the bare yard making
efforts to survive
on what remained to it.
It had its task:
to imagine the future. Steadily flying around,
patiently bearing small twigs to the solitude
of the exposed tree in the steady coldness
of the outside world.

I had nothing to build with.
It was winter: I couldn't imagine anything but the past.
I couldn't even imagine the past, if it came to that.

And I didn't know how I came here.
Everyone else much farther along.
I was back at the beginning
at a time in life we can't remember beginnings.

The bird
collected twigs in the apple tree, relating
each addition to existing mass.
But when was there suddenly *mass*?

It took what it found after the others
were finished.
The same materials—why should it matter
to be finished last? The same materials, the same
limited good. Brown twigs,
broken and fallen. And in one,
a length of yellow wool.

Then it was spring and I was inexplicably happy.
I knew where I was: on Broadway with my bag of groceries.
Spring fruit in the stores: first
cherries at Formaggio. Forsythia
beginning.

First I was at peace.
Then I was contented, satisfied.
And then flashes of joy.
And the season changed—for all of us,
of course.

And as I peered out my mind grew sharper.
And I remember accurately
the sequence of my responses,
my eyes fixing on each thing
from the shelter of the hidden self:

first, *I love it.*
Then, *I can use it.* (*Vita Nova* 37)

"Nest" is, as Stevens would put it, a "poem of the act of the mind." Like "Of
Modern Poetry" it is an *ars poetica,* and for all its thematic concern with states
of utmost humility, intends an assertion no less momentous than those of
Stevens or Keats. In fact, the poem addresses Keats's claim that beauty is truth
by asking a corollary question: where does beauty begin? "How did it weave? It
weaved, / carefully but hopelessly." By identifying this place of hopelessness,
Glück distinguishes hope from desire, formulating the claim that even in hopelessness a basic impetus to make persists. Her bird, then, is Stevens' "Dove in
Spring," struggling to make something of "the little there, / the little and the
dark" (461). The only available material is random and damaged, "brown twigs,
/ broken and fallen." From these "cold copulars" of hopelessness and damage a
particular rapture nonetheless springs. It takes its form in the poem's first instance of positive beauty: "And in one, / a length of yellow wool." As late-
Stevensian as the poem is, however, this yellow wool stands in sharp contrast to
the sublime beauty of the "fire-fangled feathers" in Stevens' "Of Mere Being."

The wool's beauty is contingent, aleatory, not a part of what the bird is but of what it happens to find. It is toward such a beauty, the beauty of the found as opposed to the beauty of the made, that Glück's most recent poems turn.

Formally, this turn manifests itself in a rhetoric of recursive and casual patterning. This is evident in the first "Vita Nova" where the repetition of the poem's few central terms ("spring," "laughter," "young," "apple," "sound") take on the quality of a rueful, casual refrain. More complexly, in the poem "Castile," recursions of unsorted memory and reflection shift and waft among the more rigid structures of irony and self-interrogation.

> Orange blossoms blowing over Castile
> children begging for coins
>
> I met my love under an orange tree
> of was it an acacia tree
> or was he not my love?
>
> I read this, then I dreamed this:
> can waking take back what happened to me?
> Bells of San Miguel
> ringing in the distance
> his hair in the shadows blond-white
> I dreamed this,
> does that mean it didn't happen?
> Does it have to happen in the world to be real?
>
> I dreamed everything, the story
> became my story:
>
> he lay beside me,
> my hand grazed the skin of his shoulder
>
> Mid-day, then early evening:
> in the distance, the sound of a train
>
> But it was not the world:
> in the world, a thing happens finally, absolutely,
> the mind cannot reverse it.
>
> Castile: nuns walking in pairs though the dark garden.
> Outside the walls of the Holy Angels
> children begging for coins
>
> When I woke I was crying,
> has that no reality?

I met my love under an orange tree:
I have forgotten
only the facts, not the inference—
there were children somewhere, crying, begging for coins

I dreamed everything, I gave myself
completely and for all time

And the train returned us
first to Madrid
then to the Basque country (*Vita Nova* 28)

Manifestly, this poem centers around memory and the contemplation of a memory. Its success, however, is in representing not a state of feeling from the past but a mind acting in the present, a mind divided and oscillating between dream and waking, between the tenacious self-scrutiny and the flux of ongoing experience. If in Glück's work there is always a dialectic between opposing elements, here the frequency of the modulation is at its narrowest and most rapid. Consciousness does not have time to divide into discrete agencies or attitudes (recollection, meditation, or self-critique) or even into sustained moods. Instead, there is a blurring; dream becomes memory, and memories join to form the story of one's life. What the facts were ceases to matter (who the lover was, whether he was her lover at all), and only the inference remains.

Specifically, this inference concerns the nature of divided consciousness. The division is between the sense of internal discontinuity (signified by the perennial political conflict in the Basque country) and the sense of unity achieved through action or desire ("I gave myself for all time"). In this poem Glück is as far as she will ever be from her syllogistic approach. With punctuation thinned to a minimal presence, the lines have a tentative, suspended quality, not marching in linear progression from one idea to another but evolving on several fronts at once. The poem represents a formal extreme for Glück, purchasing its embodiment of this multifarious, divided self by relinquishing retrospection's ordering vantage. As such, it is the furthest extension of the contrastive method of her earlier books; what had played as colloquy in *The Wild Iris* and counterpoint in *Meadowlands* here manifests itself as a conjoining of disparate strains of consciousness in unfamiliar chords. The effect of unfamiliarity is of crucial import, because what is most essential to the self, Glück implies, is its strangeness, its foreignness, its unfamiliarity. What the "self in the present" encloses is not only the convergence of all past and future contingencies that intersect in the experience of the present moment, but those experiences (dreams chief among them) that maintain their own strangeness, foreignness, or resistance to intelligibility. This foreignness is preserved even though in speech one is constrained to claim a dream as *one's own*. It is in this way that the subjectivity mediated by Glück's lyrics inheres not in the experience of identity or self-contiguity, but in the acknowledgement of the persistence of the foreign. *Vita Nova* makes the point that the mark of the foreign and the unintelligible can inhere in the most subtle and delicate registrations of the unfamiliar, not only in those experiences, confronted in the earlier books, of the wholly alien.

I WAS HERE: THE SITE OF SPEAKING IN *THE SEVEN AGES.*

In *Vita Nova,* the figure for the internal foreignness is the figure of the dream. *The Seven Ages* includes among the experience of foreignness the experience of consciousness itself. And whereas *Vita Nova* had been concerned with the mimesis of the mind in the present, *The Seven Ages* is focused on the representation of the past. It is Glück's most recent book, and the first that undertakes explicitly to look back on a life beginning to near its end. While Glück's late poetry does not suffer the ravages of silence, as Larkin's late work had, or take up death as its main topic, as Stevens' late poems had, or conceive of itself as the poetry of late age, as Hardy's *Winter Words* had, it stands nonetheless as a late communication. Like *Vita Nova, The Seven Ages* confronts the relationship between consciousness and dream, between the mind-as-I and the mind-as-other, but the dream in question is perceived, as it were, after the speaker has waked from life.

The question that *The Seven Ages* seeks to answer is what to make of the past now that the majority of one's life is a part of it. The first poem, "The Seven Ages," enacts this stepping outside of one's life:

> I was human:
> I had to beg to descend
> the salt, the bitter, the demanding, the preemptive
>
> and like everyone, I took, I was taken
> I dreamed
>
> I was betrayed:
>
> Earth was given to me in a dream
> In a dream I possessed it (*The Seven Ages* 3)

The goal here is no longer to *enact* the turbulent processes of consciousness, but to look back at a world that has now receded into an inaccessible having-been. In the two poems entitled "Fable" (9, 49), Glück undertakes to imagine this past as completely separate from the speaker, uninfluenced by desire or longing. The second of these poems undertakes to construct a timeless-ness—not an eternal transcendence, but a sense of wholeness that attends upon the recognition that one's life, however "weird and full of dreams," will inevitably reach its completion. It is a poem that recapitulates Glück's own poetic ontogeny, moving from the garden, which stands for the temporal, re-curring world, through the panicked recognitions of change and loss that marked *Meadowlands* and *Vita Nova*, arriving ultimately at a new category, the "everlasting," a term for Glück both new and surprising.

> The weather grew mild, the snow melted.
> The snow melted, and in its place
> flowers of early spring:
> mertensia, chionodoxa. The earth
> turned blue by mistake.
>
> Urgency, there was so much urgency—
> to change, to escape the past.
>
> *It was cold, it was winter:*
> *I was frightened for my life.*
>
> Then it was spring, the earth
> turning a surprising blue.
>
> The weather grew mild, the snow melted—
> spring overtook it.
> And then summer. And time stopped
> because we stopped waiting.
>
> And summer lasted. It lasted
> because we were happy.
>
> The weather grew mild, like
> the past circling back
> intending to be gentle, like
> a form of the everlasting.
>
> Then the dream ended. The everlasting began.

Glück's apprehension of the everlasting recalls Stevens' apprehension of a time outside of time in "Of Mere Being" (476). Like Stevens, Glück cannot imag-ine an afterlife, but she can conceive of a way in which the past, once the fever of the present has gone, becomes something like a permanent object, a ver-sion of Lowell's Nietzschean "it was. . . ." Unlike Stevens, however, she is not concerned to purify this experience of all vestiges of pathos; the blue of spring-time is always to be registered *both* as an accident and as a surprise.

While one perceives the "everlasting" only through separation from one's worldly desires, this separation is not something to be accomplished by will; it is what time accomplishes for us. The first "Fable" conceives of this process not as *our* relinquishing of wishes, but as the process whereby wishes release *us*.

> [. . . .]
> All [wishes] different, except of course
> the wish to go back. Inevitably
> last or first, repeated
> over and over—
>
> so the echo lingered. And the wish
> held us and tormented us
> though we knew in own bodies
> it was never granted.
>
> We knew, and on dark nights, we acknowledged this.
> How sweet the night became then,
> once the wish released us,
> how utterly silent.

Once the wish has "released us," life appears with a terrible clarity. Glück imagines a speaker capable of standing outside of consciousness itself, view-ing experience as wholly discrete, as a part of what she calls in "Nest" "the steady coldness / of the outside world" (*Vita Nova* 37). Childhood, like a feverish sickness, was the moment (she writes in "Time") when "things be-came dreams; dreams became things." But time passes, childhood passes away, and the past assumes permanent forms:

> [. . . .]
> I was a child, half sleeping.
> I was sick; I was protected.
> And I lived in the world of the gray rain,
> the lost, the remembered.
>
> Then suddenly the sun was shining.
> And time went on, even when there was almost none left.
> And the perceived became the remembered,
> the remembered, the perceived. (*The Seven Ages* 61)

Glück, with Keats in the "Ode on a Nightingale," Shakespeare in *Macbeth* (III. i. 22), and Cranmer in *The Book of Common Prayer*, imagines what it

would mean to be released from the "fever of life." This is not Eliot's escape
from personality but a process whereby personality is rendered discrete from
the speaking voice, a voice not impersonal as such but radically dispassionate,
having achieved its obdurate temper by passing though passion and arriving
on its far side. The permanence of the "everlasting," then, is to be distinguished from a state of unchangingness. The past has a kind of life but a kind
distinct from the life of the speaking subject; this is why it can speak *to* the self
in the form of memories and dreams.

Glück addresses this permanent, unassailable center in "The Ripe
Peach" (*The Seven Ages* 52) and, with more satisfactory results, in one of the
volume's best poems, "The Balcony":

> It was a night like this, at the end of summer.
>
> We had rented, I remember, a room with a balcony.
> How many days and nights? Five, perhaps—no more.
>
> Even when we weren't touching we were making love.
> We stood on our little balcony in the summer night.
> And off somewhere, the sounds of human life.
>
> We were the soon to be anointed monarchs,
> well disposed to our subjects. Just beneath us,
> sounds of a radio playing, an aria we didn't in those years know.
>
> Someone dying of love. Someone from whom time had taken
> the only happiness, who was alone now,
> impoverished, without beauty.
>
> The rapturous notes of an unendurable grief, of isolation and terror,
> the nearly impossible to sustain slow phrases of the ascending figures—
> they drifted out over the dark water
> like an ecstasy.
>
> Such a small mistake. And many years later,
> the only thing left of that night, of the hours in that room.
>   (*The Seven Ages* 29)

Not comprehending the aria, the lovers could not have predicted how their
lives would come to resemble the heroine's fate. They too would make hard
acquaintance with grief, isolation, and terror. The aria, however, is not a
record or a depiction of their experience. In fact, what Glück is struggling to
write here is the opposite of a record. She separates the personal experience,

the specific ways in which the lovers' lives came to manifest the suffering in the aria, from the artwork itself. If art is the mirror, it is a mirror that has consumed the world that it reflects, so that all that remains is the aria itself, a kind of platonic ideal standing outside and above concrete history. In its standing outside, the aria embodies, in a literal, etymological way, the "ecstasy" of art.

Lyric subjectivity, Glück implies, entails a displacement of this sort. Once the aria becomes the record of a personal experience—those few days we spent together in our rented room—the experience itself is gone, is nowhere. The "here" that the aria occupies is a version of the "here" of lyric as Glück understands it, and a version to be added to those others I have described with respect to Plath, Larkin, Stevens, and Hardy. It is in "Aubade" that Glück considers this "here" most directly:

> There was one summer
> that returned many times over
> there was one flower unfurling
> taking many forms
>
> Crimson of the monarda, pale gold of the late roses
>
> There was one love
> There was one love, there were many nights
>
> Smell of the mock orange tree
> Corridors of jasmine and lilies
> Still the wind blew
>
> There were many winters but I closed my eyes
> The cold air white with dissolved wings
>
> There was one garden when the snow melted
> Azure and white; I couldn't tell
> my solitude from love—
>
> There was one love; he had many voices
> There was one dawn; sometimes
> we watched it together
>
> I was here
> I was here
> There was one summer returning over and over
> there was one dawn
> I grew old watching (*The Seven Ages* 65)

The poem is a poem of leave-taking, but the departure is not from the lover but from a myth of specificity. Each particular lover was only a single manifestation of the one love, and each dawn a part of the one dawn. Instead of a single self traversing many seasons and many changes, the many changes fold into an impersonal surface which refracts the self into many selves. The final specificity that the poem bids farewell to, then, is the specificity of a single, encompassing subjectivity. When Glück writes "I was here / I was here," the repeated line breaks into a flurry of different senses: *I* was here, I *was* here, I was *here.* The lines assert presence, the fact of having lived, while at the same time situating the life in the past—I was here and am no longer. Meanwhile, the repetition of the line undermines the precision of the designation *here*— I was here, no *here,* no *here.* The site of speech that the *I* designates is in fact a non-site. The subjectivity it denotes is one only knowable in change, in its shifting from one form to another. The path, then, that Glück traverses in her work is toward this limit point where the lyric *I,* that point of utterance from which the whole genre proceeds, is yielded up to join those other foreign elements of experience that the speaker (now no longer congruent with the *I)* finds among "the available material."

Conclusion
Other Ends of the Mind

The question of what knowledge the lyric records remains open. If the lyric is, by definition, the soul discoursing with itself, then the questions of what a soul is, and how it enters into that discourse, and what the nature of that discourse might be, and in whose benefit it is pursued, stand unresolved. If the lyric is in its essence "overheard," then what is the perspective from which such an overhearing can take place, and what is the status of the convictions or opinions developed by the overhearer? And what does it mean to speak in such a way as to intend to be overheard, rather than heard? Is there an analogous formulation that takes into account the lyric's status as a written form? If one can speak in such a way as to intend to be overheard, can one write in such a way as to be over-read? If, on the other hand, the lyric is meant as a script to be *spoken* by the reader *in propria persona,* another set of problems emerges. In this account, the angles of the writer-speaker-reader triangle shift in such a way that it is no longer the reader who stands at the greatest distance from the writer-speaker; instead, the reader and the speaker are now less distinguishable, and the writer remains remote, depersonalized, something closer to a principle of composition. Such a formulation elides the problematic persistence of the writer's role in the poem, the "living hand," in Keats' sense, still "warm and capable," that the poem extends toward the reader (albeit as a shadow which animates through presence and absence at once). Neither account of lyric speech addresses what I take to be its central problem, its essential *foreignness,* its fundamental estrangement not only from the reader (who encounters in the lyric the trace of the mind of another) but from the writer as well (who encounters, in the gap between self-knowledge and public representation, an equally irreducible ratio of difference). One way of formulating the central argument of this book is to say that the lyric and this estrangement stand in a mutually constitutive relationship to one another; the lyric, through the interplay between form and content, between the abstract closure of line and the specific utterance of voice, endlessly re-inscribes and renegotiates these terms of difference.

Among the many divisions by which the lyric can be categorized, one in particular has held a central role in this book, the distinction between poems which question the speaking subject's internal coherence—its intelligibility to itself—and those which assume this intelligibility and proceed from that assumption to address other ends in the world. The poems on which I've focused are poems whose first concern is an inquiry into the nature and possibility of the lyric "I," and only secondarily those uses to which such an "I" may be put. (I say poems and not poets because poets themselves, at any juncture in their careers, can switch from one of these modes to the other.) This present argument could be most readily expanded with reference to other poems that fit this general category; conversely, those which presume a more secure condition of utterance will not so readily reveal the phenomena that I have sought to describe here. With that in mind, I propose, by way of conclusion, to indicate some potential avenues of expansion, and to remark how such expansions might bring other questions about the nature of lyric speech into focus.

INTRANSIGENT FACTS:
LOWELL AND THE PROBLEM OF CONFESSIONALISM

If in fact the religious valence of the term *confessionalism* is relevant in a poetic context, it is so in its implicit insistence on a special seam or fault-line that traverses the human realm; this seam marks the point of juncture between the contingent, historical, unchosen facts of mortal existence (chief among them the *given* of Original Sin), and the divine realm, which is capable of redeeming the human soul from its mortal condition, a condition which resides, by definition, at a remove from divinity. What sacramental confession must ceaselessly mediate, then, is the *violent conflict* between the warring imperatives to which the human being—greater than the beasts, lesser than the angels—is subject. The violent sacrifice on which all Christian belief pivots is the localized, historically specific manifestation of this wider, non-localized, ahistorical conflict. It is not a surprise that this conflict should continue to be felt as a violence even in the waning of institutionalized religious belief, even for poets whose central concerns were never religious ones; not only did the twentieth century outstrip all its predecessors in sheer murderousness, but in it the dominant account of the "spiritual" subject was Freudian psychoanalysis, with its central postulate of an essentially violent conflict between the different agencies, or orders, of the mind. The ego, the Freudian "I," is by definition not only occupied with but *constituted within* this unending struggle between conflicting forces.

The poets for whom this struggle is most visible are those most deeply convinced of the world's essentially inherited, unchosen, and given nature; for them the world is a welter of fact. The struggle arises in the resistance the will (as imagination) mounts to this conviction; this essential givenness must in some way be deplored, rejected, resented, or grieved. Such a condition requires a labor of justification between, on the one hand, the imaginative or the figural, and on the other, the factual or the real. Such poets appeal to the resources of the lyric to accomplish this justification, even while acknowledging each attempt to be transient and provisional. The strongest poems of Lowell, Berryman, Jarrell, Sexton, and Roethke struggle with the anguish of a factually burdened past—at times the past of autobiographical history, at other times the past of cultural or historical burden, at other times the (non)past of the Freudian unconscious, the seething repository of unchosen appetites and affections. Each of these different pasts constitutes what might be called an implacable contextual reality against which the lyric affords partial or limited tools of assimilation. This partial or limited assimilability of the factual is the dominant pressure against which confessionalism takes its form. Of course, these poets have written many different kinds of poems, and any single term cannot comprehend all of the many variant aspects of their art. In the most general terms, however, the experience their work repeatedly designates is an experience of failure, specifically the failure of art to sponsor a fully and coherently imagined world.

Because it states most explicitly the conflict between paralyzing fact and the claims of the figural and of art, the emblematic poem for this complex of issues is Robert Lowell's "Epilogue":

> Those blessèd structures, plot and rhyme—
> why are they no help to me now
> I want to make
> something imagined, not recalled?
> I hear the noise of my own voice:
> *The painter's vision is not a lens,*
> *it trembles to caress the light.*
> But sometimes everything I write
> with the threadbare art of my eye
> seems a snapshot,
> lurid, rapid, garish, grouped,
> heightened from life,
> yet paralyzed by fact.
> All's misalliance.
> Yet why not say what happened?

> Pray for the grace of accuracy
> Vermeer gave to the sun's illumination
> stealing like the tide across a map
> to his girl solid with yearning.
> We are poor passing facts,
> warned by that to give
> each figure in the photograph
> his living name. (*Collected Poems*, 838)

The image can either be the mark of the painter's caress or the snapshot-photographer's "lurid, rapid, garish" grouping, "heightened from life, / yet paralyzed by fact." The image, then, occupies a position at the border of imagination and recollection, the border of fiction and fact. Lowell brings the metaphor (of graphic-representation for poetry) back to the realm of the poet in the final line, with the introduction of the term "name." The name, like the image, exists on this border as well; it is simultaneously one of the "poor passing facts" of our existence and something "illuminated," valued, imbued with a life-giving "caress," a fullness that cannot be intended so much as prayed for and received as a "grace." "Accuracy" is the form of this grace, that intersection between an inherent nature and its just representation. While a mere name can be simply imposed or assigned, a "living name" must be not only given but responsive as well, fully accountable to the life of the person. At this moment of naming, the person, the "poor passing fact," becomes the figure, imbued, caressed, solidified, and *realized* in the way that art can realize. For Lowell, however, "accuracy" is a grace sponsored by powers beyond the powers of technique. For this reason, accuracy itself is not so much what art can accomplish, but that "grace" which art can register. The "accurate" and the "living" always point toward a realm that art cannot appropriate. The lyric, as Lowell conceives of it here, always marks a division between two worlds, on the one hand the world of the name, the snapshot, the threadbare art, the map, and on the other, the world of illumination, of yearning, of sunlight. Their coming together is a grace, but they can never become one thing. "All's misalliance."

What Lowell suggests in this poem is a larger awareness to which many of his contemporaries responded as well, an awareness of a resistance to intelligibility that inheres in the "poor passing facts" that make up our contingent existence; art can order these facts provisionally, but it can never assimilate them to a greater order (the sort, for instance, of which Stevens dreamed). From *Life Studies* on, Lowell's project (a project shared in part with some of the strongest poets of the mid-century) was an extended exploration of the ends toward which this unwinnable struggle could be directed.

THE NEW METAPHYSICS:
GRAHAM, AMMONS, CHARLES WRIGHT

Lowell's world, to the extent that it reveals a persistent divide between fact and the assimilating imagination, has much in common with Hardy's world, torn by the conflict between romantic credence and modernist skepticism. Poets with a more explicitly Stevensian inheritance, such as Graham, Ammons, and Charles Wright, have a more stable belief in the continuing possibilities of a Supreme Fiction, even though the nature of that fiction differs enormously from poet to poet. What they share, to the extent that they concern themselves with the potentials of transcendent knowledge, is an interest in the secular continuation of the religious and metaphysical lyric traditions.

Jorie Graham has dedicated her career to exploring the contemporary capacities of the lyric to mediate between the spiritual and the material worlds. Her work, an intricate hybridization of skepticism and lyricism (to paraphrase the Nietzschean title of her first volume, *Hybrids of Plants and Ghosts*) explores the end of the mind at its frontier with the limits of ontological and epistemological inquiry. Indeed for her as for Stevens the lyric is in its essence an instrument of philosophical inquiry. What distinguishes her from Stevens is her willingness to subject even the foundations of thought and consciousness itself to relentless scrutiny. Her chief fascination is not so much with the contents of experience as it is with the "act of the mind" as it moves across the surfaces of the world; beneath the pressure of her interrogations the surface intelligibility of the world breaks down or refracts into a series of ever smaller conceptual units. Her lyricism, in this way, is a medium reconstituted from the fine powdery byproduct of Lowell's "nostalgia pulverized by thought." Her accomplishment is to find a way to take this radically particulated universe and turn it back into something like a plastic medium, more abstract but never entirely so, closer, perhaps, to collage. Instead of examining the sedimentation of the particles of culture, her work examines the sedimentations of the particles of thought. For her the end of the mind is to be found in the world's transcendental elusiveness, and her sinuous and intense lyric forms are devised to give an account to this form of *philosophic* resistance to intelligibility.

Charles Wright and A. R. Ammons have a place in this category as well, but they deploy the resources of lyric toward purposes fundamentally different from Graham's. Wright, like Graham but with less manifest ambition, considers in more explicitly *metaphysical* terms the world's strange mixture of ravishing seduction and intractable resistance to the mind's embrace. For him, however, moments of failure or the approach of "the big nothing" appear in terms more or less derived from a theological view of the universe, and in this regard, despite the dilated cadences he derives from (Pound's) Whitman, he shares his deepest concerns with Wordsworth and Eliot. His attempts to re-cover the divine from the quotidian bring him into engagement with those re-sistances to lyric assimilation provided by the obdurate givens of the world, even a world as familiar and intimately knowable as his back yard in Charlottesville, Virginia. For Charles Wright, however, the world, for all its myriad anxieties, comes readily to hand. He is less interested than Hardy, or Larkin, or Glück, in the unmusical capacities of a broken lyre.

Ammons, writing with relatively untroubled lyric confidence, is the in-heritor of the more optimistic and Emersonian legacy of Whitmanian and Stevensian romanticism. His sensibility is fundamentally an expansionist one. To this extent Ammons works a particularly Emersonian vein in the American lyric, sustaining an unflinching commitment to newness and flow. Wright's and Ammons' muses, in spite of their perennially elegiac explorations, are of fundamentally ample disposition, and it is this amplitude that separates them from the poets most concerned with the end of the mind in the strictest late-Stevensian sense. Graham, at the moment, is the poet exploring most vigor-ously this territory marked out by Stevens.

DIFFICULTIES OF THE PLAIN STYLE

The question of the plain style bears a unique, and uniquely complex, rela-tion to the poetics of the end of the mind. By plain style here I am indicating an approach that presumes a more-or-less complete transparency between the narrated facts of the poem and the poem's formal occasion, or to put it in Lowell's terms, a one-to-one correspondence between the "imagined" and the "recalled." It would seem that those writers who embrace the anti-rhetorical rhetoric of the plain style (which has argued forcefully for itself at least since the rise of Puritanism) would have a close kinship to those poets with a strong stake in constrained, limited, or impeded vocal registers, registers where speech admits no elaborative or decorative enhancement—as Stevens put it, "the final finding of the ear." I suggest, however, that the opposite in fact is true. Of course, the idea that what can be said *should* be said in as parsimo-nious and rhetorically inert a fashion as possible gains its authority from an apparent compliance with those principles of conservation and multiple func-tion the Enlightenment idealized in natural phenomena. It is, therefore, a temptation for the reader—and often the rhetorical demand of the writer—to consider the plain style as a necessary ascesis, an austere transaction whereby an unshakeable credibility is purchased through the repudiation of more opulent word-hoards. The rhetoric of simplicity, however, always places a deceptively simple demand upon the reader, the demand to assume, without questioning, *a common world.* Because the terms of intelligibility, transparency, and commonness are assumed and not devised within the world of the poet's practice, the lyric is engaged in an elision of those very ratios of difference which it (by my definition) presumes and is thus prevented from mounting any real engagement with what it means, or what it costs, to make sense. It is, I feel, the too-sincere avowal of the claims of a plain style that hobbles the work of James Wright, C. K. Williams, and James McMichael, poets whose accomplishment in other ways commands respect.

Of course the category of plain-style poetry, as I've defined it here, does not include all poems that present a plain surface to the world. (Some Hardy, the late Stevens, much Frost and Larkin, most Oppen, Merwin, and Glück all manifest a plainness that does not assume *a priori* this one-to-one correspondence between fact and representation.) Admittedly, it would require an extensive argument to trace out the different rhetorical uses of a plain style that does not seek to suppress its fictive aspects; at the very least, however, it may be worthwhile, by way of expanding this present argument, to consider what is at stake in such uses, and how they distinguish themselves from more coercive claims of transparency. Such an exploration could begin by defining a relatively narrow sense in which the plain style does in fact present itself for consideration as a successful ascesis, as a form of damage in its own right, a self-scourging conducted to preserve difference as opposed to sameness. Stevens' late work—in part because it becomes, in its austerity, the negative record of all his excursions into opulence—provides a seminal example, seeking as it does to converge upon a set of final austerities, those values approximating most closely to a zero-degree of articulation, achieved not for the sake of a non-rhetorical candor, but in order to isolate an irreducible element in Being, or more precisely, in Having Been. This style manifests not a self or sensibility knowable transparently or immediately, but a self, or a part of the self, apprehensible as a starkly-perceived *foreign body.* This irreducible element consists in part for Stevens in states of irreducible *difference,* not only between selves but between those distinct and increasingly eroded coherences (memory, desire, the possibilities for action, the imaginable future) from which the self aspires to wrest its form. Such a consideration might begin by focusing thematically on the poetry of very late age, where the bulk of life stands away in the past tense. It might also consider the poetry of silence or of maximally impeded utterance (examples of which may be found in Oppen) or the poetry of posthumous or disembodied voice (of which Merwin in *The Lice* and *The Moving Target* is a strong innovator).

LYRIC AND THE WRECK OF HISTORY: RICH

Those poetic undertakings I have outlined in the preceding chapters are undertakings sponsored by securely established political and economic enfran-
chisement. None of the poets I have discussed (all white, all middle-class)
write at any great remove from the mainstream of twentieth-century cultural
privilege. The first conditions of representational felicity, access to the means
of representation, are conditions the writers I have discussed have been free to
take for granted. Securely underwritten by accessible institutions of education, publication, and distribution, each writer is at liberty, in a way that other
writers cannot be, to explore the limitations and impediments—not merely
the potentials—of their craft. It may follow from this that the discontent I
have tracked—a discontent with the resources of linguistic representation and
the costs of intelligibility—is a discontent that can be contemplated only after
political and economic stability have been secured. This issue can be described
with reference to the question of whether lyric is in its essence a comic or a
tragic form; what such an account suggests is that only after lyric's comic—
unifying—potential has been assumed can its tragic implications be pursued.
Political engagement (hopefulness) requires a comic medium, one that can
contemplate a future in which present disunity might yield to unity. The lyric,
to the extent that it is a *social* form, in its tripartite structure of writer, speaker,
and reader, is in this way always at the service of the human comedy. Those
writers in a position to question the *limits* of its serviceability are only those
who can assume, and look beyond, this unifying function, toward lyric's more
tragic aspect. This book has centered around writers free to take this skeptical
stance.

However, to say, as I have, that the lyric manifests, by definition, an irreducible ratio of difference calls for an accounting of those poems that
avowedly take up the cause of political equality and the reduction of political
difference. In the interest of establishing my central terms in those contexts
where they can be most vividly illustrated, I have had to give less attention
than I would have ideally liked to that frontier where the comic and the tragic
elements in lyric consciousness fade or blur into one another. I would like to
consider as one example of this frontier the work of Adrienne Rich, whose poetry has something in common with that of Plath and Glück, but is ultimately
and fundamentally different in approach. Plath and Glück, while acknowledging as seriously as more overtly activist writers the need for a revision of
gender roles, do not, in the long run, dedicate their practice to the political
revision of those roles. In this matter, particularly with reference to Plath,
some (e.g. Rose) would maintain precisely the opposite: that Plath was more

radical in her sensibility than has previously been acknowledged. I feel, however, that her poems, while taking sometimes as their subject middle-class marriage and traditional feminine images purveyed by popular media in the mid-century, demonstrate a wholly conservative sense of the kinds of success a poem could secure; at no point did she write in a way that presumed anything other than wholehearted acceptance of those criteria for poetic value she derived (modified through Lowell) from the New Critics. What was radical and new and chillingly fresh in her later lyrics was secured within (and often in spite of) this set of values. If her poems have been used, since her death, in the service of value revisions, their adaptability to this purpose derives from the richness of their internal complexity and not from any professed contiguity with more programmatic political undertakings. Glück similarly makes unimpeded use of the lyric prerogatives she has adapted from Lowell and Plath. Her poetry begins from a confident assumption of authority and proceeds only then from that point toward an interrogation of the terms of authority. At a very early point in her career, her voice established itself on the arrogation of this particular confidence.

The poetry of Adrienne Rich, however, manifests more vividly the fraught intersection of political and lyric ambition. Her work illuminates a tension between two propositions: on the one hand, the establishment of the subject within the terms of linguistic representation is of a piece with the establishment of the subject in terms of political representation, to which Rich has dedicated herself; on the other, the sense of justice itself, and its belief in what the future must entail, tends to assume an understanding of what the social subject is, and requires a confidence about the shared interests and investments of large classes of people. It is precisely the completion or intelligibility of the subject that the poets I have discussed call into question. They tend not to address themselves directly to the possibilities of social solidarity, because they record those conditions wherein the internal solidarity of the speaking voice has broken down or remains to be established. It is one of the virtues of Rich's best work that it reveals a field of turbulence between what is unfinished in the individual and what is unfinished in the social and political world.

A corollary of my argument is that the very nature of the lyric is to postulate an inner world defined in opposition to, and in conflict with, the outer world. Because this conflict is irreducible, it can never take a form precisely isomorphic to those conflicts which progressive political action seeks to resolve. This account emphasizes the fundamentally tragic aspect of the lyric, as that form which forever instantiates a break between what is present to the mind as self-knowledge, and what stands in the field of representation always as knowledge of an *other* mind. While in one sense every lyric seeks to bridge this break, the break itself can never be removed. And while engagement in the political arena presumes that ratios of difference in political power can in fact be leveled, engagement in the field of lyric presumes that the ratio of difference between self-awareness and the knowledge of another is permanent and cannot be erased. For this reason, the lyric ambition and the political ambition of a poem can never be precisely the same. When Milton writes "Avenge, O Lord, thy scattered saints," it may in fact be true that God will hear his plea and avenge the Waldenses killed by the Duke of Savoy, thus fulfilling the political will of the poem. This accomplishment, however, will never elide the fact that Milton must make an appeal to means other than political ones, to God's means and poetic means, in order to secure the desired outcome. Of course a certain kind of revenge is enacted in the lines themselves, to the extent that they level an indictment and thereby strike a blow in the press. But while God (or other Protestants) can perform acts of vengeance and dispatch injustice into a redeemed past, the poem itself suspends resolution permanently in a subjunctive futurity: "that from these *may* grow / A hundredfold [. . . .]." This suspension permanently inscribes the poet's weakness, which inheres in the gap or difference between his desires and his worldly powers.

Within this tragic aspect of lyric, the most avid performative speech acts (Milton's "May all Catholics be forever cursed," etc.) converge with the resignation of elegy. Yeats recognized this; he is the great modern poet of conflict between, on the one hand, the limitations of mortal agency and consciousness, and on the other, the revolutionary potential of the collective. To the extent that the collective, as Allen Grossman has argued, is founded upon the destruction of the claims of individual consciousness (*Sighted Singer* 240–244), then endeavor on behalf of a collective always entails an awareness, somewhere, of the transience, vulnerability, and indeed, the expendability of the individual. Rich's poem *Eastern War Time* takes up this conflict at a level of intimate, private detail. Rich asks what it means to encounter overwhelming historical fact, not as Yeats had, as the public man, meeting other public men in the streets or school children in the "long schoolroom," but as the schoolgirl herself, with an almost excruciatingly private consciousness, her memories sealed inside an uncherished past, in a time when the street is not a place of meeting (as in "Easter 1916") but a place of death:

> Streets closed, emptied by force Guns at corners
> with open mouths and eyes Memory speaks:
> You cannot live on me alone
> you cannot live without me

> I'm nothing if I'm just a roll of film
> stills from a vanished world
> fixed lightstreaked mute
> left for another generation's
> restoration and reframing I can't be restored or framed
> I can't be still I'm here
> in your mirror pressed leg to leg beside you
> intrusive inappropriate bitter flashing
> with what makes me unkillable though killed (49)

Rich writes here, in a context of public history, something very close to what Plath approached in "Words," but in the sphere of more solitary and explicitly personal concern. (Words for Rich can never be wholly "riderless.") In each case the topic is the cost to the individual (here constituted in "Memory") of entering into the world of representation (of "stills" and "mirrors"), into a state where the voice articulates itself as simultaneously "unkillable" and "killed." The best moments in Rich are those moments where this struggle for political acknowledgement is felt as intimately entailed within the struggle of poetic representation. It is in those moments where she writes with full awareness of the complexity and compromise inherent in assuming both lyric and moral authority that her account of voice (both political and poetic) makes its most powerful claim. Her strongest music (and she has, I feel, one of the finest ears since Eliot) unfolds in a chromatics of contrast and not of assent. She is (like Bishop and Bidart, as I will presently remark) a poet with a more complex and ambivalent relationship to violence, the violence of desire, the violence of political consequence, than many writers (including sometimes herself) would readily admit. When she turns her attention fully to "the wreck and not the story of the wreck / the thing itself and not the myth," her poems know that *they themselves* stand amidst the wreckage, a wreckage which includes damage to the intelligibility of those terms on which moral authority seeks to found itself. At these moments her work engages the fullest capacity of its lyric potential.

POETS OF THE VIOLENCE OF DESIRE: BISHOP AND BIDART

My brief consideration of Rich points to the topic of violence, particularly those instances where the poet allows the poem to bear the mark of a kind a violence to intelligibility itself. (Larkin, I have argued, manifests this most clearly). When this violence is coupled with desire—as it is in Hardy, Larkin, and, differently, Plath—a special subset of the general category of damage comes into view. Freud proposed a theory wherein the drives that make up the id are by definition threats to the integrity of the self. There are, I believe, a notable number of poets who join Freud in exploring the ramifications of this proposition, poets concerned centrally with the violent potentials that desire brings into the world. Dickinson stands as the American protomodern proto- type (though of course the tradition has its roots in antiquity). Some of Rich's work, as I have argued, fits this category; Bishop and Bidart fit it as well, in ways both obvious and unexpected.

Bishop's work presents a specialized instance of what I am describing here. Rich assumes the agreement, or at least the persuadability of her reader; her work comfortably assumes a community of like-minded people. Bishop, while presenting a similarly congenial surface to the reader, nevertheless dis- turbs this surface by indicating repeatedly the subtle violence that inhabits the relation between reader and poem. This disturbed relationship is indicated by those relations between observer and observed described in the poems them- selves, most notably in "Brazil, January 1, 1502," "Crusoe in England," "The Armadillo," and "Pink Dog." In these poems the rapt, seduced stare of a viewer, both ravished and ravishing, cannot help but enact its own form of vi- olence upon what it beholds. What Bishop emphasizes in these instances, just as Rich does, is the fraught interplay of public and private at work in the con- temporary lyric. The lyric invitation to share a private space implicates the reader in an act of trespass. What is broken in this trespass, however, is not a moral or ethical precept—as is usually the case for Rich—but a delicate pri- vacy, which is ultimately the incandescent, suspended, solitary, dangerous "fire balloon" of self-knowledge, the self's intimate and unexpressed awareness of itself. For Rich, however fraught the divide between public and private ex- perience might be, the division is, for the most part, clearly delineated. The moral imperative to which she most readily responds is to point out and thereby narrow the too-wide gap between experiences of insulation and those of implication. For Bishop, the gap is almost unbearably small. Even the movement from experience to speech is a troubled crossing; the language on the far shore is never a wholly familiar dialect; something is always lost, even in this most primary of translations.

The lyric, then, for Bishop does not protect the privacy of experience, but seeks to regulate the effects of the exposure to which the lyric subjects the speaker. If it is "A man's voice" in "The Moose" that "assures us" the moose is "Perfectly harmless . . . " (173), Bishop's voice dedicates itself to the task of saying that no encounter between different parties can claim such innocence for itself. The delicacy and surface quietism of her work creates a surface still enough to register the most delicate manifestations of harm. Because this drama of harm plays itself out not only in the thematic world of the poems themselves but between the reader and the page, what becomes visible is an entirely new plane, the reader-poem plane, on which the limits and impediments to intelligibility can be conceptualized. How such a field could be described, the rules of evidence for such an account, would be the challenge, perhaps unmeetable, of an argument, related to but entirely different from, the one I have chiefly pursued. Such an argument, however, would provide an occasion to consider at its very deepest level the question that Bishop sees everywhere in lyric speech: whose experience is this, and to what end and at what costs have these words been written?

In contemporary poetry in English, Bidart is the most explicit theorist of the role of desire as it simultaneously constitutes subjectivity and calls subjectivity into question. While this conception is in some sense wholly contiguous with Freudian libidinal theory, for Bidart, desire and subjectivity are not ultimately reducible to the interplay of drives and defenses. Instead, the word *desire* as he employs it (and the book of that title provides a long gloss on the term) takes on the more Classical quality of fate or destiny, a destiny rarely, if ever, aligned with the speaking consciousness of the poems themselves. This disjunction is for Bidart an inescapable tragedy. That the "I" is precisely that which comes into being, and comes to grief, in the torrent of desire, is that epistemological and existential problem to which the speaker must address himself with greatest urgency. If one cannot say that his desires are properly his own, Bidart asks, then what are the consequences of desiring, of being a desiring "I"? And what are the further consequences of being a speaking "I"? For Bidart the disjunction between self and desire is a field of conflict, often violent, and it is also the field of lyric endeavor.

As was the case for Hardy, what often interests Bidart most about poetic writing is its capacity to demonstrate strain. This strain, dramatized in his longer poems, is that strain exerted on the psyche by opposing cultural, emotional, and instinctual claims. The shorter lyrics most often present a speaker threatened with dissolution beneath the overwhelming pressure of grief, longing, desire, remorse, or guilt; at these moments the strain is the more elemental strain of articulating *anything at all*. The contours of these strains are registered in Bidart's unblinking attention to the visual effects available through line-spacing, capitalization, italicization, and punctuation. For all the tempestuousness of Bidart's thematic world, the work achieves in its meticulousness a jewel-like precision annealed at the fault-line between the urgent compulsion to speak and the overwhelming obstacles to utterance.

These strategies have drawn inevitable attention to Bidart's struggle to record the form and pressure of the unmistakable *voice*, particularly voice heightened and intensified by extreme experience. What is yet to be given, however, is an account of those blanknesses, embodied in his use of white space, that represent not so much the voice itself but its limits. Every poem, of course, by bending itself to the multiple termini of its devised pattern, is in some sense a negotiation with the white space of its constraining perimeter. The high modernists, particularly Pound and Eliot, brought this perimeter, as a marbling of whiteness, into the poem itself. (Bidart cites Pound's use of white space as a seminal influence on his formal procedures [*Western Night,* 224].) The breaks, however, in the typically fragmented modernist poem do not embody the voice at its breaking point but rather the process of entropic cultural dispersal which the poem itself seeks to rectify. The surface unintelligibility of such difficult poems as *The Waste Land* and *The Cantos* was a necessary price to pay for the larger recovered intelligibility of higher-order truth, a truth visible, say, at the hypostasized point of intersection between such disparate documents as Kyd's *Spanish Tragedy,* Weston's *From Ritual to Romance,* Shakespeare's *The Tempest,* and the Buddha's *Fire Sermon.* White space for Bidart works fundamentally differently, as that margin of meaninglessness against which the speaker is pressed *at all times.* By *scoring* his works for voice (Vendler, *Soul Says* 74), he brackets the poems not only with reference to what the voice *can* say—its manageable, or barely manageable range—but also to those extremes of utterance beyond which human meaning disintegrates. In spite of the attention he gives to mythic and religious cosmologies, the difference that interests Bidart most is not a hierarchic one between distinct orders of being. It is rather that between the provisional coherence of the human form and those states of annihilation or obliteration that press against the human from all sides. In Bidart's bid for a state of embodiment on the page itself, there is the implicit conviction that human meaning cannot be sustained by those other institutions (religious, political, cultural) that had once held out the promise of its preservation. The dangers his speakers find themselves in are not in the long run historical dangers, but the precariousness and torment of existing nowhere but in the "lineaments of desire."

DIVINE COMEDIES AND ENDLESS MIND

Poems whose native element is only what Stevens called "the gaiety of language" give little or no access to the terms I have elaborated in this study. This does not mean to imply that such poems must, by any account, present an optimistic face to the world, only that such poems view their linguistic resource as one of fundamentally limitless possibility. John Ashbery, for instance, is the great postmodern poet of romantic despair, and his subject is an uninterrupted exploration of the world's failures to meet the demands of human desire, but Ashbery's desire, unlike Bidart's, plays itself only on a human scale;

human presence, by extension, is an ineradicable presence in the world. For Ashbery, there is no such thing as a song "without human meaning, / Without human feeling." To put it differently, then, desire for Ashbery is human-scaled because there is no scale other than the human. In this regard his aesthetic is fundamentally urban, not merely because he, with O'Hara and Schuyler and Koch, created a saucy and much-imitated brand of Manhattan regionalism, but because he understands there to be no world other than that of the human community, of which the city is the paradigm. To this extent, Ashbery's is a more resolutely humanist world than that of other poets much less likely to be held up as exemplars of postmodernism (Larkin's, for instance). His particular species of humanism is the sort that Stevens contemplated in "A Postcard from the Volcano" in which the world is in its essence a saturation and sedimentation of prior human meanings. Ashbery, however, does not share Stevens' belief in a primitive reality beneath this sedimentation, much less his desire to cut through to it; he believes instead that these meanings call for a judicious process of sorting, a process that promises the mind inexhaustible diversion, but that does not, in itself, ever come to completion.

The poetry of James Merrill, in many ways entirely unlike Ashbery's, nonetheless shares Ashbery's disenchanted steely hedonism (and for this temperament each poet owes a debt to Auden). Even in the gravity and pathos of Merrill's last poems, speech elicits from the poet only an affirmation of its ability to clarify, order, delight, and instruct. "Christmas Tree," still uncollected at the time of his death, proposed an emblem for such a speaker—a tree deracinated and therefore doomed, but jeweled and lit nonetheless. If the loss of individual life is tragic, the tragedy dissolves in the larger Divine Comedy, the unshakable knowledge that the show will, in some form, "go on." Ending with the line "still to recall, to praise," Merrill rewrites Lowell's "Epilogue" by excluding the category of the "living name" in favor not of specificity but an act, a recollective act assumable by others after the speaker's death. The unending infinitive of "still to recall" takes the place of Lowell's preterite "what happened."

For Ginsberg and the other poets of the San Francisco Renaissance, a similar Divine Comedy, more corporeal, less plangent, determines the contour of their poetic world. For all the exuberant nudism of its self-exposure, the work shares more with the religious ejaculatory mode of Blake and Christopher Smart than with the personal disclosures of Lowell and Berryman. These poets wager their whole enterprise on the twentieth-century possibilities of Whitmanian bardic speech and the fundamentally theist proposition that poetic speech and divine speech locate themselves on the same continuum. (While there is room for spiritual doubt, there is no room for non-spiritual doubt.) To the extent that the human mind is contiguous with the mind of god, it can have no end in the Stevensian sense.

When, on the other hand, it is the radical ficticity of language that is elevated to the level of transcendent truth (cf. de Man on Rilke above in Chapter Two), then a mirror-image atheism, no less devout than the credences of the Beats, comes into being in the form of the Language Poetry movement. What such an elevation denies is a distinction between language and any realm that might appear to exist outside it; the human subject is thus recognized only as a predicate of language's figural capacity, a capacity informed, manipulated, and shaped by economic and societal forces. This stance is not the radical extension of high modernist and Heideggerean impersonalisms, both of which assume—and seek to mediate between—the claims of self-presence and artistic presence. Instead, in order to decouple language from its oppressive matrices, Language poetry seeks to assert the fundamentally illusory or fictive nature of this difference. The lofty political ambition toward which its rhetoric aspires amounts to a fundamental idealism about the uses of speech in culture, an idealism which tends to exclude any skeptical inquiry into the limits of such an undertaking.

I do not mean to say that these poets, and groups of poets, have not made significant contributions to the history of lyric. The intent rather is to restrict—and by restricting clarify—my remarks in the larger context of promising poetic developments in English. In doing so I hope to provide a glimpse of a future in which my general argument has a place. Such a future would be one where human presence is acknowledged not only in its yielding to intelligibility but in its withholding from intelligibility as well, a withholding with its own role to play in the preservation of the human form.

Notes

1. Seamus Heaney, personal communication.
2. Cf. Grossman (*The Sighted Singer*, 290–300).
3. Grossman, however, does imply an approach to this question, albeit with reference to the *human* as opposed to the *body:*
   > Other modern efforts at specifying the function of language, such as those of Austin, Wittgenstein, Piaget, and Malinowski, also call attention to the necessity of presupposing a general human science, a science of the meaning-bearing speaker and the laws of such a science, prior to the linguistic science which specifies the secondary rules of construction by which the *eidos* becomes manifest in situations. (*The Sighted Singer*, 231)
4. The antecedent for this theory of incipience is of course Emerson's "Circles." Cf. Poirier (24).
5. Cf. John Vernon:
   > If language organizes the world, and the world resists language—the human body is this tension itself, and gestures are its visible vibration, the graph of its oscillations. Gestures are the key to the relationship between language and the world. (19, emphasis added)
6. Cf. Heidegger, "The Origin of the Work of Art."
7. Grossman makes note of Levinas' theory of countenance in *the Summa Lyrica:*
   > A person *(persona)* is not a mask but a countenance. That is to say, a person is not the fiction of a face but the face known always to be a fiction. Speech, as it comes into poetry, is absorbed in, centrally preoccupied with, its status as a synecdoche of the countenance. In this sense, speech is the countenance which you *can* see that *means* (points toward) the countenance that you cannot see. It is the portrait of the inner and invisible (intuitional) person. This countenance is the one great referent of art acknowledged in these pages. The philosopher of the countenance is Emmanuel Levinas. (*The Sighted Singer*, 306)

My argument in this section can be seen as an attempt to specify and localize the means by which lyric speech "points toward the countenance you cannot see."

8. This *difference* is to be distinguished from (and, I propose, profitably maintained at a remove from) Derrida's *differance*, though conceptually the terms bear a clear kinship. Cf. Derrida on Levinas in "Violence and Metaphysics."

9. Frost's interest in abstractions of orientation is visible in "The Wood-Pile" as well, where the vertical disorientation of the woods gives way to the horizontal orientation of the pile of wood—felled, cut, stacked, and (like verse itself) measured:

    [. . . .]
    The view was all in lines
    Straight up and down of tall slim trees
    Too much alike to mark or name a place by
    So as to say for certain I was here
    Or somewhere else: I was just far from home.
    [. . . .]
    It was a cord of maple, cut and split
    And piled—and measured, four by four by eight.
    Not another like it could I see. (101)

10. Why lyric then, it may be asked, and not dramatic or narrative verse? What I am describing when I suggest this special definition for the obverse is, of course, not in its essence anything more than a way of describing a role that abstract form, any abstract form, can play in a work of art—any work of art. In this way, I do not intend to consider lyric as qualitatively different from other modes of verse, or writing, or plastic media. One aspect of the lyric, however, that gives it special status for this present argument is the essential namelessness of the lyric speaker, a speaker who is only "inferential[ly] and intuitive[ly]" associated with the author (Grossman 212). It is a part of the nature of the lyric speaker, as opposed to the speaker in narrative or drama, to be unnamed. This speaker is unnamed in a way essentially different from the omniscient speaker of narrative poetry, whose namelessness is a feature of omniscience (and therefore a principle of cohesion) and not of incipience, that essential priority of the lyric speaker to a coherent state of being capable of sponsoring a name. In this way the lyric speaker articulates itself at a point prior to personhood, and it is this incipience that Blackmur designates by the term "uncreated selves."

11. This absence is different from the solitudes in Frost it anticipates and those other solitudes in Wordsworth it recalls, because the empty landscape for Frost or Wordsworth is a landscape emptied to isolate a sign or manifestation of human labor. This reference to work is so notably absent in Hardy's lyrics, at least in comparison to those great documents of work, his novels, that one can say that poetry is the medium to which Hardy turns to depict a world in which labor no longer serves successfully to manifest human presence. Cf. Scarry, *Resisting Representation.*

NOTES TO CHAPTER ONE

1. Clarke (1993) provides an indispensable compendium of these accounts; see particularly the section in volume II dedicated to the poetry. Philip Larkin is among those who would confer upon Hardy the highest honors:

    May I trumpet the assurance that one reader at least would not wish Hardy's *Collected Poems* a single page shorter, and regards it as many times over the best body of poetic work this century so far has to show? (*Required Writing* 174)

2. Published in *Lyrical Ballads,* this poem also appears, in a different version, in the 1805 version of *The Prelude*. In its first drafts, Wordsworth narrates the event in the first person.

3. Heaney offers a similar reading of this aspect of the poem in his essay on Plath (154).

4. Compare Plath's great poem of reflection, "Words," discussed in Chapter 5.

5. Paulin has made this observation as well. I disagree with him, however, to the extent that he argues that Hardy is primarily interested in creating a "tremendous sense of presence":

    In "At Castle Boterel" he describes his memory of what he once saw so adroitly that he merges actual sight with "mindsight," because by using "look behind" and "look back" both literally and figuratively he makes their meanings combine and so creates a tremendous sense of presence. The woman's form that appears to his mindsight on the sloping road is visualized so distinctly that it's as though she is actually still alive and simply receding in the distance like Fitzpiers. Her "phantom figure" is "shrinking, shrinking" as if it's being obscured by the rain and darkness as well as diminishing in the distance. Time "has ruled from sight/The substance now," and so the rain, darkness and distance become embodiments of time. They give it a spatial dimension and become physical metaphors like the action of looking back. (111)

    I argue that it is not presence but the impediments to presence for which Hardy seeks to give an account.

6. A variant of the phrase "costumed in a shroud" is "folded in a shroud." While giving less explicit emphasis to the ironic pretext of the poem, this variant phrase also connotes a containment that is also a concealing, and is preferable, I feel, to the extent that the more muted, papery, epistolary diplomacy of "folded" comments more subtly on the topos of writing and the present-absence of the circular's "inky" cloaking.

7. De Man translates the poem "as literally as the text allows":

    "My room and this wide space / watching over the night of the land— /are one. I am a string / strung over wide, roaring resonances. // Things are hollow violins / full of a groaning dark; / the laments of women / the ire of generations / dream and toss within . . . / I must tremble / and sing like silver: then / All will live under me, / and what errs in things / will strive for the light / that, from my dancing song, / under the curve of the sky / through languishing narrow clefts / falls in the ancient depths / without end . . ." (33)

8. That there are explicitly *ten* of these wounds indicates that the violin has been changed in another way, specifically into a woodwind, such as a flute or recorder, with ten stops for the player's ten fingers. What this points toward is the specific violence narrated by Elizabeth Barrett Browning in "A Musical Instrument" where Pan cuts and perforates Syrinx's body, making a flute from the reed to which she has been recently transformed. But whereas Pan (and Browning) are interested in the transformation of bodies into instruments, Hardy is interested in the transformation of the instrument back into the body.

NOTES TO CHAPTER TWO

1. This is J. Hillis Miller's primary claim in *The Linguistic Moment*. The insistence that the work of the poem is a *mise en abîme* proposes that "The Rock," and Stevens' poetry in general, is a de Manian allegory of reading. Lakritz takes a similar stance (62). I discuss this position further with respect to Stevens' uses of single alphabetical letters.

2. I refer in passing to "Local Objects" often enough to warrant including the whole text:

   He knew that he was a spirit without a foyer
   And that, in this knowledge, local objects become
   More precious than the most precious objects of home:
   The local objects of a world without a foyer,
   Without a remembered past, a present past,
   Or a present future, hoped for in present hope,
   Objects not present as a matter of course
   On the dark side of the heavens or the bright,
   In that sphere with so few objects of its own.
   Little existed for him but the few things
   For which a fresh name always occurred, as if
   He wanted to make them, keep them from perishing,
   The few things, the objects of insight, the integrations
   Of feeling, the things that came of their own accord,
   Because he desired without quite knowing what,
   That were the moments of the classic, the beautiful.
   These were that serene he had always been approaching
   As toward an absolute foyer beyond romance. (473)

3. Donoghue makes the strongest case for reading Stevens as an Epicurean (see "Two Notes" 44) in motive, if not in subject matter. For a detailed discussion of Stevens' Pragmatism (or those ways in which he makes himself available to be described as a Pragmatist) see Rae (150–216).

4. Donoghue in "Stevens' Gibberish" gives a full account of Stevens' uses of these particular outbursts:

Nonsense poetry acknowledges particular traditions of making sense, but releases the reader from the piety the traditions expect of him; as Stevens' early poems release the reader, for a while, from the claims of reason's click-clack which he will have to yield to in the end. Gibberish is superior to any official syntax in its testimony to the unknown behind the known; and it has only this disability, that it denies us the gratification of construing it. We can spend a vacation in it, but we can't live there. What can be construed has a different disability. E. M. Cioran has remarked that "it is the indigence of language which renders the universe intelligible." (168)

The difference I would like to emphasize here is, in Donoghue's context, the difference between two different forms of what cannot be construed. The first form, on which Donoghue focuses, is the sheer expressiveness or purely phatic flaring of Stevens' nonsense. The other form, on which I will dwell, could be called, by contrast, Stevens' past-sense, or beyond-sense. The former implies an intimate proximity, a shared exuberance; the latter, my concern, implies an unbridgeable (or nearly unbridgeable) distance between interlocutors.

5. Although *The Rock* was published as the final section of *The Collected Poems*, I follow the custom of treating it as an independent volume. The reader interested in a history of the texts and publications will want to consult the "Note on the Texts" (*Stevens* 970–83).

6. See Bromwich (231) for a further consideration of the absence of the Wordsworthian Other in Stevens, particularly with reference to "The Course of a Particular," (which I will discuss later in a different context):

Wordsworth, [in "Resolution and Independence"] keeps the beggar wandering, in the belief that he may some day encounter him again. A search of all Stevens' poetry will produce no such figure. The great difference between Wordsworth and his modern successors, I have begun to think, lies not so much in the "love of man" as in his simple copresence with another figure, radically unassimilable to himself, and the troubling possibilities that this brings. The egotistical sublime could reach its height when it existed in tension with such possibilities. (231)

I would add, with a view toward Stevens' late poems, that "radical unassimilability" need not define relationships solely between persons, but between the elements of the individual (but by no means indivisible) psyche. The other that vanishes from Stevens is not only "another figure" such as the leech gatherer represented for Wordsworth, but the "rider that was" Stevens himself (461).

7. See Vendler (*Extended Wings* 119–143) for an elucidation of Stevens' strate-
    gies of conflict in the conscientiously flattening and polarizing stagecraft of
    "The Man with the Blue Guitar":

    > In the *Comedian,* the world was a chastening and educative presence,
    > in itself parental, a curriculum for the marvelous sophomore. Crispin's
    > role was to be docile, and the innate foolishness of that state of tute-
    > lage provoked in the poem Stevens' unremitting irony of surface. Here,
    > the sophomore has grown up, and takes on the world as equal. If it is
    > a monster, he will be a monster; if it is antagonist, he is protagonist; if
    > it is discord, he will be chord; if it is oppressor, he will be rebel; if it is
    > land, he is ocean. (122)

8. Like "No Possum, No Sop, No Taters," this poem invokes Hardy as well.
    Compare Hardy's "During Wind and Rain," particularly "And the rotten
    rose is ript from the wall."

9. See also Vendler (in Pearce [166]), Doggett (6), and Litz (262).

10. In interpretively capitalizing and italicizing "the *The,*" I am violating the text
    in a way that points to an under-acknowledged aspect of Stevens' work,
    namely his insistence on *typographic* indeterminacy. The literal *flatness* of his
    refusal to inflect or emphasize elements of the poems' textual surface is, given
    his historical moment, no less radical a formal statement than Pound's line
    breaks, capitalizations, italicizations, and ideograms. The editors of the
    Library of America edition include this remark:

    > The first edition of *The Man with the Blue Guitar* included on its
    > colophon page a statement regarding the book's typographical design:
    > "In some of the lines appear unusual blank spaces and extra-wide spac-
    > ing of certain crucial words. By this experimental device the author
    > wishes to indicate a desirable pause or emphasis suggested by the sense.
    > In observing these rests the reader may feel so much the closer to the
    > poet's intention." Referring to this passage, Stevens wrote in a letter to
    > Ronald Lane Latimer of September 16, 1937: "This is pure nonsense.
    > I never said any such thing and have a horror of poetry pretending to
    > be contemporaneous because of typographical queerness." (*Stevens*
    > 971)

    > Stevens admits to his horror without explaining *why* horror should
    > be the appropriate response.

11. See the introductory chapter for an extended consideration of Frost's "West-
    running Brook."

12. "The Irish Cliffs of Moher" represents a parallel approach to "The Motive
    for Metaphor," one that seeks to look beyond poetry not to the elements of
    writing but to the elements of the natural world instead:

    > Who is my father in this world, in this house,
    > At the spirit's base?
    > My father's father, his father's father, his—

> Shadows like the winds
> Go back to a parent before thought, before speech,
> At the head of the past.
> They go to the cliffs of Moher rising out of the mist,
> Above the real,
> Rising out of present time and place, above
> The wet, green grass.
> This is not landscape, full of the somnambulations
> Of poetry
> And the sea. This is my father or, maybe
> It is as he was,
> A likeness, one of the race of fathers: earth
> And sea and air. (427)
>
> Because the elements are not the elements of writing, however, the
> poem is not able to include within its material presence the primaries
> of which it speaks.

13. The leaning posture is explicitly the posture of the reader, he who inclines toward sense. See "The House Was Quiet and the World Was Calm" (311) and the marvelous, uncollected "Blanche McCarthy" (c. 1915–16):

> Look in the terrible mirror of the sky
> And not in this dead glass, which can reflect
> Only the surfaces—the bending arm,
> The leaning shoulder and the searching eye.
> Look in the terrible mirror of the sky.
> Oh, bend against the invisible: and lean
> To symbols of descending night; and search
> The glare of revelations going by!
> Look in the terrible mirror of the sky.
> See how the absent moon waits in a glade
> Of your dark self, and how the wings of stars,
> Upward, from unimagined coverts, fly. (529)

14. For the best discussion of the convergence of senescence and infancy, see Vendler (*On Extended Wings* 309–14).

Stevens, in "The Sail of Ulysses" as elsewhere, refers to the self as female. This may refer most directly to the fact that in Greek the *pneuma* or spirit is always female, but even if this is the case, it raises the larger question of gender in Stevens' cast of characters, his "*personalia*" ("Somnambulisma" [269]). In "The Sail of Ulysses," Dickie sees the female as standing, by definition, for the enigmatic:

> The "self as sibyl" is the self as other, and in that metaphor the poet
> is transformed. The sibyl is unknowable, the woman as enigma and as
> the creator of enigmas. She is a seer, an even more interminable adven-
> turer than Ulysses in worlds beyond, in divinations. As the poet's self,

she has come home, returning to her source from wanderings enforced upon her by the poet's refusal to identify himself with her. Impoverished and blind, she comes arrayed in the poet's own blind imagery. As self, she has been anticipated in "Final Soliloquy" when the poet wraps tightly into one himself and his interior paramour. But the attributes of blindness, lameness, destitution, dependence, come from earlier figures of women whom the poet had deliberately distanced from himself. Here, they are reclaimed: Nanzia Nunzio's dependence, the blue woman's destitution, the fat girl's bent-over shape, Bawda's convinced blinding of her desire. (101)

The point is well taken, but I do not think that Stevens limits the enigmatic, or the unknowable, to the female; to do so would be to restrict himself to a dialectical or oppositional mode (exhaustively elaborated in "The Man With the Blue Guitar") at cross purposes with the more synthesizing goals of the final books.

15. See Chapter Two above.
16. Compare Beard, Filreis, and MacLeod.
17. "Never Again Would Birdsong Be the Same" (339) is the pre-lapsarian version, a more avowedly humanist poem than "The Oven-bird" or anything that Stevens wrote.
18. I agree with Vendler (*On Extended Wings* 177) that "bethou" and "ké-ké" are not, as Stevens maintained, opposing sounds (*Letters* 428), but that the seduction of the former and the "bloody" hostility of the latter converge into a single threat.
19. Making itself known prior to any object of desire, the dove's song is a benign recuperation of "Chaos in Motion and Not in Motion" [311] where "Ludwig Richter, turbulent Schlemihl /[. . . .] / Knows desire without an object of desire."
20. It is not clear whether Stevens composed "Not Ideas" before or after its companion poem, "The Dove in Spring," which was published in *7 Arts* in 1954, the year of the publication of *The Collected Poems*. See "Note on the Texts" (*Stevens* 973, 976).
21. This astringency is what is left out of accounts that see Stevens as wholly dedicated to finding the terms of this new reality. Miller, however, in *Poets of Reality*, a book in many ways truer to the complexity of Stevens than his later book, does indicate the importance of the category of the external:

> To walk barefoot into reality means abandoning the independence of the ego. Instead of making everything an object for the self, the mind must efface itself before reality, or plunge into the density of an exterior world, dispersing itself in a milieu which exceeds it and which it has not made.

Compare also Byers (114).

22. The deciduous tree in New England whose leaves die but do not fall from its branches is the *American* beech. Such was Stevens' attachment to local objects that even leaves that cry so far beyond human meaning still take part in a specifically regional mythology (cf. "A mythology reflects its region" 476).

23. "A Clear Day and No Memories" attributes to consciousness a similar thinness or shallowness:

    [. . . .]
    Today the air is clear of everything.
    It has no knowledge except of nothingness
    And it flows over us without meanings,
    As if none of us had ever been here before
    And are not now: in this shallow spectacle,
    This invisible activity, this sense. (475)

NOTES TO CHAPTER THREE

1. Because the whole poem "gathers to the surprise" of the stirring last lines, they complete the poem perfectly, which is to say, they transport the poem, by a kind of magical flight, to the place it seemed, in retrospect, to want to be going all along. To this degree, the poem succeeds triumphantly under its own terms. In another way, however, such magical transformations (arrows to rain, human arrangements to cleansing and irrigating natural rejuvenation) obscure the very struggles Larkin elsewhere takes to be the substance of consciousness.

2. The poem is an elegy to Larkin's recently deceased father, Sydney. See Motion (177).

3. "Church Going" demonstrates, perhaps most clearly of all Larkin's poems, the way that Larkin's topoi bear a deep affinity to those of Wallace Stevens, and at the same time, the way that Larkin can occasionally seem to be Stevens' exact opposite. "A Postcard from the Volcano" can imagine the world of the future precisely because the past is so profoundly and essentially imbedded in it. Larkin's future, (also one where the large building becomes "a tatter of shadows peaked to white, / Smeared with the gold of the opulent sun,") is tolerable to contemplate to the degree that it has shed, or nearly shed, the encumbrances of the past.

   The sumac grows in "St. Armorer's Church from the Outside," Stevens' uncannily kindred poem—though for Stevens, the chapel represents a purification of belief beyond the objects of belief. For Larkin, it is the category of belief itself which must be allowed to fade from the world.

4. It is characteristic of Larkin criticism to smooth over the complex conflicts between his figures by making recourse to a New Critical vocabulary of tension and dynamic equipoise. Ricks sees "An Arundel Tomb" as an accomplishment of such a balance:

There is many a way in which things may almost be said. Absences, as in Larkin's poem of that title, make themselves felt; and "Maiden Name" ends with a line the obvious rhyme for which has not been granted but left unsounded, silently wedded; "With you depreciating luggage laden." As with so much of Larkin, the art is a version of pastoral, an apprehension of poignant contraries. The last line of "An Arundel Tomb" functions as an inscription itself, lucid and gnomic, an oracular and honorable equivocation, its possibilities equally voiced. (123)

Larkin's poems, of course, encourage this reading strategy, in part by striving so often to balance their entire weight on the clinching gesture of the final line. What remains to be said, I feel, is how tension between assertions, between doubt and certainty, between what is said and not said, does not inevitably create "poignant contraries" and "honorable equivocation" but can express itself instead with violence and antipathy to synthesizing assimilation.

More recently, Carey (55) has asserted a vital tension between Larkin's masculine and feminine voices. Whatever we think of as a vital tension would need to encompass expressions of violent (misogynist, sadistic) hatred to refer accurately to the full spectrum of Larkin's poems. (Longley [29] and Rowe [79] offer more satisfactory analyses of the problem of gender in Larkin.)

Such violence is also elided from accounts which assert that Larkin's poetry relies upon the vigorous interplay between a pluralism of unlike voices. Osborne invokes Levinas to attribute to Larkin a dialectical "radical alterity."

In a very real sense, then, [Larkin's] poems articulate the inwardness of the other (to use the language of the postmodern philosopher Emmanuel Levinas). (155)

I would not disagree in principle, but what I am arguing here, as elsewhere in this book, is that the alterity articulated by the poems is not an "inward" one, but one whose radical nature inheres in its standing wholly *outside* of the intelligible. I discuss the concept of the *outside* in greater length in the previous chapter. See also my remarks on Levinas in the introduction.

5. The phrase is taken from the concluding remark of Larkin's review of Sylvia Plath's *Ariel* and suggests the differing uses each poet makes of despair. (*Required Writing* 281)

6. In turn the "undated" snow recalls "death's dateless night" in Shakespeare's Sonnet 31, where the speaker is caught in a usurious obligation to grief, from which only the thought of his "dear friend" can rescue him.

7. See Vendler (*Words* 72).

8. This last phrase is taken, of course, from the title of Larkin's poem "Nothing to Be Said." That poem announces, in somewhat crude form, Larkin's unfading desire to confront experiences which seem to say everything and nothing at the same time. In this regard, Larkin revises the Horatian imperative to write poems both sweet and useful. Poetic success, for Larkin, is both sweet and meaningless, like his father's jam and summer itself.

9. Everett discusses a similar issue with specific reference to Larkin's relation to Symbolism:

> He makes use, and very consistent use, of that species of literary idealism which Symbolism implies, *only* in order to record its unavailability. (66)

10. This poem suggests a place for Larkin in the topoi explored by Fried (1987) in the context of Eakins paintings and Crane's fiction.

11. Lodge indicates this dynamic in Larkin's poetry of death:

> Many of Larkin's most characteristic poems end, like "Mr. Bleaney," with a kind of eclipse of meaning, speculation fading out in the face of the void. [. . . .] Death is, we can all agree, a "nonverbal" reality, because, as Wittgenstein said, it is not an experience *in* life; and it is in dealing with death, a topic that haunts him, that Larkin achieves the paradoxical feat of expressing in words something that is beyond words. (127)

> I would add that it is not only in response to the reality of death that Larkin orients himself toward a region beyond words. I suggest that Larkin is interested more in the damage to meaning that can be sustained within life than in the inevitability of death *per se*.

12. Heaney employs the adjective "Elysian" as well, but toward a different end:

> These moments spring from the deepest strata of Larkin's poetic self, and they are connected with another kind of mood that pervades his work and which could be called elysian. [. . . .] To borrow Geoffrey Hill's borrowing from Coleridge, these [relenting moments in Larkin, these poems of light and lightening] are visions of "the old Platonic England," the light in them honeyed by attachment to a dream world that will not be denied because it is at the foundation of the poet's sensibility. ("The Main of Light" 137)

> I cannot agree with Heaney that "Larkin also has it in him to write his own version of the *Paradiso*" (138). If he had been, these moments of relenting would not, in the long run, have become the object of such merciless attack. Because Larkin cannot imagine the "endlessness" that concludes "High Windows" as intending any human redemption, these moments of lightening constitute transient phases of alleviation, in no way part of the good of a transcendental order. Heaney, however, does provide a necessary corrective to a stereotypical account of Larkin as a poet of pervasive gloom and skepticism. But

while it is true that the stereotyped gloom hides a more beneficent Larkin, it also hides a Larkin for whom such terms as "gloom" or "skepticism" are entirely too mild, entirely too compatible with what Stevens calls "human feeling" and "human meaning."

13. See Motion (188). The subject of the documentary film that inspired the poem was a single retired racehorse named Brown Jack. In turning this one horse into a pair, Larkin is suggesting a world of companionable shades, as Yeats had in "Cuchulain Comforted" (332).

14. "Obit" (*Collected Poems*, 642).

15. Motion (105).

16. The term *angel* here is especially important, connoting both its celestial and numismatic senses. On the one hand, our needs, like celestial angels, mediate between the transcendental world of the originary sun and the terrestrial world. On the other hand, our needs, like "Angel" coins (cf. John Donne, "Air and Angels" and Frank Bidart, "Coin"), are stamped with our own meanings, and are the currency of our earthly, mortal realm, not of heaven.

17. See also Larkin's account of Hull:

> People are slow to leave it, quick to return. And there are others, who come, as they think, for a year or two, and stay a lifetime, sensing they have found a city that is in the world, yet sufficiently on the edge of it to have a different resonance. Behind Hull is the plain of Holderness, lonelier and lonelier, and after that the birds and the lights of Spurn Head, and then the sea. One can go ten years without seeing these things, yet they are always there, giving Hull the air of having its face half-turned towards distance and silence, and what lies beyond them. ("A Place to Write" 74)

NOTES TO CHAPTER FOUR

1. e.g. Alvarez (38).

2. See Rose and Malcolm for two thorough and compelling accounts of the many debates that have surrounded Plath's work and estate.

3. Heaney (151). This essay is a vital and memorable description of Plath's development as a poet, but as such, is shadowed by one of the central problems in writing about Plath: the very assertions that sponsor her validity and visibility as a poet (assertions Heaney makes with aplomb) lose much of their solidity in the poetic world that Plath herself brings into being. One of the challenges facing all of Plath's critics is the problem of locating the boundary between self and other. Most biographies and critical studies attempt to locate that moment when she leapt from her old self, a self inhabited by other voices, constrained by dead stringencies, into her new self, the self possessed of her true voice. It is, however, this very idea of true voice that her work so thoroughly undermines. One of course must determine where Plath seems most like Plath, but these efforts tend to ignore the suggestion that we believe we

are seeing her most clearly when we are watching her become something else. Poems such as "Edge" notwithstanding, Plath is much less concerned with the terminal point of arrival or perfection than with the processes of becoming (cf. "Totem). (Later Glück, too, will give direct attention to the subject of change and mutability.) Plath's suicide, which so abruptly terminated her life, obscures the abiding unfinished quality of her work, the mystery of what other thing it may have become had she lived. The following passage demonstrates the paradox of a self simultaneously separate from and dwelling within a realm of otherness. In it Richard Howard claims that Plath's identification with the otherness of death is eventually "complete, resolved, irreversible" but does not explain how this can be true of her poems as opposed to her life:

> Her entire body of work can be understood best as a transaction—out of silence, into the dark—with otherness; call it death, or The Stone, or as she came to call it, "stasis in darkness" ("Ariel"), "great Stasis" ("Years"), in the first book such negotiations taking the form of a dialogue ("your voices lay siege . . . promising sure harborage"), which is to say *taking a form;* while in the later poems she is speaking from a point of identification with stasis which is complete, resolved, irreversible ("the cold dead center / where spilt lives congeal and stiffen to history")—she is on the other side, within the Deathly Paradise, so that it is the triumph of her final style to make expression and extinction indivisible ("I like black statements"). Which is why A. L. Alvarez says that her poems read as if they were written posthumously, for the very source of Sylvia Plath's creative energy was her self-destructiveness [. . . .]
>
> But as I hope I have shown, it was not herself she became, but totally Other, so that she (or the poems—it is all one now) looked back on "herself" as not yet having become anything at all. (416)

It is tempting to think of Plath as fully dedicated to passing over into a realm of otherness, but to do is to ignore the paradox that adheres in the claim that she was most herself when her self no longer had being.

4. Compare Wordsworth's and Hardy's account of reflection, discussed in the second section of Chapter 2.

5. Vendler writes: "It is in this way that "Sylvia Plath sensed that her sensual or appetitive impulses were not the single-minded component she would have liked them to be" (*Part of Nature*, p. 273).

6. Much of Plath criticism has continued this dispute, with an insistence that extends rather than illuminates a conflict in the poems themselves. For some representative examples, compare McClatchy (199), Easthope (230), Lowell (*Ariel*, vii) and Kroll (2).

7. Compare also Bronfen (95).

8. Hughes reports in the note for this poem (295) that Plath described this poem as "a pile of interconnected images, like a totem pole." The word totem

also invokes its more specifically Freudian sense as a representation signifying both life and death in a figure both dead and alive, such as the killed primal father, revived and revered in totemic representational form (cf. *Totem and Taboo*).

9. cf. Plath in her *Journals:* "That is the latent terror, a symptom: it is suddenly either all or nothing: either you break the surface shell into the whistling void or you don't" (1956). The progression in Plath's career can be seen as a shift in the valence of the word "into" in this passage. Whereas at first Plath believes that a shell can be broken through to reveal a sublime and inspiring presence (even if that presence is the "whistling void"), she arrives at a different understanding of art's shell or mask. The void, as she comes to see it, does not lie on the other side of the shell, but inheres in the shell's nature. "Into" loses the sense of "through" as in "break through to" and gains the sense of "into" as in "turn into." Art's act is not a seeing through but an acknowledgment: the void is not what lies beyond the shell, but is the fact that every shell or veil discloses another shell or veil.

10. Helen Vendler feels, as I do not, that the fish are dead when returned to the lake (personal communication). Admittedly, they "litter" the freezing mud, but I feel the poem works, if it works at all, only in the suggestion that minimally live things ("flexing," "glittering") can be placed in morgues. Compare the frozen, minimal life of the mannequins in their "morgue between Paris and Rome" ("The Munich Mannequins").

11. The necessary cost of representation is one of Allen Grossman's central assertions about the demands placed on the poet in poetic practice. Compare his remarks on Yeats in *The Sighted Singer:*

> When Yeats came to contemplate the relationship between the obligation of the poet to establish personhood, and the inevitability for the poet of his being a self, he found that personhood and selfhood were indeed in irreconcilable conflict. The problem that poetry presents us with now is the reconciliation of the strange and desolating complexities of personhood with the intimacies and gratifications of the psychological self. (21)

Of Plath he writes:

> In that way [her poetry] was like the poetry of Hart Crane, for whom the immense passion to complete the promises of desire came into catastrophic conflict with the requirements of representation; that is to say, with the abstractness and unyielding resistance of the medium of poetry itself. (34)

12. The deep establishment in Plath's psyche of this theme (or this theme of themes) is implied in a description of a "dream of dreams":

> I've a dream of my own. My one dream. A dream of dreams. In this dream there's a great half-transparent lake stretching away in every direction, too big for me to see the shores of it, if there are any shores,

> and I'm hanging over it, looking down form the glass belly of some helicopter. . . . It's into this lake people's minds run at night, brooks and gutter trickles to one borderless common reservoir . . . Call the water what you will, Lake Nightmare, Bog of Madness, it's here the sleeping people lie and toss together among the props of their world's dreams, one great brotherhood, though each of them, waking, thinks himself singular, utterly apart. (25–6)

13. This reading of "Mussel Hunter at Rock Harbor," while arriving at a conclusion somewhat different from Heaney's, is indebted to the vivid account he offers of the poem in "The Indefatigable Hoof-taps of Sylvia Plath."

14. A characteristic account of Plath's speaker is one engaged in what Sevens might have called a "cure" of the self. The cure is not to be had through mere self-disclosure, but through the costly act of annealing, the sacrifice of a "personal" self for an artistic self (recapitulating Eliot's transaction of "self-sacrifice" in the interest of achieving the impersonal "new art emotion" [*Tradition* 4].) Heaney (*Government*), Pollitt, and Kroll base their arguments on this assertion, as does Hughes himself:

> Her poetry has been called "confessional and personal," and connected with the school of Robert Lowell and Anne Sexton[. . . .]She shares with them the central experience of a shattering of the self, and the labor of fitting it together again or finding a new one[. . . .] Her poetic strategies, the poetic events she draws out of her experience of disintegration and renewal, the radiant, visionary light in which she encounters her family and the realities of her daily life, are quite different in kind from anything one finds in Robert Lowell's poetry, or Anne Sexton's. Their work is truly autobiographical and personal, and their final world is a torture cell walled with family portraits, with the daily newspaper coming under the door. The autobiographical details in Sylvia Plath's poetry work differently. She sets them out like masks, which are then lifted up by dramatis personae of nearly supernatural qualities. (85)

> Hughes claims that the shattered self or the non-self is a point on the road to renewal and redemption. The specific, contingent personal "details" are like "masks" which are lifted in the course of Plath's poems. But they are lifted by "dramatis personae." Even in Hughes' account what is revealed is not the new, or true, or redeemed self, but the fact that that self is yet another persona in a drama. The masks do not reveal the true self, but highlight the fact that the personal, the masked, is all that is ever visible.

NOTES TO CHAPTER FIVE

1. The perils of trying to subdue Glück's poetry to a unified polemic are evident in Keller's article (120–129), which relies on a cartoonish flattening of

Glück's world. At best, for a temperament such as Glück's, polemics amount to a form of romanticism, "and romance is what I most struggle to be free of" (*Proofs*, 8). At worst they replace drama with caricature.

2. Citations from *Firstborn, The House on Marshland, Descending Figure,* and *The Triumph of Achilles* refer to the single volume edition of *The First Four Books*.

3. She will not, however, reject her own poem entirely, but will save the topos of the dream of the lost love, using it again to harrowing effect in the section of "Marathon" entitled "The First Goodbye" (*Descending Figure* 176).

4. Compare Hollander on the distance of the cry from speech (10).

5. To compare Stevens' use of color, see chapter 3.

6. This is also a particularly Stevensian concern. See section 3 of Chapter 3 above for a consideration of Stevens' belief that being is predicated on desire or lack.

7. Glück's reviewers have tended to view her first and foremost as a lyric poet, often for the sake of highlighting the stylistic shifts that have marked her career. Bonnie Costello (14–19) designates *Meadowlands* as the volume that introduces new narrative elements, while Calvin Bedient implicitly claims *Ararat* for that role while maintaining outright that the book represents a further step toward "English in its most purified [lyric] form." I maintain that the tension between narrative and "purified" lyric is firmly in place at least as early as *Descending Figure*. This may be a way of saying that lyric and narrative, fused by this tension, are not for Glück meaningfully, or stably distinct categories.

8. Compare the decentralization of the *I* in Plath's "Words" (270) and the voice's outside provenance in Stevens's "Not Ideas About the Thing but the Thing Itself" (451).

9. Both Bishop and Glück share a poetic forebear in George Herbert, particularly the dialectic exchange of "Love Unknown" (120) and the elaborate self/flower conceit of "The Flower" (156). Vendler (*Music* 248) discusses this in greater detail and points out Glück's kinship with Dickinson as well.

10. Although Glück dismisses Stevens as an excluding poet, the writer of a "hermetic patois" (see *Proofs* 113–123) the phrase "critique of heaven" is undeniably Stevensian. The phrase "critique of paradise" is to be found in "Crude Foyer" (*Stevens* 270).

11. The black bough invokes not only Stevens' "The Snow Man" (8) but also Pound's "In a Station of the Metro" (*Selected* 35).

12. Compare also the transformation of yellow into green in "Nothing Gold Can Stay" (222).

13. Compare Glück's earlier treatment of this myth in "Hyacinth" (*Triumph* 167).

14. Cf. "Mock Orange": It is not the moon, I tell you. / It is these flowers / lighting the yard" (*Triumph* 155).

15. In a figuratively literal way, the flowers of *The Wild Iris* turned into the laurel branches of the Pulitzer Prize.

Bibliography

Alvarez, A. *The Savage God.* New York: Random House, 1970.

Altieri, Charles. *Self and Sensibility in Contemporary American Poetry.* Cambridge: Cambridge University Press, 1984.

———. "Why Stevens Must Be Abstract, or What a Poet Can Learn from Painting." *Wallace Stevens: The Poetics of Modernism.* Ed. Albert Gelpi. Cambridge: Cambridge University Press, 1985.

Ashbery, John. *Self-portrait in a Convex Mirror.* New York: Penguin Books, 1976.

———. *A Wave.* New York: Viking Press, 1984.

———. *The Mooring of Starting Out: the First Five Books of Poetry.* Hopewell, N. J.: Ecco Press, 1997.

Beard, Dorothea K. "A Modern *Ut Pictura Poesis:* The Legacy of Fauve Color and the Poetry of Wallace Stevens." *The Wallace Stevens Journal* 8.1 (Spring 1984): 3–17.

Bedient, Calvin. "'Man is Altogether Desire'?" *Salmagundi.* Spring-Summer 1991: 212.

Berryman, John. *The Dream Songs.* New York: Farrar, Straus & Giroux, 1969.

———. "Hardy and His Thrush." *The Freedom of the Poet.* New York: Farrar, Straus & Giroux, 1976.

Bidart, Frank. *In the Western Night: Collected Poems, 1965–90.* New York: Farrar, Straus & Giroux, 1990.

———. *Desire.* New York: Farrar, Straus & Giroux, 1997.

Bishop, Elizabeth. *The Complete Poems of Elizabeth Bishop.* New York: Farrar, Straus, & Giroux, 1979.

Blackmur, R. P. "Language as Gesture." *Language as Gesture.* New York: Harcourt, Brace and Co., 1952.

Blake, William. *The Poetry and Prose of William Blake.* Ed. David Erdman, commentary by Harold Bloom. Garden City: Doubleday, 1970.

Bloom, Harold. *The Poems of Our Climate.* Ithaca: Cornell University Press, 1977.

———, ed. *Contemporary Poetry.* New York: Chelsea House, 1986.

Bromwich, David. *The Choice of Inheritance: Self and Community from Edmund Burke to Robert Frost.* Cambridge: Harvard University Press, 1989.

———. *Skeptical Music.* Chicago: University of Chicago Press, 2001

Bronfen, Elisabeth. *Sylvia Plath.* Plymouth: Northcote House. 1998.

Brooks, Jean. *Thomas Hardy: The Poetic Structure.* Ithaca: Cornell University Press, 1971.

Brown, George Mackay. *Fishermen with Ploughs.* London: The Hogarth Press, 1971.

Byers, Thomas M. *What I Cannot Say: Self, Word, and World in Whitman, Stevens, and Merwin.* Urbana: University of Illinois Press, 1989.

Carey, John. "The Two Philip Larkins." *New Larkins for Old.* Ed. James Booth. London: Macmillan, 2000.

Clampitt, Amy. *A Silence Opens.* New York: Knopf, 1985.

Cook, Eleanor. "The Decreations of Wallace Stevens." *The Wallace Stevens Journal* 4 (1980): 46–57.

Costello, Bonnie. "Effects of an Analogy: Wallace Stevens and Painting." *Wallace Stevens: The Poetics of Modernism.* Ed. Albert Gelpi. Cambridge: Cambridge University Press, 1985.

———. "*Meadowlands:* Trustworthy Speakers." *PN Review* 128.6 (July-August 1999): 14–19.

Culler, Jonathan. "On the Negativity of Modern Poetry." *Languages of the Unsayable: The Play of Negativity in Literature and Literary Theory.* Eds. Sanford Budick and Wolfgang Iser. New York: Columbia University Press, 1989.

cummings, e. e. *Complete Poems.* New York: Liveright, 1991.

Davie, Donald. *Thomas Hardy and British Poetry.* New York: Oxford University Press, 1972.

de Man, Paul. *Allegories of Reading.* New Haven: Yale University Press, 1979.

Derrida, Jacques. *Writing and Difference.* Chicago: University of Chicago Press, 1978.

Dickie, Margaret. *Lyric Contingencies: Emily Dickinson and Wallace Stevens.* Philadelphia: University of Pennsylvania Press, 1991.

Dickinson, Emily. *The Complete Poems.* Boston: Little, Brown, 1960.

Doggett, Frank. *Stevens' Poetry of Thought.* Baltimore: The Johns Hopkins Press, 1966.

Donoghue, Dennis. "Two Notes on Stevens." *The Wallace Stevens Journal* 9 (Fall 1980): 40–45.

———. "Stevens' Gibberish." *Reading America: Essays on American Literature.* New York: Knopf, 1987.

Donne, John. *The Complete English Poems.* New York: Knopf, 1991.

Easthope, Anthony. "Reading the Poetry of Sylvia Plath." In *English* 43.177 (Autumn 1994): 223–35.

Eliot, T. S. *After Strange Gods.* New York: Harcourt, Brace and Company, 1934.

———. *The Complete Poems and Plays of T. S. Eliot.* London: Faber and Faber, 1969.

———. *Selected Prose of T. S. Eliot.* New York: Harcourt, Brace, Jovanovich, 1975.

Ellmann, Richard. "The Story of Modern Poetry." *New York Times Book Review* 27 (April 1980): 34.

Emerson, Ralph Waldo. *Journals.* (10/8/1837). Vol. IV. Ed. Edward Waldo Emerson and Waldo Emerson Forbes. London: Constable, 1910.

———. *The Collected Works of Ralph Waldo Emerson.* Cambridge: Belknap Press, 1971.

Erasmus, Desiderius. *Des Erasmi Roterod. de utraque verborum ac rerum copia lib. II ad sermanem & stylum for. mandum utilissimi.* Londini: Impensis Johannes Wright, 1650.

Everett, Barbara. "Philip Larkin: After Symbolism." *Philip Larkin.* Ed. Stephen Regan. London: Macmillan, 1997.

Filreis, Alan. "'Beyond the Rhetorician's Touch': Stevens's Painterly Abstractions." *American Literary History* 9 (Summer 1992): 230–63.

Fisher, Philip. *Making and Effacing Art.* Oxford: Oxford University Press, 1991.

Fried, Michael. *Realism, Writing, Disfiguration: on Thomas Eakins and Stephen Crane.* Baltimore: Johns Hopkins University Press, 1987.

Friedrich, Hugo. *The Structure of Modern Poetry: from the Mid-nineteenth to the Mid-twentieth Century.* Evanston: Northwestern University Press, 1974.

Freud, Sigmund. *Beyond the Pleasure Principle.* Vol. 18. *The Standard Edition of the Complete Psychological Works of Sigmund Freud.* Ed. James Strachey. London: Hogarth, 1995.

———. *Totem and Taboo.* Vol. 13. *The Standard Edition of the Complete Psychological Works of Sigmund Freud.* Ed. James Strachey. London: Hogarth, 1995.

Frost, Robert. *Collected Poems, Prose & Plays.* New York: Library of America, 1995.

Glück, Louise. *Ararat.* New Jersey: The Ecco Press, 1990.

———. *The Wild Iris.* New Jersey: The Ecco Press, 1992.

———. *Proofs And Theories.* New Jersey: The Ecco Press, 1994.

———. *The First Four Books of Poems.* New Jersey: The Ecco Press, 1995.

———. *Meadowlands.* New Jersey: The Ecco Press, 1996.

———. *Vita Nova.* New Jersey: The Ecco Press, 1999.

———. *The Seven Ages.* New Jersey: The Ecco Press, 2001.

Graham, Jorie. *The End of Beauty.* New York: Ecco Press, 1987.

Green, André. *Le Travail du Negatif.* Paris: Editions de Minuit, 1993.

Grossman, Allen. *The Ether Dome: New and Selected Poems.* New York: New Directions Press, 1991.

———, with Mark Halliday. *The Sighted Singer: Two Works on Poetry for Readers and Writers.* Baltimore: The Johns Hopkins University Press, 1992.

———. *How to Do Things with Tears.* New York: New Directions, 2001.

Grundy, Isobel. "Hardy's Harshness." *The Poetry of Thomas Hardy.* Eds. Patricia Clements and Juliet Grindle. London: Vision Press, 1980.

Gunn, Thomas. *The Occasions of Poetry: Essays in Criticism and Autobiography.* San Francisco: North Point Press, 1985.

Handy, W. C. "St. Louis Blues." *The Complete Works of Esther Bigeou, Lillyn Brown, Alberta Brown & the Remaining Titles of Ada Brown in Chronological Order (1921–1928).* Document Records. DOCD-5489.

Hardy, Thomas. *The Complete Poems of Thomas Hardy.* Ed. James Gibson. London: Macmillan, 1976.

Heaney, Seamus. *The Government of the Tongue.* New York: Farrar, Straus & Giroux, 1989.

Herbert, George. *The Complete English Poems.* London: Penguin Books, 1991.

Heidegger, Martin. *Poetry, Language, Thought.* New York: Harper & Row, 1971.

Hollander, John. *The Work of Poetry.* New York: Columbia University Press, 1997.

Hopkins, Gerard Manley. *The Poetical Works of Gerard Manley Hopkins.* New York: Oxford University Press, 1990.

Howard, Richard. *Alone With America: Essays on the Art of Poetry in the United States Since 1950.* New York: Athenaeum, 1969.

Howe, Irving. *Thomas Hardy.* New York: Macmillan, 1967.

Hughes, Ted. "Notes on the Chronological Order of Sylvia Plath's Poems." *Tri-Quarterly* 7 (Fall 1966): 81–88.

Hynes, Samuel. "On Hardy's Badness." In *Critical Essays on Thomas Hardy's Poetry.* Ed. Harold Orel. New York: G. K. Hall, 1995.

Jarrell, Randall. *The Complete Poems.* New York: Farrar, Straus & Giroux, 1969.

Keats, John. *The Letters of John Keats.* Ed. Hyder Edward Rollins. Cambridge: Harvard University Press, 1958.

―――. *The Poems of John Keats.* Ed. Jack Stillinger. Cambridge: The Belknap Press, 1978.

Keller, Lynn. "'Free / of Blossom and Subterfuge': Louise Glück and the Language of Renunciation." *Word, Self, Poem: Essays on Contemporary Poetry from the "Jubilation of Poets."* Ed. Leonard M. Trawick Kent: The Kent State University Press, 1990.

Koch, Kenneth. *Selected Poems, 1950–1982.* New York: Random House, 1985.

Kroll, Judith. *Chapters in a Mythology: The Poetry of Sylvia Plath.* New York: Harper and Row, 1976.

Larkin, Philip. *Required Writing.* New York: Farrar, Straus & Giroux, 1983.

―――. "A Place to Write." *Philip Larkin, 1922–1985: A Tribute.* Ed. Hartley, George. London: The Marvell Press, 1988.

―――. *Collected Poems.* New York: Farrar, Straus & Giroux, 1990.

―――. *Selected Letters of Philip Larkin.* Ed. Anthony Thwaite. London: Faber and Faber, 1992.

Leavis, F. R. "Hardy the Poet." *Southern Review* 6 (1940–41): 85–98.

Levinas, Emmanuel. *Totality and Infinity.* Tr. Alphonso Lingis. Dordrecht: Kluwer Academic Publishers, 1991.

Litz, A. Walton. *Introspective Voyager: The Poetic Development of Wallace Stevens.* New York: Oxford University Press, 1972.

Lodge, David. "Philip Larkin: the Metonymic Muse." *Philip Larkin: The Man and His Work.* Ed. Dale Salwak. Iowa City: University of Iowa Press, 1989: 118–128.

Loewald, Hans. *Papers on Psychoanalysis.* New Haven: Yale University Press, 1980.

Longley, Edna. "Larkin, Decadence and the Lyric Poem." *New Larkins for Old.* Ed. James Booth. London: Macmillan, 2000.

Lowell, Robert. "Forward." In Plath, Sylvia. *Ariel.* New York: Harper and Row, 1966.

———. *Selected Poems.* New York: Farrar, Straus & Giroux, 1977.

———. *Day by Day.* New York: Farrar, Straus & Giroux, 1977.

———. *Collected Poems.* Eds. Frank Bidart and David Gewanter, with the editorial assistance of DeSales Harrison. New York: Farrar, Straus & Giroux, 2003.

MacLeod, Glen. *Wallace Stevens and Modern Art: from the Armory Show to Abstract Expressionism.* New Haven: Yale University Press, 1993.

MacLeish, Archibald. *Collected Poems, 1917–1982.* Boston: Houghton Mifflin, 1985.

Malcolm, Janet. *The Silent Woman.* New York: Knopf, 1994.

McClatchy, J. D. *White Paper.* New York: Columbia University Press, 1989.

McMichael, James. *The World at Large: New and Selected Poems, 1971–1996.* Chicago: The University of Chicago Press, 1996.

Melville, Herman. *Moby-Dick, Billy Budd, and Other Writings.* New York: Library of America, 2000.

Merrill, James. *Collected Poems.* Ed. J. D. McClatchy and Stephen Yenser. New York: A. A. Knopf, 2001.

Merwin, W. S. *The Second Four Books of Poems.* Port Townsend, Washington: Copper Canyon Press, 1993.

Moran, Richard. *Authority and Estrangement.* Princeton: Princeton University Press, 2001.

Milton, John. *The Complete Poems and Major Prose.* New York: Odyssey Press, 1957.

Motion, Andrew. *A Writer's Life.* New York: Farrar, Straus, Giroux, 1993.

Nietzsche, Friedrich. *The Birth of Tragedy* and *the Genealogy of Morals.* Tr. Francis Golffing. Garden City: Doubleday & Co., 1956.

O'Connor, Francis V. *Jackson Pollock.* New York: Museum of Modern Art, 1967.

O'Hara, Frank. *The Collected Poems of Frank O'Hara.* Ed. Donald Allen. Berkeley: University of California Press, 1995.

Olson, Charles. *Selected Writings.* New York: New Directions, 1966.

Oppen, George. *Collected Poems of George Oppen.* New York: New Directions Publishing Corporation, 1975.

Osborne, John. "Postmodernism and Postcolonialism in the Poetry of Philip Larkin." *New Larkins for Old.* Ed. James Booth. London: Macmillan, 2000.

Ovid. *Metamorphoses.* Tr. Rolfe Humphries. Bloomington: Indiana University Press, 1955.

Paulin, Tom. *The Poetry of Perception.* London: Macmillan, 1975.

Pearce, Roy Harvey and J. Hillis Miller, eds. *The Act of the Mind: Essays on the Poetry of Wallace Stevens.* Baltimore: Johns Hopkins University Press, 1965.

Perkins, David. *A History of Modern Poetry.* Cambridge: The Belknap Press, 1987.

Plath, Sylvia. *Johnny Panic and the Bible of Dreams and Other Prose Writings.* Introduction by Ted Hughes. London: Faber & Faber, 1979.

———. *The Collected Poems.* New York: Harper & Row, 1981.

————. *The Journals of Sylvia Plath.* Ed. Frances McCullough; Consulting Ed. Ted Hughes. New York: Random House, 1982.

Poirier, Richard. *Poetry and Pragmatism.* Cambridge: Harvard University Press, 1992.

Pound, Ezra. *Selected Poems of Ezra Pound.* New York: New Directions, 1957.

————. *The Cantos of Ezra Pound.* New York: New Directions Publishing Corporation, 1995.

Rae, Patricia. *The Practical Muse: Pragmatic Poetics in Hulme, Pound, and Stevens.* Lewisburg: Bucknell University Press, 1997.

Rich, Adrienne. *An Atlas of the Difficult World: Poems 1988–1991.* New York: Norton, 1991.

Ricks, Christopher. "Like Something Almost Being Said." *Larkin at Sixty.* Ed. Anthony Thwaite. London: Faber and Faber, 1982.

Riddel, Joseph N. *The Turning Word: American Literary Modernism and Continental Theory.* Philadelphia: University of Pennsylvania Press, 1996.

Roethke, Theodore. *Collected Poems.* Garden City: Doubleday, 1966.

Rose, Jacqueline. *The Haunting of Sylvia Plath.* Cambridge: Harvard University Press, 1991.

Ross, Andrew. *The Failure of Modernism: Symptoms of American Poetry.* New York: Columbia University Press, 1986.

Rowe, M. W. "Unreal Girls: Lesbian Fantasy in Early Larkin." *New Larkins for Old.* Ed. James Booth. London: Macmillan, 2000.

Sacks, Peter. *The English Elegy: Studies in the Genre from Spenser to Yeats.* Baltimore: The Johns Hopkins University Press, 1985.

Scarry, Elaine. *Resisting Representation.* New York: Oxford University Press, 1994.

Sexton, Anne. *The Complete Poems.* Boston: Houghton Mifflin, 1981.

Shakespeare, William. *The Norton Shakespeare.* Ed. Stephen Greenblatt. New York: Norton, 1997.

Shelley, Percy Bysshe. *Shelley's Poetry and Prose.* Eds. Donald H. Reiman and Sharon B. Powers. New York: Norton, 1977.

Shetley, Vernon. *After the Death of Poetry: Poet and Audience in Contemporary America.* Durham: Duke University Press, 1993.

Skelton, John. *The Complete Poems of John Skelton.* London: Dent, 1957.

Stevenson, Anne. *Bitter Fame: A Life of Sylvia Plath.* New York: Houghton Mifflin, 1998.

Stevens, Wallace. *The Letters of Wallace Stevens.* Ed. Holly Stevens. New York: Knopf, 1966.

————. *Collected Poetry and Prose.* New York: The Library of America, 1997.

Thomas, Dylan. *Collected Poems, 1934–1953.* Ed. Walford Davies. London: Dent, 1988.

Vendler, Helen. *On Extended Wings: Wallace Stevens' Longer Poems.* Cambridge: Harvard University Press, 1969.

————. "The Poetry of Louise Glück." *The New Republic.* June 17, 1978.

———. *Part of Nature, Part of Us: Modern American Poets.* Cambridge: Harvard University Press, 1980.

———. *Wallace Stevens: Words Chosen Out of Desire.* Knoxville, University of Tennessee Press, 1984.

———. "An Intractable Metal." In *Ariel Ascending: Writings about Sylvia Plath.* Ed. Paul Alexander. New York: Harper and Row, 1985.

———. *The Music of What Happens.* Cambridge: Harvard University Press, 1988.

———. *The Given and the Made: Strategies of Poetic Redefinition.* Cambridge: Harvard University Press, 1995.

———. *Soul Says: On Recent Poetry.* Cambridge: Harvard University Press, 1995.

Vernon, John. *Poetry and the Body.* Urbana: University of Illinois Press, 1979.

Walsh, Thomas F., ed. *Concordance to the Poetry of Wallace Stevens.* University Park: The Pennsylvania State University Press, 1963.

Wordsworth, William. *The Poems.* Vol. 1. Ed. John O. Hayden. New Haven: Yale University Press, 1977.

Wright, Charles. *Negative Blue: Selected Later Poems.* New York: Farrar, Straus & Giroux, 2000.

Wright, Jay. *Transfigurations: Collected Poems.* Baton Rouge: Louisiana State University Press, 2000.

Yeats, W. B. *The Collected Poems.* Ed. Robert J. Finneran. New York: Macmillan, 1983.

Zabel, Morton Dauwen. "Hardy in Defense of His Art: The Aesthetic of Incongruity." In *The Southern Review,* VI (1940–1): 624–45.

Index

Printed in Great Britain
by Amazon